GAi SO-ADE-270

**Prentice-Hall Series
in the Philosophy of Medicine**

Samuel Gorovitz,
Series Editor

MAN, MIND, AND MORALITY: the ethics of behavior control, *Ruth Macklin*

ETHICAL ISSUES IN SUICIDE, *Margaret Pabst Battin*

Ethical

in

Prentice-Hall, Inc., Englewood Cliffs, New Jersey 07632

Issues

Suicide

MARGARET PABST BATTIN

Department of Philosophy
University of Utah

Library of Congress Cataloging in Publication Data

BATTIN, M. PABST.
　Ethical issues in suicide.

　(Prentice-Hall series in the philosophy of medicine)
　Includes bibliographical references and index.
　1. Suicide—Moral and religious aspects.　I. Title.
II. Series.
HV6545.B26　　　179'.7　　　81-17813
ISBN　0-13-290155-2　　　AACR2

For M. R. P.
1910–1962

© 1982 by Prentice-Hall, Inc., Englewood Cliffs, N.J. 07632

Printed in the United States of America

10　9　8　7　6　5　4　3　2

Ethical Issues in Suicide

Margaret Pabst Battin

ISBN 0-13-290155-2

PRENTICE-HALL INTERNATIONAL, INC., *London*
PRENTICE-HALL OF AUSTRALIA PTY. LIMITED, *Sydney*
PRENTICE-HALL OF CANADA, LTD., *Toronto*
PRENTICE-HALL OF INDIA PRIVATE LIMITED, *New Delhi*
PRENTICE-HALL OF JAPAN, INC., *Tokyo*
PRENTICE-HALL OF SOUTHEAST ASIA PTE. LTD., *Singapore*
WHITEHALL BOOKS LIMITED, *Wellington, New Zealand*

Gail Downward

Contents

Suicide and the Value of Life *112*

PART TWO: CONTEMPORARY ISSUES IN SUICIDE *129*

The Concept of Rational Suicide *131*

Paternalism and Suicide *154*

Suicide and Rights *176*

CONCLUSION: Suicide and Moral Rules *192*

Index 196

Preface to the Series

It is a commonplace observation that there have been dramatic increases both in public and professional concern with questions of bioethics and in the role of philosophers in addressing those questions. Medical ethics is a well established area of inquiry; not only does it include journals, widespread courses, professional specialists, and the other features of established fields, but philosophers now participate regularly in the deliberations of public agencies at both state and federal levels. Nonetheless, there is considerably more to the philosophy of medicine than medical ethics, and even within the area of medical ethics, there are many issues that have not been adequately explored.

The Prentice-Hall Series in the Philosophy of Medicine has been established in large measure in response to these two points. Some volumes in the series will explore philosophical aspects of medicine that are not primarily questions of ethics. They thereby contribute both to the subject matter of the philosophy of medicine and to an expanding appreciation of the breadth and diversity of the philosophy of medicine. Other volumes in the series will illuminate areas of ethical concern which, despite the recent prominence of medical ethics, have been inadequately considered.

Each volume is written by a philosopher, although none is written primarily for philosophers. Rather, the volumes are designed to bring the issues before an intelligent general readership, and they therefore presuppose no specific background in either the philosophical literature or the literature of the specific areas of medical practice or health policy on which they focus.

The problems considered in this series are of widespread public importance. We suffer from no delusions that philosophers hold the solutions; we do, however, share the conviction that these problems cannot be adequately addressed without an informed appreciation of their philosophical dimensions. We must always reach beyond philosophy in addressing problems in the world, but we should be wary of reaching without it. The volumes in this series are thus addressed to all those concerned with the practices and policies relating to medicine and health, and committed to considering such policies in a reflective and rational way.

SAMUEL GOROVITZ

ACKNOWLEDGMENTS

Some of the material in Chapter V has appeared in my paper "Manipulated Suicide," first published in the volume David Mayo and I have edited, *Suicide: The Philosophical Issues* (St. Martin's Press, 1980), and reprinted in the *Bioethics Quarterly* for Summer 1980. A section from the final chapter is based in part on my paper "Suicide: A Fundamental Right?", which also appeared in the volume of edited essays. I'd like to thank a number of people who have stimulated or commented on various portions of this book: Virgil Aldrich, Brian Barraclough, Corrine Bayley, James Bogen, Pearl Bronz, Ric Charnov, Mendel Cohen, Glendy Culligan, Gary Ferrin, Leslie Francis, Sam Gorovitz, David Hansen, Brooke Hopkins, Bruce Landesman, Mark Lehman, Michael Martin, David Mayo, Glenn Olsen, Doris Portwood, Rolf Sartorius, Alan Sullivan, Daniel Wikler, and Peter Windt. Alphabetical listing does not do justice to the generosity of their contributions, however, and so I'd like to mention Leslie Francis, David Mayo, and Daniel Wikler twice. In addition, I'd like to thank the University of Utah Counseling Center and the Family Health Program for stimulating workshops with their clinical staffs. I'd also like to thank, gratefully but anonymously, a number of people—young and old, male and female—who have talked with me openly and freely about their intentions and attempts at suicide; it is through these people, who actively contemplate suicide, that I have tried to avoid the philosophers' "armchair" view. I am grateful to the University of Utah for leaves and partial leaves as the Biology Department's Resident Humanist and as a David P. Gardner Faculty Fellow. I wish to thank the Utah Endowment for the Humanities for support as Philosopher-in-Residence at the Veterans Administration Medical Center in Salt Lake. Finally, I would particularly like to thank the National Endowment for the Humanities for a Fellowship for Independent Study and Research in 1977–78, which made possible a great deal of this book.

M.P.B.

Introduction:
Suicide –
The Current View

In recent years, suicide has attracted increasing attention as a large-scale social phenomenon. In the United States, at least 25,000 people kill themselves every year.[1] Worldwide, the number of completed suicides is well over 500,000, equivalent to the population of a city the size of Edinburgh, Scotland, or Jacksonville, Florida, and as many people attempt to kill themselves as live in London or Los Angeles. In the U.S., an individual is three times as likely to kill himself as to be killed by someone else, and the risk of death from suicide is greater than if there were a fully-loaded jumbo jet air disaster *every fifth day.*

Awareness of the problem of suicide has caused both increased scrutiny of the phenomenon by sociologists, psychologists, and researchers in many other disciplines, as well as increased efforts to reduce its incidence by physicians, counselors, social workers, social planners, and police. Efforts to discover the causes of suicide and to reduce its frequency have gone hand in hand; many countries now have suicide research institutes or centers, as well as suicide-prevention services staffed by volunteers. The technical and counseling literature has grown rapidly.

Some data are now fairly well established: for instance, that suicide rates increase with age; that they are higher for males, though suicide attempt rates are higher for females; that seasonal upswings occur in the late spring months; that men typically use guns and hanging, while women use pills and gas.[2] Sophisticated

---

[1]World suicide rates are about 13 per 100,000, or 520,000 per year in a world population of 4 billion. Conservative estimates of suicide incidence in the United States run from 25,000 to 50,000 per year. There are believed to be approximately ten times as many suicide attempts as completed suicides.

To save space and yet provide easy access to bibliographic information, later references to a work cited earlier in the notes are given in the following form: Smith, *Suicide* (*op. cit.* II/37), p. 86. This indicates that Smith's book is first cited in Chapter II, footnote 37, where the complete reference can be found. "i" indicates the Introduction.

[2]Accessible sources for "facts and figures" concerning suicide include Jacques Choron, *Suicide* (New York: Charles Scribner's Sons, 1972); J. Wallace McCulloch and Alistair E. Philip, *Suicidal Behaviour* (Oxford and New York: Pergamon Press, 1972); Edwin S. Shneidman's 1973 entry "Suicide" in the

data-gathering techniques are beginning to counteract distortion introduced by coroners' varying practices in reporting deaths and by the different working definitions of suicide employed by researchers. Nevertheless, the picture is still a sketchy one, and it is widely agreed that much suicide and suicidal behavior is unreported, unstudied, and misunderstood.

However, another element is entering this picture. Very recently, due primarily to technological developments within medical science which make it possible to extend the lives of the dying and the severely ill well beyond the point at which they would otherwise have died, there has been increasing attention to the issues of euthanasia and the so-called "right to die." Considerable popular and professional sentiment supports increased autonomy of the patient vis-à-vis the physician, and the patient's right to refuse treatment when it will only prolong suffering. But resistance to routine medical prolongation of life brings with it a problem: if life is not to be prolonged, *someone* must determine when life-prolonging measures are to be withheld or withdrawn, and at precisely what point medical care, other than palliative treatment of suffering, is to cease.

Traditionally, this responsibility has been delegated to the physician, with the tacit understanding that he or she will cease treatment or, possibly, perform euthanasia at whatever moment professional judgment deems appropriate. However, this is changing, both as patients seek increased autonomy and as physicians become increasingly aware of the legal and moral implications of such acts. It is not that physicians are only now refusing to withhold treatment or practice euthanasia; a great many have always done so and continue to do so, but both physician and patient are beginning to insist that such practices be a matter of choice on the part of the patient. But voluntary euthanasia is itself a species of suicide: the deliberate and knowing choice of death by the person whose death it is to be. Whether this choice is put into effect by the patient himself or by physicians or others who administer the means of death is peripheral; the central issue concerns the choosing of one's own death.

Between these two broad social concerns—on the one hand, increased interest in suicide and its prevention, and, on the other, an increased attention to self-determination in matters of medical care—the philosophical issues begin to arise. The scientific view has tended to regard suicide as an evil or illness, to be contained, reduced, or eradicated; the newer patients'-rights view tends to regard voluntary death as an option to be welcomed in preference to continued, hopeless suffering. This may appear to be a conflict of limited scope, since it seems confined to cases in which an individual is suffering from a terminal medical condition. But although the impetus for this problem may arise in these limited circumstances, the issues it raises are of much wider scope: is suicide, or the deliberate choice of death over continued life, ever morally permissible, or is suicide always wrong?

This is a moral question, one which lies at the base of any further medical, legal, or scientific treatment of suicide. It is a question which has been answered in vastly different ways at different times in the history of western culture. Stoic philosophy in classical Greece and Rome, for instance, held that suicide was to be permitted or even encouraged when undertaken for reasons such as ill health,

Encyclopaedia Brittanica; L. D. Hankoff and Bernice Einsidler, eds., *Suicide: Theory and Clinical Practice* (Littleton, Mass: PSG Publishing Co., Inc., 1979); Louis Wekstein, *Handbook of Suicidology: Principles, Problems, and Practice* (New York: Brunner/Mazel, 1979); and various World Health Organization reports.

poverty, slavery, or insanity, or to protect the welfare of one's family or nation. Some post-Enlightenment thinkers of the eighteenth century held an even more liberal view: suicide for them was among the fundamental rights of man, to be abridged in no way save perhaps where it might seriously damage the well-being of others. Romantics of the nineteenth century glorified suicide as the heroic choice of the truly free man, an act of final self-assertion against the claims of the world. But this is only one strand of our complex cultural legacy; in contrast to this liberal view, the Christian religious tradition has maintained an increasingly negative position towards suicide. Patristic thinkers of the early Catholic Church held that suicide was permissible only to protect one's virginity or to avoid forced apostasy; since Augustine, the Church has held and continues to hold that suicide, except when excused in cases of mental illness, is gravely morally wrong.

Of these two principal strands, it is the post-Augustinian, characteristically Christian attitude towards suicide which prevails in contemporary western culture, both religious and secular. However, the recent developments in patients'-rights advocacy tend to suggest the reawakening of a Stoic or eighteenth-century liberal view of suicide. The conflict between these two fundamental views has not yet extended very far, but it is clear that contemporary western culture is entering a period of renewed interest in the issue of suicide, and that substantial changes in popular moral attitudes, professional strategies, and legal treatments of suicide are already beginning to occur.

Suicide: The Scientific View

One modern view of suicide suggests that these earlier historical attitudes toward suicide—both those which are strongly permissive, like that of Stoicism or eighteenth-century liberalism, and those which are strongly intolerant, like that of medieval Catholicism—are naive, and based on an unsatisfactory conception of the nature of suicide and its causes. In particular, it cites the lack of methods and theoretical apparatus for any thorough scientific appraisal of suicide during these earlier eras, when it was assumed that suicide was the product of deliberate, voluntary choice. As deliberate and voluntary, it could be considered sinful or not, criminal or not. If suicide is, however, held to be involuntary and nondeliberative, the outcome of factors over which the individual has no control, then one cannot properly consider it a moral choice. If suicide is not the kind of thing which can be chosen or rejected by the victim, rational or moral arguments are unlikely to have any effect on his acts. Rather, suicide is something which *happens* to the victim, a symptom of an illness or derangement which he cannot himself control. Consequently, it is irrelevant and misleading to speak of the moral issues facing him, and he cannot be held responsible for his death. The only moral issue, if there is one, concerns the role to be taken by individual or institutional bystanders to the act.

The secondary moral issues, on this view, are easy to resolve. Since suicide is an evil or an injury that happens to the victim through no fault of his own, the proper role of the bystander—be it family, physician, custodial institution, or police—is to save the victim from the damage he cannot help inflicting upon himself, at least where this can be done without incurring other severe social costs. The moral problem involves weighing these costs against the obligation to prevent the suicide in cases, probably infrequent, where such conflict occurs.

This view that suicide, although it may appear to be a voluntary act, is caused by factors beyond the individual's control, is sometimes called the "determinist" view of suicide. It is prevalent among modern scientific approaches to suicide; in the popular consciousness, it coexists, however uneasily, with the more traditional, religiously-based attitudes which consider suicide sinful or wrong, and therefore a matter of choice. Our public policies, prevention services, and treatment programs for suicide are virtually all based on the deterministic view; this is true also of research programs and decriminalizing amendments to the law. We live in a culture which regards suicide as an occurrence, not as a choice.

There are three principal types of determinist view which have been prevalent in contemporary scientific theories of suicide: the so-called medical model, which views suicide as a consequence of mental illness; the "cry for help" interpretation, according to which suicide attempts are adaptive behavior; and Durkheim's sociogenic account. Much of the work done under these three views can be subsumed under developmental models of suicide, as for instance in the recent work of Ronald Maris, but it is these three views which have been of most crucial importance in the development of suicidology.

Suicide and Mental Illness

It is widely assumed, both in scientific thinking and in the popular view, that suicide is associated with mental illness and is the product of a sick or disordered mind. But it is by no means easy to reach a scientific consensus on the incidence and extent of mental illness in suicide, or to confirm the popular belief that all suicides are insane. Two major difficulties present themselves.

First, there are definitional difficulties: not only is it not widely agreed what sorts of deaths count as suicide, but different researchers and clinicians employ different criteria for mental illness. Some investigators, for instance, limit their conceptions of mental illness to include only psychoses, psychoneuroses, and clinical depression; other investigators broaden the concept of mental illness to include neuroses and psychopathic reactions to stressful situations. It is agreed by most researchers that comparatively few suicides are genuinely psychotic, but agreement ends quickly thereafter, and there is no uniformity of opinion on whether, for example, transitory reactive depression in strongly disadvantageous situations is to be classified as "illness" or as a "normal" response to circumstances which are in themselves very bad.

Second, severe problems are encountered in gathering the kind of data required to establish the presence or absence of mental illness at the time of a suicidal act. Mental illness is a condition of the individual's mind, but after suicide the individual is obviously no longer available for examination. To deal with this difficulty, a retroactive diagnostic method known as "psychological autopsy"[3] is

---

[3]The method of "psychological autopsy" was developed by Edwin Shneidman and his colleagues at the Los Angeles Suicide Prevention Center. Fuller descriptions are available in Choron, Suicide (op. cit. i/2), pp. 86–90; Edwin S. Shneidman, "Suicide, Lethality, and the Psychological Autopsy," International Psychiatry Clinics, 6 (1969), 225–80; Robert E. Litman et al., "The Psychological Autopsy of Equivocal Deaths," in Edwin Shneidman et al., eds., The Psychology of Suicide (New York: Science House, 1970), pp. 485–96; and Edwin Shneidman, "The Psychological Autopsy," in his Deaths of Man (Baltimore: Penguin Books, 1973), pp. 131–49.

employed to retrace an individual's psychiatric history: it uses physicians' records, diaries, suicide notes, interviews with survivors, and other clues to ascertain the mental condition of the individual at the time of his act, but of course its findings are difficult to confirm. Data are also available from individuals who have made serious attempts but survived, but it is not clear that such interviews provide an accurate picture: the experience of surviving a serious suicide attempt may radically alter one's psychiatric condition, so that the post-attempt examination does not indicate one's earlier state.[4] The same may be true for interviews of those whose attempts are fatal but not immediately so. Data from what might seem to be an obvious source— the many less serious suicide attempters who do survive—is not reliably informative, not just because of the impact of the attempt, but because suicide completers and suicide attempters form two quite different groups.

Despite the difficulties of evaluation and verification of the evidence, however, many recent studies assert that all, or almost all, cases of completed suicide are associated with some form of mental illness or abnormality. For instance, in a recent study of suicides in England, Brian Barraclough and his coworkers found that 93% of completed suicides in the sample population exhibited evidence of diagnosable mental illness.[5] In this study three psychiatrists independently examined medical records, personal records, and notes, and interviewed surviving family members; with quite high mutual confidence, they delivered diagnoses of depression in 70%, alcoholism in 15%, other mental disorders in 8%, and in only 7% of the cases found insufficient clinical information to make a diagnosis. In only one case of the hundred reviewed, they report, was there no evidence of illness at all.

On the other hand, a study of suicide attempters in Edinburgh, Scotland, suggests that, at most, 70% suffer from identifiable psychiatric illness,[6] which means that nearly a third of those who attempt suicide are "sane" or clinically well. There is clearly no consensus on the frequency of mental illness in suicide or suicide attempts; one author claims that there is "general agreement" that the percentage of "clearly mentally ill" among suicides is about 35%, but observes that estimates have ranged from as low as 20% to as high as 100%.[7]

Clinical methods involving direct examination of prior attempters or postmortem autopsy of completed suicides are not the only way of determining the incidence of mental illness. A quite different method is used in Charles Miles' "Conditions Predisposing to Suicide";[8] here, Miles reviews the causes of death

[4]Survival of a serious suicide attempt has also been observed to produce a remarkably quick end to depression, even depression of quite long standing. See Herbert Hendin, M.D., "Suicide," in "Psychiatric Emergencies," *A Comprehensive Textbook of Psychiatry,* ed. Alfred M. Freedman and Harold I. Kaplan (Baltimore: Williams and Wilkins, 1967), p. 1173.

[5]Brian M. Barraclough, J. Bunch, B. Nelson, and P. Sainsbury, "A Hundred Cases of Suicide: Clinical Aspects," *British Journal of Psychiatry,* 124 (1975), 355-73.

[6]McCulloch and Philip, *Suicidal Behavior (op. cit.* i/2); see Chapter 2, "Psychiatric Findings", pp. 30-43, and Chapter 3, "Psychological Findings", pp. 44-64, for a review of the literature on psychopathology and psychological characteristics in suicide. The study which finds over a third of self-poisoning cases in Edinburgh to have no psychiatric illness at all is Kessel's study of 1965, discussed by McCulloch and Philip on pp. 30ff.

[7]Calista V. Leonard, *Understanding and Preventing Suicide* (Springfield, Ill.: Charles C. Thomas, 1967), p. 273.

[8]Charles P. Miles, M.D., "Conditions Predisposing to Suicide: A Review," *The Journal of Nervous and Mental Disease,* 164, no. 4 (April 1977), 231-246.

among groups of patients afflicted with a variety of disease conditions, and finds that a majority of suicides are associated with just a few of these conditions. The conditions for which rates of suicide are extremely high include endogenous and reactive depression, schizophrenia, psychopathic personality, alcoholism, and drug addiction. Brain trauma, organic brain syndrome, epilepsy, Huntington's chorea, parkinsonism, and multiple sclerosis are also associated with appreciable numbers of suicides, and rates are high among patients on renal dialysis, homosexuals, and jailed prisoners. But computing the number of suicides which can be predicted from the incidence of suicide in a given disease cohort and the frequency of that disease in the population as a whole yields a total very nearly equal to the actual reported incidence of suicide. Miles thus infers that all or almost all of the suicides occurring in the United States are secondary to specific diseases, conditions, or personality disorders. Since these conditions, if not in themselves mental illnesses, are often associated with depression or severe mental stress, suicides which occur in connection with them may be described as sequelae or consequences of mental illness. Thus, Miles infers, virtually all suicide is of this sort.

Further complicating this picture is the fact that suicide attempts or completions are often taken as *de facto* evidence of mental illness: "anyone who'd try to kill himself must be crazy," one perhaps apocryphal psychiatrist is reputed to have said. Historically, this sort of view has been encouraged by the Catholic Church's traditional practice of not withholding burial and funeral rites from suicides who were insane and by the English common law's policy of not declaring *felo de se* an individual who killed himself "while the balance of his mind was disturbed": since the ecclesiastical and legal penalties for suicide or suicide attempts were severe and involved considerable hardships for survivors, the tendency of coroners, judges and priests was to assume that insanity was involved.

Is the person who attempts or commits suicide mentally ill? The scientific answer, clearly, is "not necessarily," but there agreement ends. In this situation, one might hope for more informative data. One might attempt to distinguish more clearly between what counts as "sanity" in a suicide act and what counts as "insanity."[9] Or one might even dispute, as do Szasz and Menninger, the underlying conception of mental illness altogether.[10] But to attempt to resolve the issue only in this way might, I think, distract us from the philosophical problems involved.

We must keep two things clearly in mind. First, the fact that in contemporary western culture a very large proportion of suicide is associated with mental illness should not lead us to assume that the connection is a necessary one. In numerous other western and nonwestern cultures the association of suicide with mental illness seems to be much less strong, and in some cultures is quite low. The Stoics considered suicide a mark of greatness of soul; it was the choice of the wise man, and only very rarely in this literature do we find accounts of suicide in circumstances in which mental illness is clearly present.[11] Nor does suicide appear to be

---

[9]We will undertake a somewhat similar project in Chapter 4.

[10]Thomas S. Szasz., M.D., "The Ethics of Suicide," *The Antioch Review*, 31 (Spring 1971), 7–17, reprinted in M. Pabst Battin and David J. Mayo, eds., *Suicide: The Philosophical Issues* (New York: St. Martin's Press, 1980), pp. 185–98; also London: Peter Owen, 1981; Karl A. Menninger, *Man Against Himself* (New York: Harcourt Brace, 1938).

[11]Fedden reviews the four major types of suicide in classical literature—the suicide for honor, the suicide committed to avoid the pains and ignominy attendant on disease and old age, the bereavement suicide,

strongly associated with mental illness in those cultures in which institutional suicide is widely practiced—pre-European India, Japan, and numerous other cultures. There, suicide is often the result of "normal" responses to standard social expectations.[12] Of course, our knowledge of the precise psychological conditions of suiciding individuals in these various cultures is limited, and we cannot know what other factors may have been at work in particular cases. But all of these cultures have ways of describing what we recognize as mental illness, and we see that many cases of suicide are described without reference to these characteristics at all. At the very least, the primitive evidence we do have can lead us to question the prevalent popular and scientific assumption that suicide is always and necessarily connected with mental illness. In fact, Miles, although holding his own study to show that mental illness is found in virtually all suicides in present American and European culture, recognizes this point:

> It is also possible that a percentage of suicides do not correlate with any specific illnesses or personality disorders. To put this thesis in other words, it is possible that a substantial fraction of "normal" individuals under similar stressful circumstances or in response to social dictates would commit suicide. This might be true in some cultures but not in others.[13]

Second, the mere correlation of suicide with mental illness or disturbance does not prove that it cannot be voluntary or even rational. It is true that suicide is often associated with imprisonment, for instance; but this does not establish that criminality or imprisonment "causes" suicide, but may be due to the fact that prison is such a terrible place. In other words, prison doesn't *make* a person commit suicide, though it might furnish a *reason* to do so. Similarly, a schizophrenic might decide that it is better to be dead than to remain schizophrenic; here, the mental illness has the same role in a rational deliberation about suicide as any physical illness which is judged to be similarly unbearable and incurable. The same could even apply to depression: a depressed person who thought, on the basis of the evidence, that he would always be depressed, might voluntarily and deliberately choose death over life; the suicide of Virginia Woolf may be a case in point.[14] Thus, to establish that suicide is strongly associated with mental illness, as seems to be the case in our culture, is not to establish that suicide is nonvoluntary, nondeliberative, or irrational, nor that suicide involves no moral issues. One may be ill, physically or mentally, and still be capable of real moral choice.

---

and the suicide to advance one's state, cause, party, or family—and remarks that "what is particularly interesting is that two types common to-day—suicide from economic change, and suicide from depression—are extremely rare, too rare in fact to form categories of their own" in classical literature. Henry Romilly Fedden, *Suicide: A Social and Historical Study* (London: Peter Davies, 1938), pp. 49-54.

[12] With the westernization of many of these cultures, traditional suicide practices have radically changed. See the various articles in Norman L. Farberow, ed., *Suicide in Different Cultures* (Baltimore: University Park Press, 1975).

[13] Miles, "Conditions Predisposing to Suicide," (*op. cit.* i/8), p. 241.

[14] See Chapter Four, footnote 38, on Virginia Woolf.

Suicide as a "Cry for Help."

This second medically-oriented view of suicide[15] interprets an attempt at suicide not primarily as an action intended to result in death, but as a strategy for altering one's immediate social environment: it is, so to speak, a "cry for help," an elaborate attention-getting device. It is almost always "dyadic" in character, having reference to some other person who is central in the suicide attempter's life, and in this odd way it is often a kind of communication or interpersonal action. Sometimes it is fatal; nine times out of ten it is not, and it is often remarkably effective in mobilizing family or community resources to assist in the circumstances which require help. The suicide attempt is therefore a symptom not so much of underlying mental disease, but of the individual's basically healthy attempt to change the painful circumstances in which he finds himself. It is a final, last-ditch attempt to alter one's world.

If survived, the suicide attempt is often quite a successful maneuver, at least temporarily. Family, friends, and others often respond to suicide attempts with much greater concern than to other attempts by the individual to change his world, and in some cases the attempt may bring about enough change so that it is not repeated. Thus the suicide attempt is often a highly adaptive strategy. But it is a risky one: the means are potentially lethal, and the cry for help will rarely be heard unless the means are seriously used.

That a suicide attempt is a kind of calculated risk to improve his life is rarely consciously understood by the individual; most often, he believes he wishes to end his life. But the clinician detects in that intention a thoroughgoing ambivalence: although the individual believes he really wants to die, in fact he wants to live, but change his life.[16] It is this characteristic of the "cry for help" which provides a direct rationale for suicide-prevention activities. Since the prospective suicide doesn't really want to die, any bystander—whether physician, therapist, suicide-prevention worker, police officer, or family member—is justified in interfering with a suicide attempt: Suicide-prevention activities honor what the individual *really* wants, not what he at the moment is engaged in trying to get. As Edwin Shneidman says:

> *Individuals who are intent on killing themselves still wish very much to be rescued or to have their deaths prevented. Suicide prevention consists essentially in recognizing that the potential victim is "in balance" between his wishes to live and his wishes to die, then throwing one's efforts on the side of life.*[17]

[15]The term "cry for help," according to its coiners Norman L. Farberow and Edwin S. Shneidman, "is meant to convey our feelings (from our work with suicidally disturbed persons) about the messages of suffering and anguish and the pleas for response that are expressed by and contained within suicidal behaviors." See p. xi of the Preface to Farberow and Shneidman, eds., *The Cry for Help* (New York: McGraw-Hill, 1961, 1965).

[16]Sylvia Plath's suicide, last in a long series of attempts, is widely regarded as an example of "cry for help" suicide which proved fatal. See A. Alvarez, *The Savage God: A Study of Suicide* (London: Weidenfeld and Nicholson, 1971; New York: Random House, 1972; also see VI/23), especially Part One: "Prologue: Sylvia Plath." Also see Plath's novel *The Bell Jar* (New York: Harper & Row, 1971). Mary Savage's *Addicted to Suicide: A woman struggling to live* (Santa Barbara: Capra Press, 1975), provides another autobiographical account of ambivalence in suicide.

[17]Edwin S. Shneidman, "Preventing Suicide," *American Journal of Nursing*, 65, No. 5: 10–15 (1965), p. 10.

Some theorists, most following the lead of Erwin Stengel, hold that earnestness of intent to die is highly correlated with the lethality of the attempt at suicide, so that suicide attempters and those who actually do kill themselves form two radically different motivational groups. Those who are most ambivalent about death choose means which are least lethal, and those who are least ambivalent are most likely to die.

Shneidman's canon instructs suicide-prevention workers first to recognize the ambivalence of any prospective suicide and then to "throw one's efforts on the side of life." But it is at this point that philosophic issues arise: if the underlying rationale of suicide-prevention is to honor the *real* wishes of the individual, then when the individual is genuinely ambivalent, some further justification is needed for the onlooker's partisanship for one course of action rather than the other. If the surface ambivalence of the prospective suicide victim only poorly conceals a deep, genuine, eager desire to live, then—on the announced criterion of honoring the individual's real wishes—active suicide prevention would be indicated. But there are cases, too, in which the real inclination of the individual is to die. Both St. Paul and John Donne, for instance, speak of their deep desire to die, both, presumably, for religious reasons. A large proportion of the elderly, it is sometimes said, no longer wish to live; and a sensitive questioner of nursing home residents will discover that many consciously and actively wish for death. In cases where the real desire of the individual is to die, apparent ambivalence may be merely the product of socially or religiously imposed obstacles; by the justification advanced above, suicide workers should here be committed to facilitating suicide by removing these obstacles, rather than preventing the death.

Of course, this account is somewhat oversimplified; in most actual cases, it may not be at all clear either to the individual or to bystanders whether that ambivalence is weighted towards life or death, or not weighted at all. This suggests that the appropriate initial stance of bystanders is neither prevention nor facilitation *per se*, but "counseling," that is, any activity which is designed to reduce an individual's ambivalence by helping him to discover what his real wishes are. This stance, however, may prove extremely uncomfortable for many counseling personnel, since counseling may reveal that an ambivalent individual's real wishes, after all, are for death. Thomas Szasz remarks:

> *I consider counseling, persuasion, psychotherapy, or any other voluntary measure, especially for persons troubled by their own suicidal inclinations and seeking such help, unobjectionable, and indeed generally desirable, interventions. However, physicians and psychiatrists are not usually satisfied with limiting their help to such measures —and with good reason: from such assistance the individual may gain not only the desire to live, but also the strength to die.*[18]

The psychotherapist may also view the suicide of a patient as a failure on his own part, a case in which he was unable to help the patient adequately, or cure him of his abnormal desires. In fact, practicing therapists themselves exhibit a very wide range of attitudes about what is perhaps the most difficult issue in psychotherapy: some hold that they must support whatever choice the client genuinely makes, whereas

[18]Szasz, "The Ethics of Suicide," (*op. cit.* i/10), p. 10.

others insist that suicide, because it precludes further treatment, is the one thing they cannot allow to occur.[19]

A therapist who is unable to support a client's decision to die may nevertheless express relief if the death does occur, and admit that the client might have been spared considerable misery had the death occurred earlier. Sensitive therapists are well aware that insistence on continued life for a deeply troubled and psychologically impaired patient may mean insistence on continued, irremediable, and unremitting suffering for that person, when there is very little chance of his achieving anything approaching normal life-satisfaction. Most, however, would insist that the cases in which the prognosis is so dim are very, very few.

Suicide as Sociogenic

The view that suicide is a sequela of mental illness and the view that it is a cry for help treat suicide as largely the product of internal psychological forces. An alternative view, developed originally by Emil Durkheim in his landmark work *Suicide* (1897),[20] sees suicide as sociogenic, the product of social forces beyond the individual's control.

These social forces, Durkheim claims, vary with the type of social organization characteristic of a given group. In some societies, the individual is very highly integrated into the society, so that he perceives himself and is perceived by others not so much as a discrete unit, but only as a part of the whole; his life is rigorously governed by the customs of the society. In such societies, suicide occurs primarily because it is required by the society in certain circumstances. This is known as ''altruistic'' suicide; examples include institutional suicides such as India's *suttee* or self-immolation by widows, self-regicide after a fixed term of office as practiced by kings of certain African groups, and the Japanese *seppuku* or suicide of honor by disemboweling. It also includes suicides among highly structured subgroups such as military societies. For instance, the nineteenth-century military officer's suicide, *de rigeur* when unable to pay one's gambling debts, is not primarily the product of personal anguish or guilt, but of rigid social expectations. On the other hand, in some societies certain individual members are very loosely integrated into the society, so that they do not respond to social regulations and expectations: suicides by these individuals are ''egoistic.'' Finally, society may take a form in which the individual is neither under- nor overintegrated, but the society itself fails to provide adequate regulation of its members.[21] This last society produces what is termed ''anomic'' suicide, and it is, Durkheim believed, characteristic of modern industrial

---

[19]See Solomon Diamond, ''The Nondirective Handling of Suicidal Behavior,'' in Farberow and Shneidman, *The Cry for Help* (*op. cit.* i/15) pp. 281–289, for a personal discussion of the problems in a client-centered, nondirective approach to persons contemplating suicide.

[20]Emile Durkheim, *Suicide: A Study in Sociology*, trans. John A. Spaulding and George Simpson (New York: The Free Press, 1951).

[21]Kathryn K. Johnson, in ''Durkheim Revisited: 'Why Do Women Kill Themselves?' '' *Suicide and Life-Threatening Behavior*, 9, no. 3 (Fall, 1979), points out that Durkheim also mentions fatalistic suicide, a fourth type which results not from voluntary identification with society, as in altruistic suicide, but from ''excessive regulation, that of persons with futures pitilessly blocked and passions violently choked by oppressive discipline.'' (Durkheim, *Suicide* (*op. cit.* i/20), p. 276). However, Durkheim does not elaborate upon this fourth type, and most discussions of his work assume that he posits only three.

society. Thus, the types of suicide and rates of occurrence, Durkheim claims, vary as a function of the social organization of a given society:

It is not mere metaphor to say of each human society that it has a greater or lesser aptitude for suicide; the expression is based on the nature of things. Each social group really has a collective inclination for the act, quite its own, and the source of all individual inclination, rather than their result.[22]

For Durkheim, as for proponents of the medical model of suicide, no moral discredit attaches to the individual who actually commits suicide; it is, in a broad sense, involuntary, since the individual is merely responding to social forces over which he has no control. For Durkheim, however, it is fruitless to attempt to interfere with individual suicides; while success may be achieved occasionally it will be on a piecemeal basis, and the relentless social forces at work will continue to produce other suicides elsewhere. Suicide is, in a sense, the price of civilization itself.

However, according to the Durkheimian account, different forms of social organization within civilization as a whole do have different suicide rates. Thus, altering the form of social organization for a given population—if that is possible—will change its suicide rate, as well as the character of the suicides that do occur. Suicide prevention of any significant sort can be accomplished only by altering the organization of society in a way which tends to decrease the rates, and by preventing kinds of social change which are associated with increased rates. But the implications of this theory in practice may not be entirely desirable. For instance, Durkheim points out, religion has in the past operated as a considerable barrier to suicide—but only at the cost of considerable barriers to human freedom. Divorce, he observes, produces an increase in the suicide rate; but there are costs attached to making marriage indissoluble, and "what makes the problem especially disturbing and lends it an almost dramatic interest is that the suicides of husbands cannot be diminished in this way without increasing those of wives."[23] The kind of philosophical problem Durkheim's theory generates is clear: if suicide rates can be genuinely and significantly decreased only by large-scale changes in the institutions and organization of society, what changes, so to speak, are worth the gain? In contemporary industrial society, suicide rates decrease sharply in time of war; yet war itself is hardly a desirable state, and clearly not a desirable alternative to continuingly high rates of suicide. Conversely, in all societies rising educational levels are associated with increases in the suicide rate; but one can hardly argue against greater educational opportunity on the grounds that it will cause a larger proportion of the populace to kill themselves.

All three of the major scientific views of suicide have been effective in treatment and prevention. The medical model, which views suicide as a symptom or sequela of mental illness, has been extremely effective in applying standard methods of medical and psychiatric treatment to the prevention of suicide. A large proportion of suicides, for instance, suffer from recurrent clinical depression, a

---

[22]Durkheim, *Suicide* (*op. cit.* i/20), p. 299.

[23]*Ibid.*, p. 384. Durkheim thinks the solution, if there is one, lies in increased social equality of the sexes.

condition now readily recognizable and increasingly treatable, both by drug therapy and electroshock.[24] The "cry for help" model has marshaled an impressive array of support services for those who are socially isolated or suffer other psycho-social maladjustments, and has led to the establishment of numerous public suicide-prevention services. The Durkheimian model of suicide as sociogenic has had less evident public impact, perhaps because its demands—to change society—are much more difficult, but it has stimulated considerable research into suicide in different social, national, and ethnic groups;[25] particularly extensive now is research into the special characteristics of suicide among American Indians and blacks. But to say that these three views have had impressive results in the treatment and prevention of suicide is not to say that the assumptions which underlie them are sound, or that treatment and prevention are appropriate goals; that is the larger topic of this book.

The Treatment of Suicide: Prediction and Prevention

The treatment of suicide and suicide attempts usually, though not always, involves several stages; though differing workers in the field have advocated different postures in response to suicide, those outlined here are perhaps most widely followed in suicide-prevention organizations in the U.S. and England today.

Recognition

There are two central stategies for recognizing or identifying the prospective suicide *before* the attempt.[26] The first and more familiar emphasizes sensitivity to a variety of premonitory or prodromal symptoms which indicate the imminence of a suicidal episode. These include advance verbal and behavioral clues given by the prospective suicide, including both direct warnings like "I feel like killing myself," and indirect indications like "I probably won't be seeing you any more" or "well, you'll be better off without me anyway." They also include both direct and indirect behavioral clues, such as purchasing pills or a gun, making a will or setting one's affairs in order, and giving away treasured possessions to friends, family, or a charitable organization. According to some researchers, verbal or behavioral indications of oncoming suicide are given in as many as 8 out of 10 cases,[27] though most of these warnings go unrecognized by family, friends, or other associates. Even

---

[24]Peter Sainsbury, "Suicide: Opinions and Facts," *Proceedings of the Royal Society of Medicine*, 66, no. 6 (June 1973), 579-87.

[25]Works strongly influenced by Durkheim include, for instance, Herbert Hendin's *Suicide and Scandinavia* (New York: Grune & Stratton, 1964), in which Hendin accounts for the startling differences in suicide rates in neighboring Scandinavian countries on the basis of differing social organization, and William C. Swanson and Warren Breed, "Black Suicide in New Orleans," in Edwin S. Shneidman, *Suicidology: Contemporary Developments* (New York: Grune & Stratton, 1976), pp. 103-28, in which rates of black suicide are interpreted in terms of social integration among blacks in both black and white society.

[26]For a substantial collection of papers on various aspects of the recognition of potential suicides, see Aaron T. Beck, Harvey L. P. Resnik, and Dan J. Lettieri, eds., *The Prediction of Suicide* (Bowie, Maryland: The Charles Press Publishers, Inc., 1974).

[27]Shneidman, "Suicide" (*op. cit.* i/2), p. 384C.

direct verbal threats like "I'm going to kill myself, you'll see," are often dismissed as mere talk, and recognized as warnings only after it is too late to take preventive action.

A second strategy for recognition focuses on social, psychological, and psychiatric variables associated with suicide.[28] Variables which identify potential suicides include previous suicide attempts, hopelessness and depression, drug use, alcoholism, negative interaction with important others, sexual deviance, early trauma or loss, change of socioeconomic status (especially downward), conceiving of death as escape from pain, and older age and male sex. Suicide attempters also display high levels of depression, hopelessness, and dissatisfaction, but these are more concerned with sexual and marital problems, involve more anger, and are more likely to be triggered by an acute crisis. Although static profiles are perhaps less useful than typical life-histories, it is possible to describe the characteristics of the most likely suicide: he is male, white, middle-aged or older, separated, divorced or widowed, unemployed or retired, probably Protestant and not active in church; he has probably failed at a major life transition (e.g. from work to retirement) and is emotionally stagnating; he may live alone, is often in poor health, and is probably depressed and alcoholic. He has a gun or other lethal means available. In contrast, the typical suicide attempter is a young woman in her twenties or early thirties; she is likely to come from a family with multiple problems, and to have problems with her children. She is likely to make more than one suicide attempt, but comparatively unlikely to actually kill herself. Once profiles or life-histories are constructed to identify individuals at high risk for suicide, suicide prevention efforts can then be directed towards those individuals who most nearly match them.

A major problem presented by these advance-recognition techniques, however, is that of "false positives." Developed statistically by A. Rosen in a 1954 paper,[29] the problem is this: Suppose we have a test that will accurately identify 75% of the suicidal persons in a given population (for example, in a psychiatric hospital), and that effective suicide precautions might then be introduced. If the test is 75% accurate, it will correctly identify 3 out of 4 persons in the population who would commit suicide—say, in Rosen's figures, 30 out of 40 in a population of 12,000—and suicide precautions then introduced might help to save these lives. However, not only will the test fail to identify 1 in 4, or 10 persons who will commit suicide, but since it is only 75% accurate it will also incorrectly label one quarter of those persons who would *not* commit suicide as suicide risks. In Rosen's population of 12,000, this is 2,990 people[30] who may then be inappropriately subjected to

[28]McCulloch and Philip, *Suicidal Behavior* (*op. cit.* i/2). Also see many of the papers in Beck, Resnik, and Lettieri, *The Prediction of Suicide* (*op. cit.* i/26).

[29]A. Rosen, "Detection of Suicidal Patients: An Example of Some Limitations in the Prediction of Infrequent Events," *Journal of Consulting Psychology*, 18 (1954), 397–403.

[30]These figures are taken from David Lester's reconstruction of Rosen's argument, in his "Demographic versus Clinical Prediction of Suicidal Behaviors: A Look at Some Issues," in Beck, Resnik, and Lettieri, eds., *The Prediction of Suicide* (*op. cit.* i/26), pp. 71–84. In the same volume, George Murphy also discusses Rosen's problem, and considers some of the issues in false-positive prediction; see his "The Clinical Identification of Suicidal Risk," pp. 109–18. Also see the classic paper by Joseph M. Livermore, Carl P. Malmquist, and Paul E. Meehl, "On the Justifications for Civil Commitment," *University of Pennsylvania Law Review*, 117 (November 1968), 75–96, and Rolf E. Sartorius, "Paternalistic Grounds for Involuntary Civil Commitment: A Utilitarian Perspective," in B. A. Brody and H. Tristram Engelhardt, Jr., eds., *Mental Illness: Law and Public Policy* (The Hague: D. Reidel, 1980), pp. 137–45.

suicide precautions. The best predictor of completed suicide, for instance, is previous suicide attempts; the rate here is 140 times that of the general population. But 85–90% of previous attempters do *not* kill themselves, and restrictive precautions would be inappropriate. Clearly, the less accurate the predictor or the test employed, the greater the dimensions of the "false positives" problem.

Prevention

Suicide prevention, closely tied to the recognition of potential suicides, focuses on relieving the psychological and situational conditions in association with which suicide is most likely to occur. For instance, the "befriending" policy used by some groups is a type of suicide prevention technique, since its objective is to overcome the loneliness and social isolation so strongly associated with suicide. Medical treatment of depression often serves as a form of suicide prevention, since depression, too, is very strongly associated with suicide. In addition to direct medical treatment of the depressed person, suicide prevention may also involve long-term therapy with other family members, both in order to discover and treat the underlying emotional and situational disturbances with which the individual and his family live, and to alert the family to the symptoms and prognoses of depression. Since most suicide associated with depression occurs as the individual is beginning to recover from that depression, it is particularly important in suicide-prevention work to exercise special caution at this time.

If suicide prevention is the effort to alter those psychological and situational factors which are strongly associated with suicide, it is an enormous and extremely complex business: as Edwin Shneidman puts it, it is "almost tantamount to preventing human unhappiness."[31] But one may not always view large-scale suicide prevention efforts in a benign way. Jean Baechler, the French writer who argues that suicide represents a positive act to resolve an existential problem, speaks of the "inquisitorial passion" with which such policies can be pursued. He describes such efforts in this way (emphases his):

> To eliminate suicide, an official [*French ministry of public health*] commission proposes a systematic hunt for suicide candidates through obligatory examination of the mental health of students in schools and of all workers under twenty-five; a strict surveillance of young workers who work in isolation, of first-year students, and of unattached young people; an increased surveillance during exams; the creation of social hygiene centers in each arrondissement of Paris, in each large city, on university campuses, and in certain large lycees; a sustained attention to the problem on the part of teachers; a close surveillance during the years after suicide has been attempted in order to avoid a repeat; incarcerating the most serious cases in special hospitals; the creation of professional chairs of social hygiene; the nomination in each university medical center of a teacher responsible for collecting information and coordinating the means of prevention. My hair is still standing on end from all this.[32]

Perhaps the French ministry's proposal is extreme, and Baechler's reaction severe. But it does point out that suicide prevention is often something more than the mere

[31]Shneidman, "Suicide," (*op. cit.* i/2), p. 385.

[32]Jean Baechler, *Suicides,* (New York: Basic Books, 1979), trans. Barry Cooper, p. 35. Baechler's reference is to a publication of the French ministry of public health and social security, dated January 1971.

"prevention of human unhappiness," and that its costs as well as its accomplishments may be worth consideration.

Intervention

Perhaps established in the public mind under the rubric "suicide prevention," suicide intervention includes those procedures designed to interrupt a suicide attempt which is immediately imminent or already underway. Now often designated by the term "crisis intervention," the most familiar practical form of suicide-intervention activity is the "help-line" telephone service.[33] Help-line crisis intervention is usually offered on a 24-hour basis; the individual who feels himself to be at risk of suicide can telephone, usually anonymously, to a crisis center for first-aid counseling help. The objective of most such services is to help the caller overcome his immediate suicidal impulses, which are typically of relatively short duration, and to encourage him to seek counseling help on a continuing basis. The prototype of U.S. suicide-intervention services is the Los Angeles Suicide Prevention Center, established in 1955 by Edwin Shneidman and Norman Farberow. There are now crisis-intervention services dedicated to suicide prevention in most cities in the United States. In England, suicide-intervention work has been undertaken primarily by the Samaritans, founded in 1953 by Chad Varah; there are suicide-prevention and crisis-intervention services in many other countries.

There has been considerable dispute in the recent literature about whether such telephone help-line services do in fact *prevent* suicide; several studies suggest that most help-line callers are not genuinely suicidal, and that persons who do in fact commit suicide rarely call help-lines. In the U.S. and England, studies have shown that the existence of a suicide-prevention center in a given city when compared with similar cities not having such services, has no statistically significant effect on its suicide rate, though there is some conflicting data.[34] Whether such centers are actually effective in reducing the rates of completed suicide or not, what is *not* disputed is that such centers are often extremely effective in bringing first-aid psychiatric care to persons who tend to announce their difficulties by suicide threats, whether genuine or theatrical. But suicide intervention services vary quite widely in the services they offer and in their practices regarding direct interference in a suicide attempt; it is here that the philosophical issues begin to arise. At one end of the range, a service may simply provide a nondirective "listening ear"; at the other, a service may summon rescue or police services in cases where the likelihood that a potentially fatal attempt will actually be initiated is quite high, with or without the consent of the caller.

The range of practices is illustrated in a study by R. K. McGee, who described

---

[33] Two brief accounts of suicide-prevention services are contained in Hankoff and Einsidler, eds., *Suicide: Theory and Clinical Practice* (*op. cit.* i/2): Albert R. Roberts, "Organization of Suicide Prevention Agencies," pp. 391–99, and Irene Trowell, "Telephone Services," pp. 401–9. See also R. K. McGee, D. Berg, G. W. Brockopp, et. al., "The Delivery of Suicide and Crisis Intervention Services," in H. L. P. Resnik and B. C. Hathorne, eds., *Suicide Prevention in the 70's* (Bethesda, Md.: National Institute of Mental Health, 1973).

[34] David Lester, "Effect of Suicide Prevention Centers on Suicide Rates in the United States," *Health Service Reports,* 89, no. 1 (Jan–Feb. 1974), 37–39.

the following hypothetical case to the coordinator of various suicide prevention centers, and asked how help-line volunteers should respond. The case:

> A call is received from an elderly man who states that he is a burden to his family and wants to explain why he must kill himself. He intends to carry out his plan in two days. It is 2:30 p.m.

The responses, from the various center coordinators:

> "Ask what method he plans to use for his suicide. Contact the relatives as soon as the call is finished."
> "Call back early in the evening and see how he is feeling then. Notify relatives."
> "Encourage man that life is worthwhile."
> "Try to determine how open he is to the suggestion of seeking professional help. Contact relatives."
> "Depend primarily on significant others. Suggest activities for retired people."
> "If he is over 70 take him to a nursing home."[35]

Coercively interventionist practices seem on the whole to be diminishing, perhaps because of the finding that most help-line callers are not in fact likely to kill themselves; most crisis intervention centers now see themselves as offering help on a voluntary basis, guaranteeing not only anonymity but freedom from coercive rescue attempts—except, of course, where they are directly or indirectly requested by the caller.

Postvention

Postvention, a term introduced by Shneidman in 1971, refers to a variety of counseling and therapy services offered to the person who has attempted suicide but survived, or to the survivors of a person who has actually killed himself. In cases in which the individual has attempted suicide but survived, postvention is generally viewed both as repair of the psychological injury sustained in the attempt and as prophylaxis against a future attempt. In cases in which the individual did kill himself, postvention involves grief therapy for the survivors—the widowed spouse, the parents, the children—with particular attention to the stigma and sense of failure produced by association with death in a socially disapproved fashion. Postvention therapy among survivors is also prophylactic in intent, since after the suicide of a particular individual, the likelihood of suicide among immediate survivors is statistically increased, especially during the first year.

In all areas of the treatment of suicide—recognition, prevention, intervention, and prophylactic postvention among survivors—the underlying assumption is quite clear: it is to prevent the occurrence of suicide. Whether and when such an aim is morally legitimate, however, depends on the issues to be discussed in this book. What we must do, then, is to examine the underlying philosophical issues, before we can get a clear view of our current practices in the treatment and prevention of

[35]Richard K. McGee, *Crisis Intervention in the Community* (Baltimore: University Park Press, 1974).

suicide. These practices may indeed be successful; but that does not mean that they are right.

Suicide: The Legal Dilemma

One might turn to the law for some resolution of the immediate moral issues generated by the varying views of suicide, but here one finds that the legal issues concerning suicide are almost equally unresolved. Clearly, the legal status of suicide has undergone considerable transition, but what its future status will be is by no means evident.

Suicide was treated as a felony offense in early English and continental law; it was subject to harsh civil as well as religious penalties, including forfeiture of the decedent's property to the crown, public desecration of his body, and refusal of burial in consecrated ground. France relaxed its sanctions against suicide at the time of the 1789 revolution; suicide remained a felony in England until 1961, and has been a criminal offense in many states of the United States.[36] Generally, however, the trend in contemporary Europe and America has been to drop or not exercise criminal sanctions against suicide; this results largely from increasing acceptance of the deterministic models of suicide, according to which suicide is an involuntary symptom of illness and/or psychosocial pressures, and therefore is a candidate for treatment rather than punishment. To assist the suicide of someone else, however, remains a criminal offense in almost all areas, and in some is an offense of considerable gravity.[37]

American law retains an extremely strong precedent against the legal permissibility of suicide. A large number of court decisions at all levels have referred to "the State interest in preventing suicide" (e.g., the recent *Superintendent of Belchertown* v. *Saikewicz*[38]); this interest, suggested in *In re Quinlan,* is rooted in the state's interest in the preservation of life.[39] In *Maycock* v. *Martin,* a Connecticut court refused to grant release from a state hospital to a man with explicit intentions of suicide but without (other) evidence of mental illness.[40] In some jurisdictions, for example the District of Columbia, a person who has attempted to end his life may be involuntarily confined for psychiatric treatment for a period of up to forty-

---

[36]See Helen Silving, "Suicide and Law," pp. 79–95 in Edwin S. Shneidman and Norman L. Farberow, eds., *Clues to Suicide* (New York: McGraw-Hill, 1957); Norman St. John-Stevas, *Life, Death and the Law: Law and Christian Morals in England and the United States* (Bloomington: Indiana University Press, 1961), especially Chapter Six; Glanville Williams, *The Sanctity of Life and the Criminal Law* (New York: Alfred A. Knopf, 1974), especially Chapter Seven; "The Prohibition of Suicide."

[37]For surveys of the legal status of suicide and assisted suicide in various U.S. jurisdictions, see Donald M. Wright, "Criminal Aspects of Suicide in the United States," *North Carolina Central Law Journal,* 7, no. 1 (Fall 1975), 156–63; R. E. Schulman, "Suicide and Suicide Prevention: A Legal Analysis," *American Bar Association Journal,* 54 (Sept. 1968), 855–62; and Leslie Pickering Francis, "Assisting Suicide: A Problem for the Criminal Law," in Battin and Mayo, eds., *Suicide: The Philosophical Issues* (*op. cit.* i/10), pp. 254–66.

[38]Mass., 370 N.E.2d 417 (1977), at 425–26.

[39]355 A.2d 647.

[40]157 Conn. 56, 245 A.2d 574, cert. denied, 393 U.S. 1111 (1969).

eight hours without a court order, seven days with an order, and indefinitely after commitment proceedings, if he "is mentally ill, and because of that illness, is likely to injure himself or others . . ."[41] In no state is it a legal wrong to prevent a suicide.[42]

But it is not clear that the law's posture towards suicide is uniformly paternalistic. Contrasting with announced state interests in preserving life are assertions of the individual's constitutionally guaranteed right to privacy of his person and body.[43] In *Schloendorff* v. *Society of New York Hospital,* a 1914 case upholding a patient's refusal of medical treatment on religious grounds even though it was certain he would die, the court stated:

> *Every human being of adult years and sound mind has a right to determine what shall be done with his own body.*[44]

This principle was restated in the 1960 case *Natanson* v. *Kline:*

> *Anglo-American law starts with the premise of thorough-going self-determination. It follows that each man is considered to be master of his own body, and he may, if he be of sound mind, expressly prohibit the performance of life-saving surgery, or other medical treatment.*[45]

In the 1965 contraceptives case *Griswold* v. *Connecticut,*[46] and again in the 1973 abortion case *Roe* v. *Wade,*[47] the U.S. Supreme Court asserted what it calls the "penumbral" constitutional right of privacy, a right not explicitly mentioned in the Bill of Rights, but nevertheless implied by it. In the language of *Griswold,* the unwritten constitutional right of privacy is found to exist in the "penumbra" of specific guarantees of the Bill of Rights "formed by emanations from those guarantees that help give them life and substance";[48] it is this right which is reflected, though not asserted, in the refusal-of-lifesaving-treatment cases cited above. In *Roe* v. *Wade,* the Court described this right as "a right of personal privacy, or a guarantee of certain areas or zones of privacy";[49] this has been interpreted both as

[41]The District of Columbia Hospitalization of the Mentally Ill Act, quoted by Gerald Dworkin in "Paternalism," *The Monist* 56, No. 1 (June 1972), pp. 64–84; reprinted in Samuel Gorovitz et al., eds., *Moral Problems in Medicine* (Englewood Cliffs, N.J.: Prentice-Hall, 1976), pp. 185–200, and Richard Wasserstrom, ed., *Morality and the Law* (Belmont, Calif.: Wadsworth, 1971), pp. 10–26.

[42]Leslie Francis, personal communication.

[43]This interpretation is based on the account by Alan Sullivan, "The Constitutional Right to Suicide," in Battin and Mayo, eds., *Suicide: the Philosophical Issues, (op. cit.* i/10), pp. 229–53.

[44]211 N.Y. 125, 105 N.E. 92 (1914), overruled on other grounds.

[45]185 Kan. 393, 350 P.2d 1093; rehearing denied 187 Kan. 186, 354 P.2d 670 (1960).

[46]381 U.S. 479, 85 S.Ct. 1678, 14 L.Ed.2d 510 (1965).

[47]410 U.S. 113, 93 S.Ct. 705, L.Ed.24 147 (1973).

[48]381 U.S. at 484, 85 S.Ct. at 1681, 14L.Ed.2d at 514.

[49]410 U.S. at 152, 93 S.Ct. at 726.

the right to privacy of the person (for example, in information-disclosure cases) and as the right to privacy of the body (in *Roe* v. *Wade* itself). Although the Court stopped short of enunciating a broad right to do with one's body or person as one pleases,[50] *Roe* has frequently been cited as precedent for refusal of medical treatment even in circumstances where death will certainly result, at least when there are no minor dependents, and "no clear and present danger to public health, welfare or morals."[51] Legal support for choices of nontreatment resulting in death has been enunciated in such cases as *Perlmutter, Saikewicz,* and *Quinlan,* and numerous states have enacted "right to die" laws.[52] Because these decisions appear to recognize the right of a person to choose to allow himself to die, some observers believe that these cases will supply the basis for a future major court decision on suicide.[53]

The outcome of this projected future case, whenever it may be brought and whatever the particular circumstances with which it deals, can by no means be predicted. Such a case might try to draw a distinction, for instance, between suicide as the product of mental illness or emotional disturbance, and euthanatic rational suicide in the case of painful terminal illness, though many persons who are in a medical sense "mentally ill" or "disturbed" are nevertheless legally competent. It might take into account cases where death is not imminent or inevitable, and where mere refusal of continued medical treatment will not produce death, but where continued life is nevertheless expected to be painful or subject to severe physical or other limitations. Such a case will surely also need to consider the possibilities of abuse, manipulation, and self-interest on the part of observers, advisors, or assisters to a suicide. Or it might even take into account the growing philosophical conviction, argued by such authors as Robert Kastenbaum and Mary Rose Barrington, that suicide, because it allows one to control the time, place, style, cause, purpose, and painfulness of death, will or should become the preferred way of death.[54]

But this decision has not yet been considered or rendered. In lieu of an actual court case, attorney Alan Sullivan has constructed a hypothetical situation which presents some of the features such a case might involve.

A man whom we shall call Harris is a chronically ill patient living at a Veterans Administration hospital. He is 54 years old with no family, and no one depends upon him for financial support. His illness—it does not matter for our purposes whether it is cancer or emphysema or tuberculosis—will probably kill him before old age, but is not

---

[50]In fact, the Court appears to have rather sharply limited the right to do with one's body or person as one pleases in certain other areas: in the 1976 case *Doe v. Commonwealth's Attorney* (90 S.Ct. 1489 (1976)), it upheld a Virginia statute restricting private homosexual activity between consenting adults. See also Kent Greenawalt, "The Burger Court and Claims of Privacy," *The Hastings Center Report* 6, no. 4 (August 1976), pp. 19–20, and Note, "Informed Consent and the Dying Patient," *Yale Law Journal* 83 (1974), 1644, footnote 75.

[51]In re Yetter, 62 Pa. D & C.2d 619 (C.P., Northampton County Ct. 1973).

[52]A summary of various state right-to-die laws can be found in the annual *Manual* published by The Society for the Right to Die, 250 West 57th Street, New York, N.Y. 10019.

[53]Alan Sullivan, "The Constitutional Right to Suicide," (op. cit. i/43).

[54]Robert Kastenbaum, "Suicide as the Preferred Way of Death," in Shneidman, ed., *Suicidology: Contemporary Developments (op. cit.* i/25), pp. 425–41; Mary Rose Barrington, "Apologia for Suicide," in *Euthanasia and the Right to Death,* ed. A. B. Downing (London: Peter Owen, 1969), pp. 152–70, reprinted in Battin and Mayo, eds., *Suicide; The Philosophical Issues (op. cit.* i/10), pp. 90–103.

imminently terminal. In the meantime Harris's illness prevents him from earning a living and caring for himself. Harris is mentally competent in the usual sense of the term. But because his illness has deprived him of the capacity to do what he considers worthwhile, Harris wants to end his life. He does not want to die in pain or alone, but would prefer to end his life at the hospital where the only people he knows would care for his remains. He does not ask that anyone administer the means of death to him, but only that those around him refrain from preventing him from doing so himself. However, the Veterans Administration personnel who care for him have already intervened in one attempt at suicide, and they continue to watch him closely.

Does Harris have a constitutional basis to enjoin these agents of the federal government from preventing his suicide?[55]

However such a case might be decided, it is clear that it rests on the fundamental philosophical issues we are about to discuss, for it is these philosophical issues which lie at the root of the central legal question concerning the bases both for a state interest in preventing suicide, and an individual's right to self-determination in matters of life and death. Whether the state in fact has such an interest, or the individual such a right, will rest, in the end, on the moral and practical issues we shall confront here.

The Suicide Taboo

In discussing both medical and legal attitudes toward suicide, we discover that similar tensions are developing in both areas. In medicine, on the one hand, we discover a growing friction between those who practice suicide prevention and those who support voluntary euthanasia or euthanatic suicide. In law, on the other hand, we find conflict between assertions of state interests in preventing suicide and individual rights to privacy and self-determination. These parallel developments suggest that there is a larger issue here, one which is not merely medical or legal, but which is a general philosophic issue concerning individual autonomy in one's own death.

However, this issue of autonomy in death has been concealed by a strong modern taboo against the discussion of death at all, and in particular against the discussion of suicide. Only recently has the taboo against the discussion of death been effectively broken, largely by Elizabeth Kübler-Ross' highly influential work with terminally ill patients in hospital settings.[56] Nevertheless, the taboo against discussion of suicide has remained relatively intact. It dates from about the time of Durkheim in the latter part of the nineteenth century, when a rapid increase in interest in sociological and scientific data concerning suicide and an increasing acceptance of the deterministic view led to an eclipse of the philosophic and moral issues. This, in turn, permitted the reestablishment of the originally Christian cultural prohibitions against suicide, which we now find firmly entwined in popular culture with the deterministic view. Contemporary culture still largely considers suicide a sin, an illness, and even a crime, and has been not at all willing to explore the bases (or the coherence) of this view.

[55]Sullivan, "The Constitutional Right to Suicide," (*op. cit.* i/43), p. 230.

[56]Elizabeth Kübler-Ross, *On Death and Dying* (New York: Macmillan, 1969).

If we probe back beyond the immediate taboo, however, we find an extraordinarily long and complex philosophical tradition concerning the moral permissibility of suicide. This book examines the major arguments offered within this long tradition, both for and against, as a basis for reaching a considered, contemporary conclusion. Some of these traditional arguments may seem stilted or out-of-date, especially in a post-religious culture. And they are not always the sorts of argument which persuade or dissuade people who are actually considering suicide; only rarely does suicide occur as the outcome of reasoned philosophic argument. But these arguments are extremely important nevertheless: it is they which are for the most part responsible for the attitudes towards suicide characteristic of the society in which we live. They have enormous formative influence on our values and beliefs, and consequently on the institutions, policies, and legal structures we have established to deal with suicide. For instance, one sometimes hears that suicide is wrong because it is a "trust violation," or the breaking of the faith one has with God. Another frequently offered justification for our attitudes towards suicide is that because we did not "put ourselves here," we have no right to "take ourselves away"; these are versions of the early religious argument asserting God's dominion over life and death. On the other hand, one sometimes hears a right to suicide defended on the grounds that "it's *my* life"; this is a contemporary version of the traditional argument from private ownership. Because the post-Durkheimian taboo has inhibited critical inspection of these traditional arguments, they have continued to exert much more influence on contemporary attitudes than one might expect.

One technical question which immediately confronts us concerns the definition of suicide. There is growing discussion in the academic philosophic literature on this topic, and attempts to formulate a satisfactory definition of suicide are numerous. Some writers count all cases of voluntary, intentional self-killing as suicide. Others include under the term only cases in which an individual's *primary* intention is to terminate his life. Still others recognize that much of what we call suicide is neither voluntary nor involves a genuine intention to end one's life. For coroners, though their practices are not uniform, suicide is one of the four possible modes of death, along with homicide, accident, and natural death; a suicide is any death in which the proximate cause of death is deliberately (not accidentally) inflicted upon oneself, whatever its moral character. In contrast, writers in the Catholic tradition emphasize the motivation or moral signification under which the act is done; they tend to use the term "suicide" synonymously with "morally repugnant self-killing," and reserve the terms "self-sacrifice," "martyrdom," and "heroism" for cases judged praiseworthy. Still other authors, beginning with Durkheim, include under "suicide" any action which an individual takes knowing that it will result directly or indirectly in his own death; this includes not only heroic self-sacrifice and martyrdrom among the suicides, but also those actions which involve mere failure to rescue oneself from impending destruction. Even broader definitions, primarily in the tradition of Karl Menninger, include activities involving severe risks, dangerous lifestyles, and any activity which the agent performs although he knows it increases his chances of death. Anthropologists tend to use as a working definition of suicide "a death for which the responsibility is socially attributed to the dead person";[57] this may also include ritual sacrifices and killings

---

[57]Jean La Fontaine, "Anthropology," in Seymour Perlin, ed., *A Handbook for the Study of Suicide*, (London, Toronto, New York: Oxford University Press, 1975) pp. 77–91.

not initiated but consented to by the individual. No one definition is generally accepted by all speakers of English; the narrower definition used in the Catholic tradition seems closest to much ordinary usage, but the broader, Durkheimian definition is often used in research.

If we were to phrase the guiding concern of this inquiry as "whether suicide is morally permissible" (something which we shall frequently but loosely do), then much might depend upon reaching a satisfactory definition of suicide. But we can avoid these disputes by describing our inquiry as one concerned with the issue of whether it is morally permissible for an individual to choose to die, to determine that he shall die, to acquiesce in death, or to bring about his own death. This more flexible description will allow us both to concern ourselves with the central cases of suicide in the narrower sense, and to consider other forms of self-killing where relevant. This in fact has its advantages: the term "suicide" carries extremely negative connotations,[58] whereas alternative locutions like "elective death," "self-determined death," and "voluntary death" are neutral, and still others, such as the nineteenth century German *Freitod* ("free death"), have strong positive connotations. By extending our inquiry beyond the confines of a single term, we may be able to avoid some of the bias that might otherwise be introduced.

In this book we shall be considering arguments for and against the moral permissibility of (as we shall loosely say) suicide. Such considerations will have bearing on the roles we assign to bystanders of suicide, and in particular whether we regard secondary persons as obligated to intervene, assist, or do neither. But we cannot simply assume that if we find suicide impermissible on moral grounds, we must then also maintain that it should always be prevented, or that if it is morally permissible, bystanders ought to permit or encourage it. One can hold that suicide is morally permissible but should not be tolerated by law or custom (because of the risk of abuse, for instance), or that a right to suicide should be legally respected (because no behavior which concerns only oneself should be interfered with by law), even though it is not morally right. One might also want to ask what effects our findings concerning the moral status of suicide might have on various codes of professional ethics, including the Hippocratic Oath,[59] upon suicide-prevention or-

---

[58]Interestingly however, the term "suicide" appears to have been devised (along with other pseudoclassical compounds like "autocheiria") in order to avoid the negative connotations of terms then in use in the European languages: "self-murder," "self-slaughter," and the like in English, *"Selbstmord"* in German. The word *Suicide* appears in English in 1637 in Walter Charleton, *The Ephesian and Cimmerian Matrons* (London: for Henry Herringman, 1668), in the following context: "To vindicate ones self from extream, and otherwise inevitable Calamity, by *Sui-cide* is not (certainly) a Crime, but an act of Heroique Fortitude." (p. 73); it is also used by Thomas Browne. See Edwin Shneidman, entry "Suicide," (*op. cit.* i/58), p. 384, for a brief discussion of the word, and for a more extensive discussion of terms for suicide in various languages, David Daube, "The Linguistics of Suicide," *Philosophy & Public Affairs* 1, no. 4 (Summer 1972), pp. 387–437.

[59]Voluntary self-administered euthanasia, using poisons provided by one's physician, was apparently in widespread practice in cases of irreversible illness in classical Greek times. The Hippocratic Oath takes what is clearly a minority stand against this practice. See Ludwig Edelstein, "The Hippocratic Oath: Text, Translation, and Interpretation," in *Supplements to the Bulletin of the History of Medicine* no. 1 (1943), and in *Ancient Medicine: Selected Papers of Ludwig Edelstein*, Owsei and C. Lillian Temkin, eds. (1967), both Baltimore: The Johns Hopkins Press. Also see Danielle Gourevitch, "Suicide Among the Sick in Classical Antiquity," *Bulletin of the History of Medicine* 43 (1969), 501–18; Darrel W. Amundsen, "The Physician's Obligation to Prolong life: A Medical Duty without Classical Roots." *Hastings Center Report* 8, no. 4 (August 1978), 23–30; and M. Pabst Battin, "Philosophers' Death and Intolerable Life: Plato on Suicide," unpublished paper, University of Utah.

ganizations, upon organizations supporting voluntary euthanasia and right-to-die legislation, and upon social planning schemes, particularly those concerned with institutionalized and geriatric populations. We shall treat only some of these questions here; it should be obvious that even if we do make some progress toward resolving the issue of whether suicide is morally permissible, we shall still have many interesting questions left.

PART ONE

Traditional Arguments Concerning Suicide

CHAPTER 1

Religious Views
of Suicide

In an increasingly secular age, it may seem curious that the opening chapter of this book is devoted to views of suicide based on explicitly religious assumptions. In part, this reflects the fact that arguments against suicide originated within religious contexts, and that present legal and social practices regarding suicide arose from medieval religious law. But it also underscores the fact that because of the extremely strong taboo to which the issue of suicide has been subject, the religious issues in suicide have not been talked about very much, and only very rarely submitted to careful criticism. We tend, correctly, to assume that it is Christianity's opposition to suicide which is the basis of much of our cultural and legal disapprobation of suicide. But what we do not stop to examine is whether the scriptural and theological foundations of this tradition in fact provide adequate support for this opposition. On what basis is the Christian religious tradition opposed to suicide, and why is its opposition so strong? That is a question almost never asked, at least in recent times; it is the question we shall approach here.

In this chapter, we will examine the traditional and contemporary religious arguments concerning suicide. Almost all of these arguments presuppose the existence of a divine being, and almost all of these arguments could be defeated by denying this belief. In a secular society, this is often the approach taken: the argument that suicide is wrong because life is a gift from God, for instance, is often said to be unsound because there is no God. But to discard these arguments in this summary way is to ignore what is interesting and significant about them. Here, we shall treat the religious arguments against suicide as seriously as any others, particularly since they remain so strongly influential in forming public attitudes, and attempt to see what is illuminating about them.

To do this, we shall grant for the duration of this chapter the central assertions of western Christian theology: that there is a God; that this God is omnipotent, omniscient, and benevolent; that this God is the creator of the world and its inhabitants; and we will use the notions of salvation, retribution, and sin. This we will do, however, only in the first chapter of this book; when in the later chapters of this volume we consider other traditional and contemprary arguments concerning suicide, we will do so without reference to matters of religious belief.

In this discussion of religious attitudes toward suicide, we shall be concerned primarily (though not exclusively) with western, Christian views. There are two reasons for this: first, it is western, Christian-influenced attitudes towards suicide which have historically led to the development of modern psychological, sociological, and legal views of suicide, which now form the basis for the study and treatment of suicide throughout the world; and, second, it is only Christianity (and, derivatively, Islam and Judaism)[1] which has promulgated a strict, thoroughgoing doctrine prohibiting suicide. Other religious cultures do have teachings concerning the permissibility and impermissibility of suicide, but these are nowhere as strict as in the traditional Christian doctrine and do permit self-killing in various circumstances. Consequently, other religious cultures have not developed the elaborate theological, argumentative machinery for defending strict prohibitions. Nor do other cultures contain anything resembling the ongoing discussion and debate concerning the morality of suicide that is to be found during some periods of Christian and Christian-influenced culture. If this chapter seems excessively oriented towards Christian theology, this is because it is the Christian tradition which has first and foremost made suicide a matter of severe dispute, and is in large part responsible for the attitudes towards suicide taken by the scientific and professional community throughout the contemporary world.

The Religious Arguments Against Suicide

We shall begin by examining those arguments explicit within the Christian tradition that lead to conclusions denouncing or prohibiting suicide. These arguments fall into four main groups: those based on Biblical texts; those based on analogies to everyday objects and relations, or the so-called religious analogies; the natural-law arguments; and arguments concerning the role of suffering in Christian life. In examining these arguments, we shall be acquainting ourselves with the central aspects of the Christian case against suicide, which culminates in the claim made by some members of that tradition that suicide is a greater sin than any other; these are the arguments which have served as the theoretical basis for strict ecclesiastical penalties for suicide and the corresponding civil penalties in medieval and modern law.

But the religious arguments against suicide are only half the story; as we examine the positions Christianity takes against suicide, we also begin to observe

---

[1] Judaism's prohibition of suicide appears to develop in response to, or perhaps simultaneously with, that of Christianity. See Fred Rosner, "Suicide in Biblical, Talmudic and Rabbinic Writings," *Tradition: A Journal of Orthodox Thought*, 11, no. 3 (Fall 1970/71), 25–40, for a detailed account of the development of Jewish thought on suicide. Though Rosner does not compare this development with that of Christianity, the perceptive reader will observe that both traditions exhibit simultaneous increases in the severity of their suicide prohibitions, beginning with Augustine and the Tractates of the Talmud. Islam contains a thoroughgoing prohibition of suicide from its beginning; but this too is postAugustinian. Buddhism contains a very strong principle of respect for life, but is not strictly prohibitive of suicide; it permits suicide when one has reached the highest possible spiritual state. (See L. De La Vallée Poussin, entry "Suicide (Buddhist)," in *The Encyclopaedia of Religion and Ethics*, ed. James Hastings (New York: Charles Scribner's Sons, 1925), XII, 24–26.

the remarkable way in which Christian theology lends itself to arguments *in favor of* suicide. These arguments favoring suicide, of course, have almost never been explicitly stated; in the second part of the chapter, we shall attempt to formulate them. It is the persuasiveness of these covert arguments favoring suicide, one may suspect, that has led to the energetic formulation of explicit, theologically-based arguments against and prohibitions of suicide, which survive in contemporary society under the protection of the taboo. Christianity *invites* suicide in a way in which other major religions do not; it is for this reason, we may suppose, that Christianity has been forced to erect stringent prohibitions against it.

The nonreligious reader may wish to skip this first chapter and move directly on to those chapters in which other moral arguments concerning suicide are discussed. But I do not think it will be possible to fully understand contemporary western attitudes towards suicide without understanding something of the religious climate from which they arise, and, more important, without understanding something of the way in which Christian theology necessitates development of a case against it. It is this which may provide insight into contemporary moral views.

Suicide as a Violation of Biblical Commandment

It is one of the more prevalent assumptions of western religious culture that the Bible prohibits suicide; inspection of the Biblical texts, however, shows that this is by no means clearly the case. To begin with, there is no explicit prohibition of suicide in the Bible. There is no word anywhere in the Bible, either in Aramaic, Hebrew, or Greek, which is equivalent to the English term "suicide," either in its nominal or verbal form, nor is there any idiomatic way of referring to this act which suggests that it is a distinct type of death.[2] Nor is there any passage in either the Old or New Testament which can be directly understood as an explicit prohibition of suicide; those passages which are often taken to support such a prohibition require, as we shall see in a moment, a considerable amount of interpretation and qualification.

However, the Biblical texts do describe a number of cases—eight in the Old Testament, two of which are in the Apocrypha, and one in the New Testament[3]—of the phenomenon most contemporary English-speakers would call "suicide." None of these passages offers explicit comment on the morality of suicide, nor is there anywhere in the Bible an explicit discussion of the ethical issues. Neverthe-

[2]David Daube, "The Linguistics of Suicide," (*op. cit.* i/58).

[3]These include Abimelech (Judges 9:54); Samson (Judges 16:30); Saul and his armor-bearer (I Samuel 31:4, II Samuel 1:6, I Chronicles 10:4); Ahitophel (II Samuel 17:23); Zimri (I Kings 16:18) in the Old Testament; Razis (II Maccabees 14:41) and Ptolemy Macron (II Maccabees 10:13) in the Apocrypha; Judas (Matthew 27:5) and Paul's jailor (an attempted suicide) (Acts 16:27) in the New Testament. See L. D. Hankoff, "Judaic Origins of the Suicide Prohibition," in Hankoff and Einsidler, eds., *Suicide: Theory and Clinical Aspects* (op. cit. i/2), p. 6 and passim for dating and further information on the old Testament suicides. See also the Church [of England] Assembly Board for Social Responsibility's study, *Ought Suicide To Be a Crime? A Discussion of Suicide, Attempted Suicide and the Law* (Westminster: Church Information Office, 1959), p. 42 and O. Kirn, entry "Suicide," *Schaff-Herzog Encyclopaedia of Religious Knowledge,* ed. Samuel Macauley Jackson (Grand Rapids, Mich.: Baker Book House, 1964), 11, 132–33. There may also be several borderline cases in which intent to suicide cannot be determined, for example Lot's wife and Jonah.

less, these passages are of considerable importance in establishing the moral stance of the scriptural texts towards suicide.

Consider, for instance, the passage in I Samuel which describes the deaths of Saul and his armor-bearer in battle against the Philistines:

> *The Philistines fought a battle against Israel, and the men of Israel were routed, leaving their dead on Mount Gilboa. The Philistines hotly pursued Saul and his sons and killed the three sons, Jonathan, Abinadab, and Malchishua. The battle went hard for Saul, for some archers came upon him and he was wounded in the belly by the archers. So he said to his armour-bearer, "Draw your sword and run me through, so that these uncircumcised brutes may not come and taunt me and make sport of me." But the armour-bearer refused, he dared not; whereupon Saul took his own sword and fell on it. When the armour-bearer saw that Saul was dead, he too fell on his sword and died with him. Thus they all died together on that day, Saul, his three sons, and his armour-bearer, as well as his men.*[4]

It is clear that Saul kills himself only after all hope of victory is lost, after his sons are dead and his army destroyed, and after it is certain that he will be captured, tortured, and will die either of torture or the wounds in his belly. Saul's act could be interpreted as one of cowardice. Yet it could equally well be maintained that Saul killed himself in order to avoid degradation at the hands of the enemy, since the treatment to which these "uncircumcized brutes" would subject him would not befit the Lord's anointed; to avoid this would be to defend the honor of Israel. In either case, however, it is clear that the Biblical narrator makes no overt condemnation of Saul's act. Furthermore, the populace of the surrounding area is said to have accorded both Saul, a suicide, and his sons, who were not suicides, identical anointment, burial, and fasting rites; this further suggests that no moral disapprobation attached to suicide.

Other Old Testament suicides include Ahitophel, the wise counselor of Absalom, who hanged himself not so much because his pride was wounded when Absalom refused to follow his advice, but because he recognized that Absalom's cause was therefore lost; the usurper Zimri, who burned the royal citadel over him in what is apparently viewed by the redactor as a self-imposed judgment for the sins he had committed; Abimilech, whose suicide also appears to be viewed as a punishment for sins; and Samson, who in destroying the Philistines pulled the temple down upon himself. The only completed New Testament suicide is that of Judas, who hanged himself;[5] the Matthean narrator implies that the motive is remorse over the betrayal of Jesus, and seems to see Judas' death as appropriate in the context. Again, there is nowhere, in either the Old or New Testament, an explicit discussion of the moral status of suicide. There are cases in which a Biblical figure expresses despair or weariness of life, often from persecution or physical affliction—e.g., Elijah, Job, Jonah, Sarah the daughter of Ragnel, and possibly Jesus at Gethsemane—but although these figures all recover an earlier enthusiasm for life,

---

[4] I Samuel 31:1–6, trans. *New English Bible*. See the analysis of this case by George M. Landes of Union Theological Seminary in his unpublished paper "Some Biblical Perspectives Relating to the Matter of Suicide," p. 1.

[5] Matthew 27:5; Judas is said to have hanged himself by a halter. At Acts 1:18, however, Peter is quoted as saying that Judas "swelled up" and died.

there is no condemnation of any consideration of suicide they may have made.[6] On the whole, however, suicide seems to be a comparatively rare phenomenon in Biblical times.

An explanation frequently offered in the secondary literature for the paucity of reference to suicide in early Hebrew sources is that because the Jews were "joyously fond of life" and believed that human life is sacred, suicide virtually never occurred; hence explicit discussions of its morality and injunctions against its practice were unnecessary.[7] This is said to explain the fact, for instance, that there is no mention of suicide in the 613 Precepts, although this code attempted to regulate all aspects of the Jews' everyday and religious lives in minute detail. However, there is no independent evidence to substantiate the claim that suicide was virtually unknown, and we do not know whether suicide prohibitions are absent from early Hebrew literature because suicide did not occur, or because suicide was not prohibited. What we do know is that those few suicides which do occur in the Old Testament literature are not subject to obvious moral censure.

Scholarly views have been expectedly diverse. L. D. Hankoff, although acknowledging that no explicit Biblical prohibition exists, argues that independent evidence concerning the notions of blood ties, sacrifice, and other elements of early Hebrew culture "suggest that suicide would have been strongly opposed because it represented a dangerous form of the spilling of blood, a loss of community control over the blood of a tribal member, and the possibility of an unattended corpse in the wilderness."[8] In the view of another commentator, however, the Hebrews, at least until late post-Exilic times, "must be counted among those races to whom suicide is simply one of the various possible forms of death and calls for no special comment."[9]

The earliest explicit negative moral evaluation of suicide in the Jewish tradition is to be found in the first century A.D. Josephus, attempting to dissuade his own army from a mass suicide in which he would be forced to include himself,[10] argues that suicide is cowardly, repugnant to nature, and an act of impiety to God; he says that it violates the will to live, that it rejects God's gift, that it misuses God's entrustment of an immortal soul, and that it would be to "fly from the best of masters." He further asserts that the souls of suicides go to the darker regions of the

[6]Except perhaps in the case of Sarah (Tobit 3:10, in the Apocrypha). Sarah decides not to hang herself, as she had intended, but instead begs the Lord to let her die. That the Old Testament contains no explicit discussion of the morality of suicide is not in itself surprising; particularly before the prophetic period, the Jews did not approach ethical questions in a philosophically explicit manner.

[7]G. Margoliouth, entry "Suicide (Jewish)," *The Encyclopaedia of Religion and Ethics* (*op. cit.* i/1), XII, 37–38 (New York: Charles Scribner's Sons, 1925). "The ancient Hebrews were, on the whole, a naive people, joyously fond of life, and not given to tampering with the natural instinct of self-preservation." (p. 37) See also Jacob Hamburger, *Real-Encyclopädie für Bibel and Talmud,* II (Leipzig: In Commission von R. F. Koehler, 1886–92), 1110, on the rarity of suicide among the early Jews.

[8]L. D. Hankoff, "Judaic Origins of the Suicide Prohibition," (op. cit. I/3) p. 18. Hankoff grants that the earliest period of Hebrew civilization, up until the Exodus, may have had—like its Egyptian, Greek, and Babylonian neighbors—no prohibition of suicide (p. 5).

[9]H. J. Rose, entry "Suicide (Introductory)," in *Encyclopaedia of Religion and Ethics* (*op. cit.* I/1) XII, (New York: Charles Scribner's Sons, 1925), 24.

[10]Flavius Josephus, *The Jewish War* III 316–391 (London: William Heinemann, New York: G. P. Putnam's Sons, 1927), 2, 664–87), describes the events at Jotapata; a similar mass suicide, that at Masada, is described in *The Jewish War* VII 320–406 (1928), 3, 594–619.

nether world, and that one's descendants will be punished for this act. But this is probably not authentically Hebrew; much of Judaism had become quite hellenized, and Josephus himself had Greek assistants and was familiar with Greek literature. Many of the arguments he presents against suicide can be discovered in Plato and other Greek sources.[11]

With the development of the Talmud in the first several centuries A.D., later rabbinic tradition begins to make explicit a prohibition of suicide, both in stories condemning suicide and by means of mourning and funeral restrictions. The Talmud, unlike earlier Hebrew sources, contains numerous stories of suicide and suicidal martyrdom, and in many of these disapproval of the act is clearly indicated by the narrator or author. The major Talmudic discussion of rules governing suicide appears in the tractate *Semakhot;* this text forbids one to rend one's garments or bare one's shoulders as signs of mourning for a suicide or to say a eulogy at the funeral.[12]

In the developing Talmud, the Old Testament passage at Genesis 9:5 begins to be cited as the fundamental basis of Judaism's prohibition of suicide. What follows is the text, in which the verse considered relevant is emphasized:

> *And God blessed Noah and his sons, and said to them, "Be fruitful and multiply and fill the earth. The fear of you and the dread of you shall be upon every beast of the earth, and upon every bird of the air, upon everything that creeps on the ground and all the fish of the sea; into your hand they are delivered. Every moving thing that lives shall be food for you; and as I gave you the green plants, I give you everything. Only you shall not eat flesh with its life, that is, its blood. For your lifeblood I will surely require a reckoning; of every beast I will require it and of man; of every man's brother I will require the life of man. Whoever sheds the blood of man, by man shall his blood be shed; for God made man in his own image. And you, be fruitful and multiply, bring forth abundantly on the earth and multiply on it."*

The Talmudic reading of this phrase as a prohibition of suicide, however, is much later than the original text, and it is possible to read the original text in several ways. Most plausibly, it is read as a prohibition of the wrongful killing of other human beings,[13] and not as a prohibition of suicide *per se.*

Whatever the scriptural basis, however, medieval and contemporary Judaism maintains very strong prohibitions of suicide. However, sanctions are not applied for suicides of children, for those under extreme physical or mental stress, for those not in full possession of their faculties, or for those who kill themselves in order to atone for past sins,[14] and the position is, therefore, much less strict than that of

---

[11]For instance, the argument that we should not "fly from the best of masters," i.e. God, is reminiscent of Plato's argument against suicide at *Phaedo* 62B, where Socrates describes men as the property of the gods, and argues that "one should not escape from a good master." Tr. Hugh Tredennick, in Edith Hamilton and Huntington Cairns, eds., *Plato: The Collected Dialogues* (Princeton: Princeton University Press, 1961).

[12]*Semakhot,* Chapter 2. Chapter 2, Rule 2 also provides a definition of suicide, excluding cases of possible accident or murder. "A willful suicide is one who calls out: 'Look, I am going to the top of the roof or to the top of the tree, and I will throw myself down that I may die.' When people see him go up to the top of the tree or roof and fall down and die, then he is considered to have committed suicide willfully. A person found strangled or hanging from a tree or lying dead on a sword is presumed not to have committed suicide intentionally and none of the funeral rites are withheld from him." See Fred Rosner, "Suicide in Biblical, Talmudic, and Rabbinic Writings," (*op. cit.* I/1), pp. 33–34.

[13]Louis Zucker, private conversations, University of Utah.

[14]Fred Rosner, "Suicide in Biblical, Talmudic and Rabbinic Writings," (*op. cit.* I/1), p. 39.

Christian orthodoxy. Indeed, Judaism, unlike Christianity, recognizes the sanctity of self-destruction to avoid spiritual defilement; this is known as *Kiddush Hashem*.[15] And, again unlike Christianity, the Jewish tradition cites several mass suicides, notably the suicide of 960 Jews at Masada, who are still very much venerated.

Much like Judaism, Christianity does not rely on particular stories of suicide told in the Bible to justify its assertion that the Bible prohibits suicide; rather, it points to a passage which is held to provide the basis for a general, lawlike prohibition. For Christians, this text is Exodus 20:13, the Sixth (Fifth)[16] Commandment, "Thou shalt not kill." Christian authorities do not in general take Genesis 9:5, which serves the Jewish tradition as the central passage, to provide a prohibition of suicide, nor do Jewish authorities interpret a prohibition of suicide in the Sixth Commandment; this is particularly odd considering that the Old Testament is scriptural for both traditions and that each tradition claims its scripture to provide a direct and unmistakable condemnation of suicide. Both traditions cite many other Biblical passages in support of their anti-suicide claims, although selection and interpretation of these passages also often differs.

The Christian use of the Sixth Commandment as the basis for the prohibition of suicide originates with St. Augustine;[17] prior to the early fifth century A.D., the Church had no unified position on the moral status of suicide, and was widely divided on whether various forms of self-killing, including deliberate martyrdom and religiously motivated suicide, were to be allowed. Like the Genesis passage, the Sixth Commandment also presents severe interpretational problems; these involve both the meanings of the words employed, and the scope of the prohibition stated.

First, the semantic difficulties. The term usually translated "kill" actually means "wrongful killing"; the commandment is best translated "Thou shalt do no wrongful killing," or perhaps "Thou shalt do no murder."[18] Nowhere in the Old Testament does the term "wrongful killing" appear in connection with suicide, and there is no philological reason to think that suicide is included under this term. The commandment thus does not serve as a general prohibition of self-

---

[15]For an example of *Kiddush Hashem,* see Chapter Five, of this volume, on the self-poisonings of the 93 maidens of the Beth Jacob School, pp. 166-67.

[16]"Thou shalt not kill" is the Fifth Commandment in the Roman Catholic numbering system; it is the Sixth Commandment for Protestants.

[17]Augustine's discussion of suicide in the *City of God* appears to draw quite heavily from Lactantius' comments in the *Divine Institutes* a century earlier (c. 314-317), particularly in its direct arguments against the suicides of Cleombrotus and Cato. However, Lactantius does not rely on the Sixth Commandment as a basis for the prohibition of suicide, but on the Orphic/Platonic argument that "just as we came into this life not of our own accord, so departure from this domicile of the body which was assigned to our protection must be made at the order of the same One who put us into this body, to dwell therein until He should order us to leave." Use of the commandment as the basis for the suicide prohibition appears to be wholly original with Augustine. See Lactantius, *The Divine Institutes,* Book III, Chapter 18, trans. Sister Mary Francis MacDonald, Fathers of the Church, vol. 49 (Washington, D.C.: Catholic University of America Press, 1964), see esp. p. 214.

[18]See Joseph Fletcher's discussion of the language of the commandment in his chapter "Euthanasia: Our Right to Die," from his *Morals and Medicine* (Princeton University Press, 1954), pp. 195-96. Also see, on the linguistic basis of this commandment, *The Interpreter's Bible* (New York: Abingdon Press, 1952), 1, 986, and David Daube's thorough account of Hebrew and Greek terms which are used for suicide, in "The Linguistics of Suicide," (*op. cit.* i/58).

killing, since self-killing may not always be wrongful killing. That suicide is *wrongful* killing would need to be established independently; only then could the Sixth Commandment be used to confirm the centrality of a suicide prohibition in the Christian scriptures.

Second, the scope problems. Augustine claims that "Thou shalt not kill" means not only that one should not kill others, but that one ought not kill oneself. But Augustine's conclusion is not immediately evident. For one thing, not only is "Thou shalt not kill" almost universally relaxed to permit the killing of plants and animals, it is usually also interpreted to allow the killing of human beings in self-defense, capital punishment, and war. However, one might argue, if under this commandment the killing of human beings is permitted in these situations, it is hard to see why it should not also be permitted in the case of suicide. Indeed, suicide would seem to have a stronger claim to morality, since suicide alone does not violate the wishes of the individual killed.

To meet such an objection, Augustine draws a distinction between "private killing" and killing which is carried out at the orders of a divine or divinely constituted authority.[19] Private killing, or killing undertaken "on one's own authority," is never right; it is wrong whether one kills oneself or someone else, and it is wrong whether the victim is innocent or guilty of crime in any degree. Consequently, private killing of oneself—that is, self-initiated suicide—is wrong whether one kills oneself in order to declare one's innocence (like Lucretia), or to punish oneself for a crime (like Judas).

However, according to Augustine, not all killing is private. God may command a killing, and when this is the case, full obedience is required. The command may take either of two principal forms: it may be a direct command from God, like the commandment to Abraham to sacrifice Isaac, or it may be required by a just law. In these two cases, the individual who performs the killing does not do it "on his own authority" and is not morally accountable for it; he is "an instrument, a sword in its user's hand."[20] This accounts for the permissibility of both killing in war and in capital punishment, since both types of killing are performed by persons acting under law. Augustine appears not to permit killing in self-defense, though present-day Catholic moral theology does permit it for persons not capable of attaining the "higher way" of self-sacrifice.

While suicide is almost always a matter of private killing, in Augustine's view there can be cases in which it is not: an individual may be ordered to kill himself by law (as Socrates was ordered to drink the hemlock by the Athenian court), or he may be directly commanded to do so by God. Just as Abraham's sacrifice of Isaac would not have been wrong, had not God supplied the ram instead, Samson's causing his own death by pulling the temple down does not violate the commandment against suicide because—at least so Augustine conjectures—it was required by God.

And when Samson destroyed himself, with his enemies, by the demolition of the building, this can only be excused on the ground that the Spirit, which performed miracles through him, secretly ordered him to do so.[21]

---

[19]Augustine, *Concerning the City of God Against the Pagans,* ed. David Knowles, trans. Henry Betten-son (Harmondsworth: Penguin, 1972), Book I, Chapter 21.

[20]*Ibid.,* I, 21.

[21]*Ibid.,* I, 21.

Suicide is permitted under divine command; otherwise, it is not.

Indeed, to say that suicide under divine command is *permitted* is itself short of the truth; suicide in these circumstances is not merely optional or supererogatory but *required*. Inasmuch as most discussion of the religious view of suicide has centered on whether suicide can ever be allowed within the Christian faith, it is crucial to see that the kind of account of suicide adopted by Augustine and followed by virtually all later Catholic writers, at least until recently, holds suicide to be obligatory in specific situations. Killings of oneself or of others committed at the orders of God, whether by direct divine command or under law, may not be avoided. When a soldier kills in war, says Augustine, "he is punished if he did it without orders," but it is also the case that "he will be punished if he refuses when ordered."

> ... And so one who accepts the prohibition against suicide may kill himself when commanded by one whose orders must not be slighted.[22]

Since God is "one whose orders must not be slighted," the individual does not have an option to kill himself, but *must* do so if he is to remain religiously devout.

Augustine's explanation of the legitimacy of Samson's suicide has seemed to some entirely *ad hoc*. In the seventeenth century, John Donne points out that the traditional view is clearly embarrassed by the need to accommodate Biblical suicides and those of the later saints—for instance, St. Pelagia—who are portrayed without condemnation and are believed to have attained salvation. Augustine had acknowledged that external observers cannot tell with certainty whether any given suicide, Biblical or otherwise, is commanded by God, since the issuance of divine command is not always a public event;[23] Donne disputes the likelihood of such mechanisms altogether. He agrees with Augustine that it is permissible to commit suicide only upon the command of God: "Whensoever I may justly depart with this life," he says, "it is by a summons from God."[24] But Donne supplies a different interpretation of how that command may occur:

> Yet I expect not ever a particular inspiration, or a new commission such as they are forced to purchase for Samson and the rest, but that resident and inherent grace of God, by which He excites us to works of moral, or higher, virtues.[25]

What Donne was referring to is *conscience,* that faculty in human beings by which, according to seventeenth-century thinkers, the promptings and admonishments of divinity are known. Since conscience, according to these thinkers, is the voice of primary reason, and so provides direct access to the will of God, if one's rectified conscience permits or recommends suicide, then suicide is in accord with the will of God. If one's conscience is troubled or repelled by the idea, then no matter how

---

[22] *Ibid.,* I, 26.

[23] *Ibid.,* I, 26. "We have only a hearsay acquaintance with any man's conscience; we do not claim to judge the secrets of the heart."

[24] John Donne, *Biathanatos.* (New York: Arno Press, 1977, a photoreprint of the edition of 1647); also Michael Rudick and M. Pabst Battin, eds., (New York: Garland Publishing Co., 1981).

[25] *Ibid.,* II. iv. 7: 3076-80.

difficult the circumstances in which one finds oneself, the act would count as disobedience to the will of God. For Donne too, as for Augustine, suicide is not merely permissible, but obligatory at the divine command—though for Augustine this occurs in vision, for Donne at the prompting of conscience. Donne writes:

> *And this obligation which our conscience casts upon us is of stronger hold and of straiter band than the precept of any superior, whether law or person. . . . If then, a man, after convenient and requisite diligence, despoiled of all human affections and self-interest. . . do in his conscience believe that he is invited by the spirit of God to do such an act as Jonas, Abraham, and perchance Samson was, who can by these rules condemn this to be sin?[26]*

Despite Donne's reinterpretation, Augustine's original reading of the Sixth Commandment remained the basis of the prohibition of suicide not only in Catholicism, but also in much of Protestant Christianity, and the notion of obligation in suicide has been barely examined. The twentieth-century Catholic writer J. Eliot Ross, for instance, admits that it may be "lawful" for a person who is a condemned criminal to act as the state's executioner and take his own life;[27] but he does not recognize that, if ordered by the appropriate authority, self-execution would be not merely "lawful" but obligatory. Nor does Ross consider the possibility that God might directly order self-killing in nonjudicial contexts. Similarly, Joseph V. Sullivan, also defending a contemporary Catholic position, claims:

> *For a man to take the life of an innocent person directly, even his own life, for any reason whatsoever, apart from a divine command, has always been against the conscience of the West.[28]*

But what is not explored in recent religious writing is the obligation of the individual to kill himself under divine command. No doubt this has a great deal to do with the frequency of psychotic delusions and imaginings of "divine command"; a feeling of being "ordered to kill myself" is a very frequent concomitant of suicide and attempted suicide in those who suffer from delusional psychoses. Assertions of divine command have also accompanied both individual and mass suicide in contemporary religious cults. But, for the religious, these facts merely underscore the difficulty of distinguishing genuine divine command from hallucination or cult coercion; they do not alter the principle that genuine divine command is always to be obeyed. However, Augustine's distinction between private and divinely ordered suicide has given way in recent Catholic literature to distinctions made on the basis of the doctrine of the double effect (to be discussed later in this chapter), and the notion of suicide as the possible product of divine command is rejected: if suicide is intrinsically evil, it is argued, God could not command it, and suicide can be excused

---

[26]*Ibid.,* II. vi. 8: 3842–55.

[27]J. Eliot Ross, *Ethics from the Standpoint of Scholastic Philosophy* (New York: The Devin-Adair Company, 1938), p. 143.

[28]Joseph V. Sullivan, *Catholic Teaching on the Morality of Euthanasia,* Studies in Sacred Theology (Second Series), no. 22 (Washington, D.C.: Catholic Univeristy of America, 1949), p. 54.

only by attributing it to inculpable ignorance[29] such as that which occurs in mental illness.

In addition to the Sixth Commandment, numerous other Biblical passages are also cited as authority for the Christian prohibition of suicide. These include Deuteronomy 33:39, "I kill and I give life"; I Samuel 2:6, "The Lord killeth and maketh alive"; and a number of similar passages which assert God's power over life and death.[30] Some Biblical episodes are said to show awareness of the prohibition of suicide: Paul prevented the suicide of his jailor (Acts 16:27-28); Elijah and Job considered suicide and rejected it; wicked figures like Judas do not respect the prohibition. The evidence for such a prohibition, however, is far from compelling.

A number of later interpreters have agreed that the Bible does not prohibit suicide, either in the central Genesis 9:5 and Exodus 20:13 passages, or at other loci throughout the Old and New Testament. John Donne, for instance, after a meticulous analysis of both the Biblical texts and the then-current secondary interpretations, concluded that "in all the judicial and ceremonial law, there was no abomination of self-homicide."[31] A century and a half later, in 1773, Caleb Fleming also admitted that the Scriptures do not expressly prohibit suicide, but offered as an explanation the suggestion that suicide is "too deformed" to be mentioned in the Bible.[32] In recent years, a committee of the New York Presbytery has concluded that the Bible does not prohibit suicide; rather, "it is clear that for some Christians, as a last resort in the gravest of situations, suicide may be an act of their Christian conscience."[33] With increasing popular attention to voluntary euthanasia and the "right to die," the issue of whether the Bible does contain an implicit prohibition of suicide is of increasing importance to those with traditional religious commitments. Numerous scholars suggest that renewed examination of the texts will not support the view held by both Judaism and Christianity that the Bible prohibits suicide; but results of such investigations are still forthcoming. In the interim, one interpreter reads the texts in this way:

> *The Bible tends to be life oriented, life protecting and life affirming. Even in trial and adversity, life is good, and one awaits God's will in the taking of a life, including one's own. But there are times and circumstances when biblical tradition views suicide as*

[29]T. C. Kane, entry "Suicide," *The New Catholic Encyclopaedia* (New York: McGraw-Hill, 1973), 13, 782. It is instructive to compare this account with that of the 1908 edition of the same work; of particular interest is the more recent version's explicit statement that in cases in which it is doubtful whether the person was responsible for his act—"and frequently such doubt exists because the person is often mentally deranged"—the doubt is to be decided in his favor, and consequently no ecclesiastical penalties are to be imposed, at least provided no scandal is likely to ensue. In contemporary practice, suicide cases are almsot always treated in this way.

[30]Donne's *Biathanatos* (*op. cit.* I/24), Part 3 passim, provides a thorough compilation of Biblical passages sometimes interpreted as prohibiting suicide, and argues a nonprohibitive interpretation for each of them.

[31]*Ibid.*, II, v. 1: 5002-04.

[32]Caleb Fleming, *A Dissertation upon the Unnatural Crime of Self-Murder Occasioned by the Many Late Instances of Suicide in this City, etc.* (London: Printed for Edward and Charles Dilly, 1773), p. 7.

[33]Presbyterian Senior Services, The Presbytery of New York City, pastoral letter on euthanasia and suicide, March 9, 1976, p. 3.

within the divine will: when it guards, protects, or allows a larger good; when it constitutes a divine judgment for human sin; and when it prevents a greater evil.[34]

The Religious Analogies

In addition to the claim that suicide is prohibited by the Scriptures, the Judaeo-Christian religious tradition also brings several other kinds of argument against the permissibility of suicide. The most informal and casually propounded among these, though nonetheless interesting, is a loose group of arguments I shall call the religious analogies, or the analogy-based arguments, to denote the fact that they all depend on analogies drawn between the person who commits suicide and some particular everday circumstance or object. But despite the apparent informality of these arguments and the often superficial way in which they are put forth, they are among the most influential of the religious arguments against suicide, and probably much more operative in the thought and behavior of ordinary persons— both the religiously inclined and the nonreligious—than are more sophisticated arguments developed by Christian theologians. Although these analogy-based arguments are one of the oldest forms of argument against suicide in the western tradition, many of them considerably antedating the scriptural and natural-law arguments, most of them are still quite alive in popular thought.

In practice, religious analogies are often found intermixed with more formal natural-law arguments; Thomas Aquinas, for instance, uses one religious analogy—the gift argument—together with two natural-law arguments in his central statement against suicide. Also, in practice, we find that the religious analogies are often propounded by thinkers not generally associated with religious thought, although these arguments do all depend on the belief in the existence of God. Indeed, some of these arguments are given their classic formulations by thinkers not primarily concerned with religious matters, including Plato, Josephus, Locke, and Kant.

The analogy-based religious arguments against suicide may be very roughly divided into two major groups: those which rest on analogies to *property* relationships between man and God, or which have reference to concrete objects for use or possession, and those in which the central analogy is drawn to a particular kind of *personal* or occupational relationship between God and man. The argument based on the root analogy of life as a "gift" from God, for instance, is probably best classed among the property relationships, since (at least initially) it concerns the treatment and disposal of the gift object; the argument based on the root analogy of man as a "sentinel" stationed by God trades on a particular kind of interpersonal relationship. However, the distinction between property and personal analogies is rarely sharp. In some arguments, such as Plato's claim that man is slave to God and hence ought not run away, both property and personal relationships are involved. In others, an argument that begins with one kind of relationship may conclude with another, as when the initially property-related gift argument becomes an argument concerning the personal relationship of gratitude.

---

[34]Landes, "Some Biblical Perspectives Relating to the Matter of Suicide," (*op. cit.* I/4), p. 3.

The list below presents the central analogy-based arguments in the Christian religious tradition. A brief statement of the argument is accompanied, whenever possible, by its *locus classicus* in the history of thought; this is usually its most explicit or extended statement, though not necessarily the earliest, and not always from authors whose interests were primarily religious.

A. The property analogies:

life is a gift from God, and so
should not be destroyed

> . . . life is a gift made to man by God, and it is subject to Him who is master of death and life. Therefore a person who takes his own life sins against God. . .
> *Thomas Aquinas*[35]

life [or, the soul] is loaned or
entrusted to the individual by God, and so
should not be destroyed

> Know you not that they who depart this life in accordance with the law of nature and repay the loan which they received from God, when he who lent is pleased to reclaim it, win eternal renown. . . *Josephus*[36]

> Humanity in one's own person. . . is a holy trust. *Kant*[37]

the human being is made in the image of God
[and should not destroy God's
likeness]

> So God created man in His own image; in the image of God He created him. . .
> *Genesis* 1:27

the body is the temple of God, and
should not be destroyed

> Surely you know that you are God's temple, where the Spirit of God dwells. Anyone who destroys God's temple will himself be

[35]Thomas Aquinas, *Summa Theologiae* 2a2ae64.כ (Blackfriars, New York: McGraw-Hill, London: Eyre & Spottiswoode, 1964).

[36]Josephus, *The Jewish War* III 374 (*op. cit.* I/10).

[37]Immanuel Kant, *Lectures on Ethics,* tr. Louis Infeld (New York: Harper Torchbooks, 1963), p. 151.

destroyed by God, because the temple of
God is holy; and that temple you are.

I Corinthians 3:16–17

*The human being is the handiwork of God, and should not
destroy what God has created*

For men being all the workmanship of one
omnipotent, and infinitely wise maker...
they are His property, whose workmanship
they are, made to last during His, not
one another's pleasure.   *Locke*[38]

B.   *The personal-relationship analogies*

*The human being is God's possession [i.e., slave], and
should not destroy himself because he is
his owner's property*

I believe that this much is true; that the
gods are our keepers and we men are one of
their possessions....

Then take your own case; if one of your
possessions were to destroy itself without
intimation from you that you wanted it to
die, wouldn't you be angry with it and
punish it, if you had any means of doing so?
Certainly.
So if you look at it in this way I
suppose it is not unreasonable to say that
we must not put an end to ourselves until
God sends some compulsion like the one
which we are facing now.   *Plato*[39]

*the human being is imprisoned by God [or,
the body is the prison of the
soul], and should not escape*

... we men are in a kind of prison and
must not set ourselves free or run away...
Plato, quoting Orphic doctrine[40]

*the human being is the servant of God, and
should do his master's bidding*

---

[38]John Locke, *The Second Treatise of Government* Chapter II, Paragraph 6, ed. Thomas P. Peardon
(Indianapolis: Bobbs-Merrill, 1952), p. 5–6.

[39]Plato, *Phaedo* 62B-C, (*op. cit.* I/11) p. 45.

[40]*Ibid.*, 62B; my translation.

> For men being. . . all the servants of one
> sovereign master, sent into the world by
> His order, and about His business. . .
>
> *Locke*[41]

*the human being is stationed as a sentinel on earth
by God, and should not desert his post*

> So the aged ought neither to cling too
> greedily to their small remnants of life
> nor, conversely, to abandon them before
> they need. Pythagoras forbids us desert
> life's sentry-post till God, our commander,
> has given the word.   *Cicero*[42]

> This duty [of self-preservation] is upon
> us until the time comes when God expressly
> commands us to leave this life. Human
> beings are sentinels on earth and may not
> leave their posts until relieved by another
> beneficent hand.   *Kant*[43]

*the human being is the child of God, and should
trust and obey his father in all
things.*

> "Your heavenly father [says] 'Thou
> shalt not kill' [yourself]."

All of these arguments make reference to concrete, everyday objects, such as gifts, loans, images, temples, and the objects fashioned by craftsmen, or to particular human relationships, such as that between master and slave, prisoner and jailer, master and servant, military superior and subordinate, or parent and child. Since these are familiar objects and relationships, we tend to have a fairly well-developed set of ordinary moral beliefs and practices surrounding them: we believe that gifts ought to be preserved, loans repaid, temples respected, commanders obeyed, and parents loved. It is on these ordinary moral beliefs and practices that the analogy-based arguments rely.

If we isolate these tacit premises, however, we discover that the arguments may not after all succeed in supporting the general Christian prohibition of suicide. First, many of these arguments produce trivial and sometimes rather amusing surface difficulties in interpretation. For instance, it is often claimed that life is a gift from God, and therefore ought not be destroyed. But this invites us to ask who it is who receives God's gift, if that individual does not yet have life; mainstream Christian theology does not assert the antecedent existence of nonliving individuals

---

[41]Locke, *Second Treatise of Government* (*op. cit.* I/38) Chapter II, Paragraph 6.

[42]Cicero, *On Old Age,* VII: "Death Has No Sting," tr. Michael Grant (Baltimore: Penguin Books, 1960), p. 242.

[43]Kant, *Lectures on Ethics* (*op. cit.* I/37) p. 154.

upon whom such gifts might be bestowed. Or, if life is construed as a "loan" from God to man, one might suggest that suicide can be no more wrong than ordinary death: in either case, life is ended, and is not "repaid" to God. On the other hand, if it is the soul which is said to be loaned, it cannot *not* be returned: since in standard Christian theology the soul is immortal, it will thus be "repaid" whether death occurs by suicide or in some other way.

But these are trivial objections, and should not distract us from the central concern in each of these analogy-based arguments, since it is on this central concern that the analogy actually rides. The analogy to life as a loan, for instance, though indeed subject to surface difficulties, is centrally concerned with what we might call the "entrustment" feature of loans—the notion that the borrower of an object assumes an obligation to protect and care for the loaned object while it is in his possession—and it is on this feature that the serious argument against suicide is based. In analyzing this and other analogy-based arguments against suicide, then, we must be careful not to discredit them on the basis of superficial objections: serious attention to these arguments requires a careful search for the central concern beneath its surface. Even so, as we shall see, the analogy-based arguments do not seem to succeed in supporting the traditional blanket prohibition of suicide.

Unfortunately, we have space here to examine only one of these arguments in detail; our specimen will be the argument that suicide is wrong "because life is a gift from God, and ought therefore not be destroyed." There are several reasons for selecting this argument from among the others. It is as complex as any, and very clearly displays the way in which deeper issues emerge from trivial surface difficulties. It involves both property and personal-relationship notions. And because it is used by Thomas Aquinas as one of three central reasons why suicide is wrong, it occupies an influential place among the analogy-based arguments in the history of dispute concerning suicide.

THE GIFT ARGUMENT. The argument that because life is a gift of God, one ought not destroy it by suicide is open to a very simple objection, first formulated by the eighteenth century Swedish philosopher, Johann Robeck.[44] Robeck, who composed a lengthy treatise defending suicide and later drowned himself, argued that if life is a gift, then it becomes the property of the recipient, who may therefore do with it as he wishes. In giving a gift, the donor relinquishes his rights and control over the gift item; if he does not, then the item is not a genuine gift. Thus if life is really a *gift* from God to the individual, it is that a person's to do with as he chooses.

The tacit premise involved in this first part of the gift argument, that based on notions of property, holds that it is wrong to reject or destroy a gift; thus, to assess the argument, we must examine this premise. Is it wrong to reject or destroy a gift? Generally, we think not. We are, of course, aware of circumstances in which it would indeed be wrong to destroy a gift—for instance, if it is an object like a peck of wheat, a warm coat, or a fifty-dollar bill, which could be useful to others. However, although we might find it wrong to *destroy* such items, we would not think it wrong to decline such gifts if they were then to be given to others instead. Similarly, although we are aware that some gift objects may have intrinsic aesthetic or historical value—a painting or a rare book, for instance—and that it would therefore be wrong to destroy these gifts, we need not also hold that it would be wrong to reject them.

[44]Johannes Robeck, *Exercitatio philosophica de... morte voluntaria....* Recensuit J. N. Funccius, Rintelii, 1736. See also Fedden, *Suicide* (*op. cit.* i/11), pp. 210–11.

Since to decline or reject the gift of life by suicide is tantamount to destroying it, these counterarguments may seem to support the initial thesis that suicide is wrong. Even so, these counterarguments show only that it is wrong to destroy an item if it is useful to someone else, or if it has intrinsic value of its own; they do not show that it is wrong to destroy something *because it is a gift.* Suicide may be wrong because one's life is or could be useful to someone else, or because life is of intrinsic value; but this is not to say that suicide is wrong *because* life is a gift.

There is another, deeper aspect to this analogy. Though our ordinary conventions may suggest that it is permissible to destroy a gift when it is not of intrinsic value or value to others, there is an additional component of gift-giving which is not recognized either in the original statement of the argument or in Robeck's initial reply. The receiving of a gift usually, though not invariably, involves *gratitude:* gratitude felt towards the donor, which can be expressed in a variety of ways. Sincerely felt and appropriately expressed gratitude we take to be commendable; we often evaluate people morally on the basis of their capacity to feel and express gratitude. It is this feature of ordinary gift-giving to which the central analogy in the gift argument is drawn, involving now a personal rather than property relationship, and it is here that the anti-suicide argument has a foothold. The wrongness of failure to feel gratitude is not, of course, logically entailed by the commendableness of succeeding in doing so, but we nevertheless do make this assumption in our everyday practices: since we recognize gratitude as good, we consider lack of gratitude bad. On this basis, it could be argued, if life is a gift, the expression of gratitude for life—perhaps in prayer, perhaps in enthusiastic living—is morally commendable, while the individual who displays lack of gratitude or outright ingratitude by destroying the gift by suicide is morally reprehensible. R. F. Holland suggests that this is the root of our horror of suicide: like parricide, we see it as an act of extreme, ultimate ingratitude for the gift of life.[45]

Gratitude is, of course, a moral, not a legal obligation. For example, the established patron who helps a struggling student initiate a career has no legal basis to expect later support from his protégé if he himself falls from fame—but as moral obligations go, it may be a fairly strong one. The level of expectation of gratitude is related to the magnitude of the gifts and the size of the sacrifice it requires on the part of the donor: the greater the gift on the part of the donor, the greater the obligation on the part of the recipient, and the more morally appalling we would find ingratitude, particularly for major gifts like a transplantable kidney or an entire estate. If life is the greatest gift of all—and because life is a prerequisite to any further gifts or any human experience whatsoever, it is often said to be the greatest gift—then the greatest gratitude is owed to the giver of life.

However, there are situations in ordinary gift-giving in which the recipient of a gift may be less strongly obligated to gratitude, or not obligated at all. A gift may be unattractive, ill-fitting, or spoiled. It may be damaging to one's health or one's values. It may be unnecessary, burdensome, or embarrassing. We customarily feign gratitude even in situations in which we are not actually grateful, but careful inspection of our beliefs and canons with regard to gratitude and truth-telling will reveal, I think, that we do not consider ourselves obligated to feel or express gratitude in these situations at all. If parallel reasoning applies in the case of suicide, we might

[45]R. F. Holland, "Suicide," from *Talk of God,* Royal Institute of Philosophy Lectures, Vol. 2, 1967–68 (London: Macmillan, 1969), reprinted in James Rachels, ed., *Moral Problems* (New York: Harper and Row, 1971, 1975), pp. 388–400; see p. 397.

want to say that our obligation to be grateful for the gift of life depends on the nature and characteristics of the particular gift. If it is a good life—say, one involving a healthy, handsome body, an intelligent and sane mind, reasonable financial security, a peaceful political environment, deep human relationships, and so forth—we might well consider ourselves obliged to express gratitude (whether in prayer or in enthusiastic living) to the giver of this gift. But if the life you are given is an unsatisfactory one—one involving a diseased or deformed body, severe poverty, desperate political repression, terrifying insanity, unbearable grief or deprivation—we would be very much less likely, if the analogy with ordinary gift-giving situations holds, to claim that you are obliged to be *grateful* for it. Gratitude, in such a circumstance, might seem impossible or perverse.

Nevertheless, there are circumstances in which we do find gratitude morally appropriate even for unsatisfactory or defective gifts. A perceptive recipient, although he sees a particular gift to be unsatisfactory, knows something about the intentions with which it was given. For instance, although the gift itself may be crude or ungainly, it may have involved a great deal of effort or expense on the part of the giver, and it may be appropriate for the recipient to acknowledge these. Even the strength of the giver's intention to please may itself be an appropriate object of gratitude. If your small child glues together three acorns and a rock as the gift for your birthday, your pleasure in it is not primarily a function of the characteristics of the object itself, but of your child's affectionate intentions in presenting it to you. If the analogy holds for suicide cases, then while the individual who ends his painful, misery-filled life might not be held accountable for failing to appreciate the gift-object as such, he ought nevertheless to appreciate the affection with which God has bestowed upon him this gift.

But gratitude for the intentions and affections of a giver despite the unsatisfactoriness of the gift can be expected only in a situation where the giver is subject to limitations. The acorn-rock is welcome from a child, but not from an accomplished artist. Life, however, is the gift of a giver who has no limitations: it is the gift of an omnipotent, omniscient being, one who has, presumably, the ability to fashion for any individual a pleasant and attractive life, including a healthy body, a sane mind, and comfortable circumstances. God is not a giver limited to the creative equivalent of acorn-rocks. Furthermore, God's gift is assumed to be freely given; God, presumably, is under no compulsion to bestow any gifts at all. Given these assumptions, the individual who receives from God a life disfigured by pain or deformity cannot excuse the donor on grounds of limitations, and may begin to suspect that the donor's intentions are not the best. Similarly, the individual who does receive an acorn-rock from a skilled artist may suspect hastiness, lack of interest, lack of understanding, jokesterism, or even malevolence behind the gift.

Thus the potential suicide who, because his life is so excruciatingly painful to live, considers discarding the "gift" which an omniscient and omnipotent God has given him, in effect asserts that it is the donor's and not his own intentions which are subject to moral question.[46] If he does kill himself, it is God who is at fault and not he: God clearly is not a benevolent God, and one has no obligations to be grateful to

[46]Cf. Eike-Henner W. Kluge, *The Practice of Death* (New Haven: Yale University Press, 1975): "A gift which we cannot reject is not a *gift*. It also follows that if retribution were to be visited upon us because of such a rejection, mistreatment, or destruction of the gift from God, we should have no alternative but to conclude that it would be the individual who visited the retribution and not we ourselves that would be morally guilty. In fact, the very threat to visit such retribution would be immoral, for it would be a calculated threat or actual attempt to interfere with our liberty." (pp. 124–25).

the uncaring or even malevolent donor of a horrid and painful "gift." Read in this way, the original gift argument against suicide seems to backfire, and to legitimize suicide wherever life involves unfortunate, deeply unwanted circumstances.

One might reply that what is crucial is not that life is a gift, but that it is a gift *from God.* Since God is not just any ordinary donor, and since God is worthy of utmost reverence, one cannot trifle with His gifts as one might with those of another. But this compounds rather than resolves the problem; we now see clearly that it is part of the problem of evil. Why would God, who is not only omniscient and omnipotent but perfectly good, give to some individuals the gift of good lives, and to some others desperate or painful ones?

Three principal strategies are traditionally used to answer the problem of evil: 1) *The "ultimate harmonies" defense,* according to which there must be some evil in the world in order that the goodness of the whole be apparent, just as there must be shadow in the painting or a pause in the chant, in order that their beauty be appreciated; 2) *The freewill defense,* according to which the evil that occurs in the world is the product of the human being's misuse of the free will God has granted him; and 3) *The "soul-making" defense,* according to which God permits evil to occur so that it will develop, test, and strengthen souls in their quest for salvation. There are other theodicies, of course, but it is these three which have been central in the traditional discussions of philosophy of religion.

The answer to the question with which we are concerned, whether one is morally obligated to retain a deficient or defective life, and to feel or express gratitude to God for it, depends on the type of theodicy with which one attempts to explain the occurrence of evil in the world. Suppose one, for instance, relies on a soul-making theodicy: then one explains the evil and pain which occur in Jones' life as a benevolent measure, enabling Jones to develop and perfect his soul in a way that is not possible for individuals not granted an opportunity to suffer. For this opportunity, painful though it may be, Jones is perhaps obligated to be grateful: he, unlike others, may hope for human nobility and higher celestial rewards. But while Jones clearly has a duty of gratitude for this opportunity, this still does not entail that he also has a duty to exercise it, or that he is obligated to retain his life. If, on the other hand, one uses the ultimate-harmonies defense, one may argue that though there must be some evil in the world, Jones has no reason to be grateful that it was assigned to him. Finally, if the evil and suffering that occur in Jones' life and which incline him to suicide are seen as the result of his own misuse of free will, then again, one may wish to argue that Jones has no obligation to be grateful for his life. Just as the donor of a penknife is culpable for giving it to a three-year-old child who he knows will cut himself with it, so a God who bestows life on a being who he knows will misuse and thus suffer for it is not to be praised.

The general point is this: the answer to the overriding question of whether gratitude to God is appropriate or morally required, even when the life He has bestowed is unsatisfactory, depends on the type of theodicy we employ. But there is no easy agreement among philosophers of religion or theologians as to which, if any, of these theodicies is successful; all of them are open to considerable objection. If none of them is sound, we may be led to conclude either that God does not exist, or that He does not have all three attributes of omnipotence, omniscience, and perfect benevolence. Of course, if God does not exist, then the "life-as-a-gift-from-God" argument against suicide has no substance. But if God is assumed to exist, but lacks one or more of the three properties traditionally attributed to Him, then the success of this argument may rest on the matter of which property or properties it is that God is said to lack. We pointed out earlier that in ordinary cases of gift-giving, we are sometimes led to question the motivation of the giver of an extremely inappropriate or unsatisfactory gift; it would seem here that it is benevolence, rather than omnipotence or omniscience, which would come into question. But a further question then arises: if the God from whom one receives one's gift of life is not, after all, benevolent, does one continue to owe Him duties of obedience and gratitude; or, rather, does one begin to regard him as an adversary, from whom any route of escape, including suicide, is justified? On the other hand, suppose it is omniscience or omipotence which God lacks: his bestowing dismal, defective gifts of life upon some unfortunate individuals is the result of His being able to do no better, and the defectiveness of the lives in question serves as a measure of His lack of power and wisdom. One may discover an obligation to be grateful to such a God for his benevolent intentions and well-meaning efforts, but certainly not an obligation to express it by keeping the sorry products of his unsuccessful attempts. Indeed, a God who would insist that you do so would be the one to fault, not the individual affected by those efforts.

We see, then, that if we construe life as a gift from God, we may find gratitude for life and a consequent refraining from suicide an appropriate response for lives that are good ones. But these are not, by and large, the circumstances in which suicide is considered. In cases in which an individual's life is deeply unsatisfactory, and where suicide seems preferable to continued life, gratitude is inappropriate. Thus, the gift argument against suicide backfires: it leads to the conclusion that suicide, at least in certain kinds of cases, is not on these grounds morally wrong.

OTHER ANALOGY-BASED ARGUMENTS. If we glance very briefly at the other analogy-based arguments, we see that many of the same issues begin to emerge. Josephus, for instance, had argued that suicide is wrong because God's "loan" of life ought not to be returned until "he who lent is pleased to reclaim it," yet we recognize a variety of circumstances in which a borrowed object may or should be returned early: when the borrower cannot protect or care for it, for instance, or cannot keep it from damage by outside influences. If life is construed as a loan, which the lendee may keep only as long as he can adequately care for it, then by analogy suicide may seem appropriate in those cases in which the condition of the loaned life is threatened: the beginnings of deteriorative illness, the onset of insanity, the symptoms of degenerating character.

Similarly, if it is argued that suicide is wrong because, according to the Biblical text, man is made in the image of God, we can point out that while destruction of an image—a portrait, a photograph—may be an insult to the model when the likeness is a good one, it may be an act of respect when the likeness has become distorted. We can imagine that an individual would find himself, because of his sinfulness, criminality, or physical disability, a comparatively poor likeness of God, and our ordinary beliefs concerning image-destruction might suggest that he would be justified in ending his life. (This, of course, is independent of the question of whether these self-perceptions are correct.) If, on the other hand, the "likeness" is interpreted, as is customary in Catholic theology, as the conformity of the human will to the will of God, then the tacit premise of the underlying analogy—that one ought not destroy an image or likeness of someone—no longer exerts its initial precritical pull.

There are still other analogies. Considering the body as the "temple of God," although in general we hold it right to respect temples and wrong to desecrate or destroy them, we also recognize cases when for reasons of safety or cost temples are properly deconsecrated and razed. Similarly, considering Locke's notion of man as the "workmanship" of God, analogous to the products of the craftsman, we readily grant that in general it is wrong to destroy such things; but we recognize cases in which it would be morally correct or even praiseworthy to do so: for instance, when a particular piece of craftsmanship is defective, broken, or uncharacteristically clumsy. If, when contrasted with the lives of other human beings, one's own life seems to be an example of a good craftsman's uncharacteristically bad worksmanship, ordinary practices suggest that it would not be wrong or disloyal to destroy it.

The analogies which trade on personal relationships between man and God present similar issues. Take, for instance, Plato's conception of man as the bondsman or slave of God: while the Greeks held that a slave had no right to leave his master even if seriously mistreated, contemporary moral thought—if it were to recognize the institution of slavery at all—would surely hold that although a well-treated slave might have some obligation to remain, a mistreated slave does not. Analogously, the person who escapes from an unusually cruel servitude in life cannot be said to have done wrong. The Orphic argument that the body is the prison of the soul, from which one ought not escape until one's sentence is done, is challenged by the popular (although nonSocratic) conviction that a prisoner has no obligation to remain imprisoned if his conviction is unjust. Or consider Locke's description of people as "all the servants of one sovereign master, sent into the world by His order, and about His business": though our ordinary moral beliefs honor the faithful servant of the trusted master, they also recognize cases in which the servant ought to escape: when the master is gratuitously cruel, or demands some morally repugnant task. Similarly, if we conceive of man as a sentinel, as do Cicero (apparently mistranslating Plato[47]) and Kant, we may recognize that in general, sentinels are obligated to remain at their posts—except when rendered incompetent by wounds, blindness, or perhaps pathological fear: in these cases, we hold, it is fitting that they should yield the post to somebody else. Finally, in perhaps the most contemporary of these analogies, we may conceive of God as father, man as child, and hold that man's obligation is to trust and obey; but contemporary ferment surrounding children's rights and child abuse show that we are beginning to think children ought not always trust and obey, but in some cases ought to hide, run, or rebel. In this last case, we see that a traditional moral assumption—the duty of unquestioning filial obedience—is now undergoing widespread public examination and criticism, and we might expect its use in analogy-based arguments against suicide to decline. After all, if a person is God's child, then in circumstances in which that person's life is analogous to that of the abused child, escape by suicide is not morally wrong.

All of these circumstances involve what we might generally call evil: threat to a loaned object, poorness of an image or likeness, the crumbling unsafety of a temple, the defectiveness of a craftsman's products, mistreatment by the master of the slave, unjust sentencing by the court, perversity in the orders of the master to the servant, incapacitation of the sentinel, or the father's abuse of the child. Thus, although we cannot here give full consideration to these additional analogy-based

---

[47]Cicero reads the ambiguous *phroura* as "guardpost" rather than "prison"; Plato's (Orphic) argument had been that man is in a kind of prison and ought not escape; Cicero renders this as the claim that man is stationed at a guardpost, and ought not run away. See my "Philosophers' Death and Intolerable Life: Plato on Suicide," (*op. cit.* i/59) footnote 19, and discussions by such commentators as Burnet, Hackforth, Bluck, and Gallop *ad loc*.

arguments, we may nevertheless suspect that many of them will display the same structure as that of the gift argument we have examined: serious consideration of each analogy and its central concerns will lead directly to the problem of evil, and assessment of the argument as a whole then rests upon the adoption of one or another theodicy. One may assume, of course, that we do not always understand God's ways, and that God, despite appearances, always acts in the best interests of each individual in the world; but this is to assume, not to provide, an answer to the problem of evil. One may also hold that the occasions upon which the problem of evil seems to loom largest are precisely the occasions when the believer is called to *faith*, an absolute trust in God's ultimate justice and mercy, and that to choose to end one's life would be the act of ultimate despair. As the Anglican theologian P. R. Baelz puts it, suicide would be

> *a refusal to trust in God, an embracing of death for its own sake, a form of self-justification, a desertion to the enemy. A final act of despair is substituted for a waiting in hope.*[48]

But again, this is to dictate a stance, not to show that it is the right one in circumstances such as these. Without an answer to the problem of evil or an examination of the best response to its demands, however, the analogy-based arguments used in the Christian tradition to prohibit suicide all seem to defend it instead, at least in the kinds of circumstances in which suicide (as distinct from manipulative suicide attempts) is most likely to occur.

Of course, it is always open to the defender of the analogy-based arguments to observe that our analysis has treated these analogies in a wholly literal way, and to claim that they are not in fact meant literally but "metaphorically" or in some other way. God's gift of life is not like any ordinary gift, one might claim, and so not subject to the same considerations as those operative in ordinary gift-giving; underlying considerations regarding gratitude will presumably be different as well. Similarly, one could maintain that man is not the same kind of sentinel as the military watchman, or that the individual's relation to God is not like that of a child to an ordinary father. These are important objections. But the defender of such positions must then, if he is to maintain that these traditional analogy-based arguments provide any reason for thinking one should not commit suicide, supply some new metaphorical or other interpretation of these arguments which can then be examined. It is simply inadequate to claim that the notion of "gift" in the thesis that life is a gift from God ought not to be taken literally when one cannot supply any other interpretation of this term on which an argument might be based. In the history of religious argumentation concerning suicide, these analogies have not been given careful, sympathetic and yet nonliteral interpretations. Perhaps it can be done. Our examination here shows only that these analogies do not provide a secure basis for arguments against suicide *when taken literally;* obviously, this finding should not suggest that the religiously committed thinker scrap these arguments altogether, but may rather encourage an attempt to formulate more subtle and substantial versions of these arguments.

It is equally open to the defender of the analogy-based arguments against

[48]P. R. Baelz, "Voluntary Euthanasia: Some Theological Reflections," *Theology,* Vol. 75 (May 1972), pp. 238–51; reprinted in slightly excerpted form as "Suicide: Some Theological Reflections," in Battin and Mayo, eds., *Suicide: The Philosophical Issues* (*op. cit.* i/10), pp. 71–83. Baelz does not hold that all suicides are necessarily acts of ultimate despair.

suicide to claim that although the analogies may be taken literally, our ordinary practices and beliefs regarding everyday things, relationships, and situations are morally incorrect. Ordinary gift-giving beliefs and practices, we have seen, suggest that it is not always wrong to reject the gift of life; yet, one might argue, they are mistaken, and we ought *never* reject a gift or fail to show gratitude. But just as an objection to literal interpretation of the analogies obliges the objector to produce an intelligible nonliteral interpretation, an objection to our ordinary moral practices obliges the objector to provide a thoroughgoing critique of ordinary morality, and replace it with a coherent alternative moral system.

Either defense—that the analogies are not to be taken literally, or that our everyday practices are wrong—would prove an adequate rebuttal to the argument pursued in this section that the life-is-a-gift and other religious analogies are not adequate as arguments against suicide. But neither of these defenses is an easy one to make. In the meantime, we must remember that these analogy-based religious arguments, however they were intended by the historical figures who formulated and publicized them, are very frequently understood by persons within or influenced by the religious tradition quite literally, and are understood with reference to ordinary moral practice. However these arguments may have been presented, this is the way in which they are received, and it is this common, literal, ordinary understanding of these arguments which still lies behind the western suicide taboo.

Suicide as a Violation of Natural Law

The religious analogies serve to provide easily grasped, popular arguments that suicide is wrong, and the Biblical commandments are held to provide fundamental evidence that suicide is contrary to God's will. But the *explanation* of the wrongness of suicide traditionally favored within the medieval and later Christian tradition has involved the assertion that suicide is a violation of natural law.

The concept of natural law has been understood in quite varied ways; when applied to the issue of suicide, it has given rise to at least three distinct types of interpretation. Some authors claim that suicide is contrary to the natural physical laws governing the universe, including those which facilitate God's domination over life and death; others that it defeats man's normal, basic biological will to live; still others that suicide perverts man's natural ends, or the purposes he fulfills in the universe.

SUICIDE AND NATURAL PHYSICAL LAW. That suicide is a violation of natural law is sometimes interpreted to mean that suicide disrupts the natural physical laws with which God rules the universe or which God has established to ensure the orderly functioning of the universe. As Hume, the principal critic of this view, describes it, suicide offends God ''by encroaching on the office of divine providence and disturbing the order of the universe.''[49]

---

[49]It is not easy to identify who actually held the view Hume is attacking; Beauchamp (see below) argues that Hume is replying to Aquinas, but Hume's argument is surely a misconstrual of Aquinas' views. Nevertheless, Hume's attack has given this view a conspicuous place in the later history of the discussion of suicide, hence its consideration here. See David Hume, ''On Suicide,'' in *The Philosophical Works of David Hume* (Edinburgh: Printed for Adam Black and William Tait, and Charles Tait, 1826), IV, 556–67; also, David Hume, *Of the Standard of Taste and Other Essays,* ed. John Lenz (Indianapolis: Bobbs-Merrill, 1965); Tom L. Beauchamp, ''An Analysis of Hume's Essay 'On Suicide,' '' *The Review of Metaphysics, 30, no. 1 (September, 1976), 73–95.*

If suicide is a disruption of the established order of the universe, Hume claims, so is any other action which alters the normal outcomes of natural physical or psychological processes. However, we interfere with the operations of nature in many of our everyday activities, and if we did not, we would not long survive.

> *All animals are entrusted to their own prudence and skill for their conduct in the world and have full authority, as far as their power extends, to alter all the operations of nature. Without the exercise of this authority they could not subsist a moment; every action, every motion of a man, innovates on the order of some parts of matter and diverts from their ordinary course the general laws of motion.*[50]

To bring about an earlier death by suicide is no more, and no less, a disturbance of the operations of nature than to postpone death by attempting to cure oneself of a disease, by bracing oneself against a fall, or by protecting oneself against an enemy. Hume writes:

> *If I turn aside a stone which is falling upon my head, I disturb the course of nature, and I invade the peculiar province of the Almighty by lengthening out my life beyond the period which by the natural laws of matter and motion he had assigned it.*[51]

According to this stance, it is no more wrong to shorten one's life than to extend it. Hence, this argument against suicide is wholly ineffective; in order to make the case against suicide succeed, we would have to explain why some but not others among the laws of nature ought not be disturbed. But, Hume claims, there are no relevant differences with regard to human life: "The life of man is of no greater importance to the universe than that of an oyster."[52] Consequently, if disturbing some of the laws of nature is permissible, then it is—unless some further evidence should arise—permissible to disturb any of them, and suicide cannot be held to be wrong because it is such a disturbance. He puts the point in this way:

> *It would be no crime in me to divert the Nile or Danube from its course, were I able to effect such purposes. Where then is the crime of turning a few ounces of blood from their natural channel?*[53]

Of course, Hume's argument cannot be used as a *justification* of suicide; it merely succeeds in undermining one version of the natural-law argument against it. For if Hume's argument were taken to justify suicide, it would also justify every sort of genuine moral evil which occurs in the world: murder, theft, cruelty, and so forth. These, of course, are not to be justified, but not because they are not disturbances of the universe: they are deemed wrong on other, independent grounds.

A related argument holds that since God has "dominion over life and death," it is wrong to bring about not only the death of others, but one's own death as well. The emphasis here is on God's normal causal role in creating and destroying human life; one must not interfere with it. Thomas Aquinas, for instance, refers to God as

[50]Hume, "On Suicide," (*op. cit. 1/49) p. 561.*

[51]*Ibid.*, p. 562.

[52]*Ibid.*, p. 562.

[53]*Ibid.*, p. 562.

"master of life and death," and says: "And God alone has authority to decide about life and death, as he declares in *Deuteronomy, I kill and I make alive.*"[54] This notion, that an individual must not usurp God's power to create and terminate life, is also embedded in the civil law; Blackstone, in his *Commentaries* of 1775, remarks:

> *And also the law of England wisely and religiously considers, that no man hath a power to destroy life, but by commission from God, the author of it...*[55]

And it appears to be central in the anti-abortion, anti-contraception positions of some contemporary groups, both within Catholicism and in various other pro-life groups.

However, this argument may appear flatly wrong in holding that God alone has the power to create *and* destroy life. Even if one grants that God is somehow involved in or responsible for the inception of life, it may seem obvious that God is not the cause of the termination of life: wars, murders, falling rocks, diseases, explosions, and old age are what destroy life. To claim that God creates and destroys the human soul would not answer this objection; in Christian theology the soul is eternal, whether damned or saved, and is not destroyed even by God.[56]

But one might claim that wars, falling rocks, and diseases are the instruments by which God, as agent, indirectly brings about the deaths of human beings. Although this sort of theory is generally associated with the Christian middle ages, it is characteristic of classical Greek and other theologies as well. It may occur in a general determinist form, according to which God has at the beginning of time predetermined what natural events will befall each individual in the world, so that these events simply occur as the result of causal laws designed by God. It may also take the so-called interventionist form (the form often used in naturalistic explanations of miracles): God on some particular occasion uses a particular circumstance or item from the natural world—whether a war, a falling rock, or a disease—to bring about designs of His own. In both versions, it is God, operating through natural objects and circumstances and by means of ordinary causal laws, who brings about events which occur to human beings, including their deaths. Suicide is wrong, it would then be claimed, because it preempts God's operations in this manner, and so "encroaches on God's order for the universe."

But, it may be objected, if God is able to use wars, falling rocks, or diseases as His agents to bring about the death of an individual, He is also able to use that individual to bring about his own demise. John Donne pursues this counterargument:

> *Death, therefore, is an act of God's justice, and when He is pleased to inflict it, He may choose His officer, and constitute myself as well as any other.*[57]

[54]Thomas Aquinas, *Summa Theologiae* (*op. cit.* I/35), 2a2ae64.5.

[55]Sir William Blackstone, *Commentaries on the Laws of England,* 18th edition, ed. Archer Ryland (London: Sweet, Pheney, Maxwell, Stevens & Sons, 1829), Book IV, "Public Wrongs," Chapter XIV, "Of Homicide," pp. 188-90.

[56]The metaphorical sense in which suicide and other acts held to be sinful are said to cause the "death of the soul" is usually understood as equivalent to the "loss of eternal (heavenly) life"; it means not that the soul ceases to exist, but that it is consigned to permanent damnation.

[57]Donne, *Biathanatos* (*op. cit.* I/24), II. iv. 4: 2968-70.

Under these general theological assumptions, even those deaths we label "suicides" may very well have been brought about by God—with or without the kind of direct command envisioned by Augustine. Thus, we have no basis for assuming that the suicide has acted contrary to God's plans, when he well may have been the agent, witting or unwitting, of God's designs. Hume puts the point this way:

> Do you not teach that when any ill befalls me, though by the malice of my enemies, I ought to be resigned to providence, and that the actions of men are the operations of the Almighty as much as the actions of inanimate beings? When I fall upon my own sword, therefore, I receive my death equally from the hands of the Deity as if it had proceeded from a lion, a precipice, or a fever.[58]

The claim that God has dominion over life and death may, alternatively, be understood to make a normative point about how human beings should behave with regard to life and death. One might formulate this by granting that, as a matter of fact, human beings do have "dominion" or physical control over death, since they are able to end their own or others' lives at any time; whether they *ought* ever to do so is now the issue. Obviously, this version of the question is strongly associated with the general issue of man's use of free will. Some writers argue that, although man is granted the freedom to end his life, he ought never to do so. But others reply that the very fact that man is granted free will in this matter shows that the divine imperative is for the "responsible exercise of our freedom of choice" in bringing to an end our own lives.[59] Since suicide can be moral or immoral, godly or ungodly, it is in this view the responsibility of the individual in his own particular circumstances to make the moral, devout choice.

As with the religious analogies, there are a great many additional arguments similar to or based on this first group of natural-law claims, which have been traditionally presented against suicide. Just two need be mentioned here, both originating with St. Thomas: 1) that suicide is forbidden because it attempts to usurp God's judgment over "the passage from this life to a more blessed one"; and 2) the warning that suicide is "very perilous" because it leaves no time for repentance.[60] In reply to the first of these arguments, we might point out that in Christian theology no human act fully determines God's disposition of a soul, and hence the individual cannot force his own "passage" from earthly life to that in heaven. The second argument is primarily prudential; it holds that suicide jeopardizes the individual's salvation, so that suicide is not only wrong but foolish. This latter view, that suicide leaves no time for repentance, has been extremely influential as the basis of the Church's traditional denial of Christian burial to suicides (in recent years seldom enforced, on the grounds that most suicides are mentally ill): suicides were assumed to have died unrepentant and therefore in a state of sin. However, Robert Burton claims, even the most rapid forms of suicide cannot be said to preclude repentance; in his landmark psychology, *The Anatomy of Melancholy* (1621), he says that repentance can be instantaneous, and that God's mercy may come "betwixt the

[58]Hume, "On Suicide," (*op. cit.* I/49) p. 563.

[59]Baelz, "Voluntary Euthanasia: Some Theological Reflections," (*op. cit.* I/48) p. 247.

[60]Thomas Aquinas, *Summa Theologiae* (*op. cit.* I/35) 2a2ae64.5.

bridge and the brook, the knife and the throat."[61] One might reply that the Catholic's examination of conscience does take time, and so Burton's claim can hardly be considered sound prudential advice.

SUICIDE AND BIOLOGICAL LAW: THE WILL TO LIVE. A second major type of natural-law argument against suicide appeals to the *will to live,* or man's fundamental, natural tendency to preserve his life. Josephus, for instance, claims that:

> *suicide is alike repugnant to that nature which all creatures share . . . among the animals there is not one that deliberately seeks death or kills itself; so firmly rooted in all is nature's law—the will to live.*[62]

Also often interpreted in a biological way is St. Thomas' argument that suicide is wrong because

> *. . . everything naturally loves itself, and it is for this reason that everything naturally seeks to keep itself in being and to resist hostile forces. So suicide runs counter to one's natural inclination . . . Suicide is, therefore, always a mortal sin in so far as it stultifies the law of nature. . .*[63]

A failure of the will to live, it is held, is not natural, and therefore wrong.

Biological observations concerning the absence of suicide among animals have been widely accepted by traditional writers, though with specific exceptions. St. Ambrose, for instance, believed that bees kill themselves; in the seventeenth century, it was widely believed that pelicans commit suicide; and the myth of mass suicides among lemmings has persisted in Scandinavia and other northern areas for a number of centuries.[64] Some twentieth century accounts also hold that suicide is frequent among horses and dogs.[65] Popular beliefs exist that many species stop eating when they are mortally ill or wounded, and so accelerate their own deaths. Nevertheless, despite these exceptions, it is assumed that animals in general do not kill themselves: suicide is a distinctively *human* act.

If it is true, however, that human beings do kill themselves (and although a few human societies report very low rates of suicide, there are very few or none where suicide is unknown[66]) then it is false that "everything naturally seeks to keep

---

[61]Robert Burton, *The Anatomy of Melancholy* Part I, Section 4, Member 1, "Prognosticks of Melancholy." Ed. Floyd Dell and Paul Jordan-Smith (New York: Farrar & Rinehart, 1927), quotation from p. 374.

[62]Josephus, *The Jewish War (op. cit.* I/10), III 369–70.

[63]Thomas Aquinas, *Summa Theologiae* 2a2ae64.5 (*op. cit.* I/35).

[64]Walter Marsden, *The Lemming Year* (Toronto: Clarke, Irwin, 1964), cited pp. 134–36 in Bernice Einsidler and L. D. Hankoff, "Self-Injury in Animals," in Hankoff and Einsidler, eds., *Suicide: Theory and Clinical Practice (op. cit.* i/2), pp. 131–39. This paper cites much of the literature on suicide-like behavior in various animal species. See also Donne, *Biathanatos (op. cit.* I/24), Part 1, Distinction 2, Section 2, for seventeenth-century claims concerning pelicans and bees.

[65]Einsidler and Hankoff, "Self-Injury in Animals," (*op. cit.* I/64), pp. 133–34 and passim.

[66]See S. R. Steinmetz, "Suicide among Primitive Peoples," *American Anthropologist,* 7, no. 1 (1894), 53–60; Edward Westermarck, *The Origin and Development of the Moral Ideas* (London: Macmillan and Co., 1908), esp. Vol. II, Chapter XXXV, "Suicide"; Fedden, *Suicide (op. cit.* i/11) and Ruth Cavan, *Suicide* (New York: Russell and Russell, 1965), for surveys of suicide in preliterate and nonwestern

itself in being,'' and that human suicide runs counter to ''nature's law'' at least in any biological sense. A single case of suicide is sufficient to defeat such claims.

Of course, it is still possible to treat suicide as an exception, although acting in accordance with one's innate will to live is the rule. But even this weakened claim can be disputed. For instance, John Donne, surveying widespread suicide and voluntary martyrdom practices among the early Christians, claims that while man does have a natural will to live, he is also possessed of an ardent natural desire to die. So strong is this desire to die, says Donne, that it has necessitated ecclesiastical and civil laws prohibiting suicide, for otherwise the human population would be destroyed.

> Since, therefore, to my understanding it [the prohibition of suicide] hath no foundation in natural nor imperial law, nor receives much strength from those reasons, but having by custom only put on the nature of law, as most of our law hath, I believe it was first induced amongst us, because we exceeded in that natural desire of dying so.[67]

Similarly, Freud posits the existence of a natural destructive urge in the human psyche, which may either be displaced onto others in interpersonal aggression, or—though he regards these cases as abnormal—directed towards oneself, often resulting in suicide.[68] For Donne, the desire to kill oneself is not at all abnormal, but a natural feature of the human constitution; for Freud, the impulse which gives rise to suicide is also a natural feature of man, though it is usually deflected in outward directions.

An even more recent scientific development has challenged the thesis that suicide ''runs counter to one's natural inclinations.'' New biological data, particularly that assembled under the theoretical construct known as sociobiology,[69] suggests that suicidal behavior is not uncommon among animal species, and is genetically selected for wherever the death of an individual confers upon its nearest kin benefits sufficiently outweighing the genetic value of its own survival. For instance, a given prairie dog, spotting a predator, may issue a warning cry; though this behavior markedly reduces that individual's chance of survival (since it is the individual most likely to be captured by the predator), it markedly increases the survival chances of the individual's near kin, who escape into their burrows at the

---

cultures. Cavan writes, reflecting what is probably the prevailing consensus, ''Suicides for personal motives are reported from so many sources that it must be assumed that they occur in all except the most isolated groups with extremely simple cultures,'' (p. 64), and she observes that institutionalized suicide, including suttee, self-punishment, self-senicide, and ''running amok,'' is found in widely varied societies in all parts of the world. However, the consensus also holds that suicide rates in most small-scale societies are relatively low. See also Jean La Fontaine, ''Anthropology,'' (op. cit i/57). For a perceptive analysis of the way data in such sources as the Human Relations Area Files have been influenced by the interests of anthropologists who gather them, and a conjecture that this seriously distorts findings concerning suicide, see Jean Baechler, Suicides (op. cit. i/32), pp. 38–42.

[67]Donne, Biathanatos (op. cit. I/24), II. iii. 1, 2710–15.

[68]See Sigmund Freud, Mourning and Melancholia, in The Standard Edition of the Complete Works of Sigmund Freud, ed. and tr. James Strachey (London: The Hogarth Press, 1915), 14, 250–52; also Chapter V of The Ego and the Id, and the last pages of ''The Economic Problem of Masochism.''

[69]Edward O. Wilson's Sociobiology: The New Synthesis (Cambridge, Mass.: Harvard University Press, 1975) is the central statement of this thesis; his newer On Human Nature (Cambridge, Mass.: Harvard University Press, 1978) examines claims concerning altruism in animals and human beings.

warning. But these kin share a determinate number of genes with the self-sacrificing dog, including the genes which determine this behavior; thus, in future generations such behavior in similar circumstances will occur with increasing frequency, since it is these kin who survive. Similar altruistic phenomena include broken-wing distraction displays in birds, nest defense by soldier termites and ants, and defensive but fatal stings in social bees and wasps; all of these are suicidal behaviors in that they involve substantial risk to the individual's own life or actually result in death when it could be avoided.

Of course, one may object that kin-benefiting behavior in animals is not properly termed "suicide," since it involves no conscious intention to end one's life. But the issue which concerns us is not whether animals do commit suicide; the issue, rather is whether *human* suicide—especially those forms usually called heroism and self-sacrifice—can be accounted for by the same natural-selection mechanisms. Inspection of earlier and non-western human societies shows widespread practice of self-initiated or acquiescent suicide, altruism, and self-sacrificial behavior, much of it occurring in various institutional practices like suttee, self-senicide, self-regicide, and voluntary euthanasia associated with serious illness and insanity. Of course, it may not be that such practices in fact serve to promote the survival of one's near kin (though suttee and self-senicide are often explained as practices conferring economic and hence survival benefits upon one's family or immediate community, especially in times of scarcity). Then, too, there is a tremendous amount of cultural variation in the rates and types of suicide practices; this, too, might seem to undermine the sociobiological thesis. Yet the central suggestion of the sociobiological view in its strongest form is an important one: that suicide practices, though they may seem to be only a product of cultural expectation, are in fact genetically based, and merely find more or less free expression in various cultures. Seen from this point of view, some cultures, such as Greek and Roman Stoicism or traditional Chinese culture, can be said to encourage expression of the genetically-encoded tendency to voluntary death in certain sorts of situations; others, specifically post-Augustinian Christian and Muslim culture, attempt to suppress it. This is not to say that the sociobiological thesis is correct; if it should prove to be so, however, a disposition to self-death behavior in certain types of kin-benefiting circumstances could be said to be natural, in that it has become part of the genetic heritage of the human species.

Whether suicide or suicidal behavior is "natural" in the sense that it arises from central urges in the human psyche or is genetically favored, however, may have little bearing on the moral status of the act. There is some "natural" behavior which our moral systems do not permit, and some "unnatural" behavior which our moral systems recommend. Celibacy, we might point out, is hardly a matter of natural inclination, and yet highly prized within some branches of the Christian tradition.[70] Similarly, truthtelling rather than lying, sharing in scarcity situations, monogamy, and so forth are not always matters of biologically natural inclination, and yet are morally recommended in western culture. On the other hand, stealing, intimidation, and outright aggression may be "natural" behaviors, and yet are severely discouraged. Arguments against suicide which hold that it is "unnatural" because it runs counter to ordinary human inclinations are inadequate as moral arguments against suicide; such arguments move from "is" to "ought," arguing

---

[70]For an early allusion to this point, see Donne, *Biathanatos*, (*op. cit.* I/24) I. ii. 2, 1689–97.

that because human beings do generally attempt to remain alive rather than kill themselves, they ought always to do so.

SUICIDE AS THE PERVERSION OF MAN'S NATURAL END. The previous arguments that suicide violates natural physical or biological law depend on interpreting their natural-law claims as *descriptive* natural laws, and for this reason fail as moral arguments. Another way of interpreting these claims, frequently used in reading St. Thomas, is to argue that although suicide does occur and so is not counter to any descriptive physical or biological law, nevertheless suicide is counter to *prescriptive* natural law, which describes not the way things are but the way things ought to be. To term suicide "contrary to nature" is not to say that suicide cannot or does not occur, just as to term certain sexual acts "unnatural" is not to say that they are not practiced, but rather to say that these "unnatural acts" ought not occur.

This argument holds that certain kinds of activity are "natural" to man, and so ought to occur; other acts, like suicide, are not. This version of the natural-law argument has served as the basis of much of traditional and contemporary Catholic thinking on the issue of suicide. Just as it is "natural for the sun to light and heat the earth, for flowers to grow and bloom, for fish to swim and birds to fly,"[71] as one author in this tradition puts it, so it is natural for man to live and to engage in specifically human activities: thought, communication, the performance of morally good acts, and other actions which promote the fulfillment of man's highest potential. Suicide is wrong because it precludes these activities.

Other authors have described this natural-law view in similar ways. In *Julie, or the New Heloise,* Rousseau's fictional character Lord Bomston identifies the central human function as "doing good," and uses a concrete statement of the natural-law principle as an explicit argument against suicide.[72] When Saint-Preux, the lovelorn young man who is the central figure of the novel, proposes to kill himself, his mentor Bomston raises this question:

> *Is it lawful for you, therefore, to quit life? I should be glad to know whether you have yet begun to live? What! were you placed here on earth to do nothing in this world? Did not Heaven when it gave you existence give you some task or employment? If you have accomplished your day's work before evening, rest yourself for the remainder of the day; you have a right to do it; but let us see your work. What answer are you prepared to make the Supreme Judge when he demands an account of your time? Tell me, what can you say to him?*[73]

Lord Bomston also supplies an answer:

> *Whenever you are tempted to quit [life], say to yourself, "Let me at least do one good action before I die." Then go in search for one in a state of indigence, whom you can relieve; for one under misfortunes, whom you can comfort; for one under oppression,*

[71] Austin Fagothey, S. J., *Right and Reason,* Ch. XI: "Natural Law," (St. Louis: C. V. Mosby Co., 1953) p. 152.

[72] A number of critics maintain that Saint-Preux's arguments defending suicide, rather than Lord Bomston's against it, represent Rousseau's actual views, and this is probably the case; nevertheless, the arguments voiced by Bomston in this novel remain an excellent statement of the natural-law view. The discussion between Saint-Preux and Bomston is contained in Letters 114 and 115 of *Julie, or the New Heloise;* however, these letters have been severely abridged in the only widely available English translation. The quotations used here are from pp. 166–90 of *Eloisa, or, A Series of original letters.* (London: Printed for C. Bathurst, 1795).

[73] *Ibid.,* p. 182.

whom you can defend. . . If this consideration restrains you today, it will restrain you tomorrow; if tomorrow, it will restrain you all your life. If it has no power to restrain you, die! you are below my care.[74]

As a recent writer within the natural-law tradition summarizes the point on which Bomston is relying,

> *the suicide uses or neglects to use his powers to achieve an object, viz., his death, the very contrary of that for which they are naturally disposed.*[75]

They are naturally disposed, Bomston supposes, for doing good.

But even if we accept this premise, the argument still will not yield a firm case against suicide. This is because this argument is directed, so to speak, only to the able-bodied and to those of sound temperament; it does not say how persons ought to act who are, for any of a variety of reasons, unable to perform the "natural" functions of human beings. Even if we were to grant that it is "natural" and therefore morally obligatory for human beings to think, communicate, and perform morally good acts for one another, there can be circumstances for individual human beings in which they are not able to do these things. The person in severe and unremitting pain or subject to severe mental disturbance, for instance, may be unable to reason or think in any coherent way. The person who has suffered an aphasia-producing stroke or finds himself in a medical situation involving continuous intubation may be unable to communicate. And some persons may be unable to do good for others, either because of physical disability or because of (as in Plato's recidivist temple-robber) permanent defect of character. The natural-law argument does not make clear what obligations are imposed upon individuals whose capacities to function have been seriously diminished by disease or disability; these, however, are often the situations in which suicide, or prearranged euthanasia, may be considered. Aquinas would hold, surely, that one ought to live the life of reason *as far as one is capable of it,* and to this degree is committed to remaining in being, but does not consider whether suicide might be permissible in cases where this condition cannot be met.

The religious tradition, however, has sometimes maintained that even the human "near-vegetable," although unable to think or communicate or do good for others in any sustained way, nevertheless performs a morally good action by undergoing suffering; we shall examine this claim later. It is tied to the larger issue of the significance of suffering for the Christian believer and the belief that suffering is of value.

Suicide as Avoidance of Suffering

Unlike the earlier religious arguments considered here, the claim that suffering is in itself valuable, and therefore ought not be avoided by suicide, does not depend wholly on claims concerning the nature or properties of God. The theological version does involve a religious framework in which the notion of salvation is

---

[74] *Ibid.,* p. 190.

[75] Henry Davis, S. J., *Moral and Pastoral Theology,* Vol. 2 (London: Sheed and Ward, 1936), p. 114.

intelligible, but an important secular version, emphasizing cowardice, is also possible. Most of the earlier theological arguments we have considered do not survive dismissal of the standard theological assumptions; this one may.

SUICIDE AS COWARDICE   Although later strongly associated with the Christian religious tradition, the claim that suicide is wrong because it is cowardly seems to arise from secular roots. Central among these sources is Aristotle; he says that

> ... to die to escape from poverty or love or anything painful is not the mark of a brave man, but rather of a coward; for it is softness to fly from what is troublesome, and such a man endures death not because it is noble but to fly from evil.[76]

One finds in many Greek and Roman writers the related notion that true fortitude consists in the heroic endurance of suffering, and a number of these writers point out that this precludes at least hasty suicide. This notion is adopted by Christian writers as well. Augustine, for instance, says that

> ... greatness of spirit is not the right term to apply to one who has killed himself because he lacked strength to endure hardships, or another's wrongdoing. In fact we detect weakness in a mind which cannot bear physical oppression, or the stupid opinion of the mob; we rightly ascribe greatness to a spirit that has the strength to endure a life of misery instead of running away from it, and to despise the judgment of men...[77]

Thomas Aquinas says that suicide is "the inability to bear penal afflictions."[78] Religious authors frequently cite the Biblical example of Job, who endured extraordinary misfortunes without seeking to escape. They also frequently compare the suicide of Cato with the death of Regulus: whereas Cato killed himself to avoid becoming Caesar's slave, Regulus, though undefeated, returned to keep his promise to the enemy Carthaginians, although he knew he would be tortured to death in an exceedingly cruel fashion.[79] The notion that suicide is cowardly survives today: an observer commenting on the August, 1977, suicide of Wallace Proctor, a seventy-five-year-old dermatologist afflicted with Parkinson's disease, said that it was "unfair" because Proctor "got out of what the rest of us have to go through," namely death due to a long and debilitating illness.[80]

One might point out that not all suicide is "avoidance-motivated"; self-sacrificial, altruistic suicide typically does not involve flight from personally painful circumstances, but commitment to other persons or causes. Furthermore, not all

---

[76]Aristotle, *Nicomachean Ethics* 1116a, tr. W. D. Ross, in *The Basic Works of Aristotle,* tr. Richard McKeon (New York: Random House, 1941).

[77]Augustine, *City of God (op. cit.* I/19), Book I, Ch. 22, p. 33.

[78]Thomas Aquinas, *Summa Theologiae* 2a2ae64.5 (*op. cit.* I/35).

[79]See Augustine's discussion of the suicides of Cato and Regulus at *City of God* (op. cit. I/19) Book I, Chapters 23-24; Augustine says that Regulus is a "nobler example of fortitude" than Cato, although Christians supply much nobler instances.

[80]An account of Wallace Proctor's suicide, as aided by his close friend Morgan Sibbett, is available in *The New York Times,* Dec. 11, 1977; in the Public Broadcasting System's "All Things Considered" for Friday, Dec. 2, 1977; and in Berkeley Rice, "Death by Design: A Case in Point," *Psychology Today,* January 1978, p. 71.

suicide which is avoidance-motivated is necessarily cowardly: some evils are quite reasonably avoided. Besides, suicide itself may be a supremely difficult task. Paul-Louis Landsberg writes:

> It is very customary to find all suicides condemned as cowards. This is a typically bourgeois argument which I find ridiculous. How can we describe as cowardly the way of dying chosen by Cato, or Hannibal, or Brutus, or Mithridates, or Seneca or Napoleon? There are certainly far more people who do not kill themselves because they are too cowardly to do so, than those who kill themselves out of cowardice.[81]

The Stoics claimed that real cowardice lay in fearing death, true bravery in the courage to take it upon oneself. And many contemporary first-person accounts of contemplated or attempted but not completed suicide admit a lack of courage at the last moment.

In part, those who emphasize the cowardice of suicide stress its relationship to those painful circumstances which are to be avoided, including illness, disgrace, poverty, and loss; those who emphasize its courageousness are attending to certain painful features of the performance of the act, particularly evident in suicides that involve cutting, piercing, burning, falling from heights, and other violent means. But suicide can be seen as courageous in another way: it involves entering death, a state of which the individual has no prior experience, an unknown. The most famous display of hesitation in the face of this unknown is Hamlet's:

> Who would fardels bear,
> To grunt and sweat under a weary life,
> But that the dread of something after death,
> The undiscovered country, from whose bourn
> No traveller returns, puzzles the will
> And makes us rather bear those ills we have
> Than fly to others that we know not of?
> Thus conscience does make cowards of us all.[82]

Whether one believes in a beatific afterlife or no life after death, no one has prior knowledge of what it is like to be dead.[83] Obviously, those who choose suicide to escape suffering assume that what comes after death will involve less suffering than their current circumstances; otherwise, they would not make such a choice. But, as Philip Devine argues, one cannot rationally choose death, since one lacks adequate information about one of the alternatives between which the choice is to be made: to

---

[81]Paul-Louis Landsberg, *The Moral Problem of Suicide*, in *The Experience of Death and The Moral Problem of Suicide*, tr. Cynthia Rowland (New York: Philosophical Library, 1953; original French edition 1951), p. 68. Landsberg himself once planned suicide, but changed his mind after a religious experience while under capture by the Nazis.

[82]Shakespeare, *Hamlet*, Act III, Scene 1, 76–83. (Baltimore: Penguin, 1970), pp. 89–90.

[83]There have, of course, always been claims about those "returned from the dead," most recently fueled by Raymond A. Moody, Jr.'s *Life After Life* (New York: Mockingbird Books, 1975; Bantam, 1976), but scientifically verifiable accounts of what it is like to be dead are nowhere available, and the life-after-life reports describe only experiences occurring within a very few minutes after clinical "death," not, so to speak, death on a long-term basis.

choose death is to hazard a leap into the wholly unknown.[84] Nevertheless, one might argue that to avoid something because it is unknown is itself a kind of cowardice, and that suicide is the more courageous act, while remaining alive because one fears the unknown is the act of the coward.

Death as an unknown aside, we may still question the original Aristotelian assumption that the avoidance of evils is cowardly. Mere avoidance of pain is not cowardice; we normally call someone a coward only when he avoids some painful or dangerous action which he might reasonably be expected to perform, or when avoiding pain also involves failing to meet a morally required duty. A man who avoids an attacker is not a coward, unless, say, he is a soldier on duty or a wrestler who has volunteered for the sport. To support the claim that suicide is cowardly, one would have also to demonstrate that it involves failing to do a duty which the individual can reasonably be expected to perform. Unless, as Kant claimed, this duty is to be understood as a general duty simply to continue to live (in which case we must press for further justification of such a claim), the duties the coward avoids must be particular duties, including those to himself, to other persons, and to society in general. Among these might be the duties to preserve one's health, to support one's children, to contribute useful work to society. But in many kinds of suicide undertaken to avoid painful physical conditions or social circumstances, it may be increasingly implausible to speak of such continuing duties, since these are precisely the cases in which the individual cannot continue to function in ways which would satisfy such duties. Unless there is a general duty to live, to show that the suicide of a person who has advanced and debilitating cancer is cowardly, we must show that he is defaulting upon some obligation or duty he ought to perform for himself, his family or society. But it is just that, in cases of advanced and debilitating cancer, which is particularly hard to do.

Of course, this reply does not answer the position taken by St. Thomas, that suicide is wrong because it is an "inability to bear penal afflictions." Thomas' position is similar to the Orphic doctrine enunciated by Plato: the body is the prison-house of the soul, and one ought not attempt to escape until one's sentence has been served. But Thomas' position invites consideration of a general issue in social and political philosophy: does someone who has been sentenced to "penal afflictions," whether simple incarceration or various forms of physical hardship and torture, have a moral *obligation* to submit to them, and would it be cowardly (rather than prudent) to escape them if one could? We are tempted to answer both in terms of the justice of the sentence (the innocent convict has no obligation to remain; the guilty one does) and in terms of the severity of the punishment (the guilty convict is obligated to submit to confinement, but not to torture). This would suggest that suicide is impermissible only if the "sentence" to life is just and the severity of the afflictions is not great. But again, these may not be the situations in which suicide is most earnestly considered.

THE VALUE OF SUFFERING. In the Christian tradition the argument that suicide is the coward's way of avoiding suffering has taken on an additional element. The basis of this argument is evident as early as St. Paul's assertion that "we welcome our sufferings" (Romans 5:3): this is the notion that there is some positive value in suffering itself. The full-scale argument with respect to suicide is

---

[84]Philip Devine, *The Ethics of Homicide* (New York: Cornell University Press, 1979), pp. 24–28; reprinted as "On Choosing Death" in Battin and Mayo, eds., *Suicide: The Philosophical Issues, (op. cit. i/10)*, pp. 138–43.

first made explicit by Mme. de Staël at the beginning of the nineteenth century. "Suffering is a blessing," she writes in her long essay "Reflections on Suicide," (written to refute her own libertarian treatise "On the Influence of the Passions," composed many years earlier); "it is a privilege to be able to suffer."[85]

Her argument, briefly stated, is this: it is true that life often presents us with painful circumstances, and we may be inclined to consider suicide as a way of avoiding this suffering. But for the true Christian, suffering is to be *welcomed*, not avoided. For the true Christian, mere happiness is not the goal of life; rather, the true Christian seeks the attainment of blessedness, moral elevation, and eternal life. But the way to salvation is *through* suffering: one must therefore submit oneself willingly to suffering, reenacting the life of Christ, and triumph in one's faith despite one's suffering. To commit suicide in order to avoid suffering would be to fail to see it as the means to grace. As the contemporary Catholic writer Joseph Sullivan says,

> It is rather the mark of a good and holy God that he permits so many of his children to undergo that suffering here on earth. Suffering is almost the greatest gift of God's love.[86]

For the Christian, then, suffering is not a phenomenon to be excused or explained away. Rather, for the Christian, suffering—both one's own and that personified in Christ—is real, important, and in the end redemptive: it is the way to the beatific world beyond death.

But this emphasis on the value and centrality of suffering—even of the innocent—is open to a serious objection. If suffering is of value, it would seem to follow that, rather than work to reduce suffering among one's fellows and in the world at large, one ought to impose on them as much suffering as possible. But this, of course, is a wholly repugnant conclusion. We do regard suffering as an evil; it is something which it is our duty to eradicate, not to foster. W. R. Matthews, former Dean of St. Paul's, points out that we would revolt "against a person who complacently regarded the suffering of someone else as a 'blessing in disguise' and refused to do anything about it on those grounds."[87] We use anaesthetics where they are medically appropriate, whereas if we believed all suffering to be of value, we should hesitate to do so.[88] We engage in charitable works to ease or end suffering where we can.

On the other hand, we are familiar with the attitudes of popular culture towards suffering, and in particular with the folk truth that suffering "will make a

[85]Mme. de Staël-Holstein [Anne Louise Germaine (Necker), the baroness Staël-Holstein)], "Reflections on Suicide," in George Combe, *The Constitution of Man, considered in relation to external objects*, "Alexandrian Edition" [not in other editions]. (Columbus: J. and H. Miller, 18–?), pp. 99–112 of second half of volume. The earlier work is *A Treatise on the Influence of the Passions upon the Happiness of Individuals and of Nations*, tr. K. Staël-Holstein (London: George Cawthorne, 1798).

[86]Sullivan, *Catholic Teaching on the Morality of Euthanasia*, (*op. cit.* I/28), see esp. pp. 73–76, "The Catholic Philosophy of Suffering." See also Léon Meynard, *Le Suicide: Étude morale et métaphysique* (Paris: P.U.F., 1966), p. 105.

[87]W. R. Matthews, "Voluntary Euthanasia: The Ethical Aspect," in *Euthanasia and the Right to Death*, ed. A. B. Downing (London: Peter Owen, 1969), p. 25–29, citation p. 26.

[88]Joseph Fletcher, *Morals and Medicine*, (*op. cit.* I/18), points out in Chapter I that anaesthetics, especially in childbirth, were in fact opposed on these grounds when first introduced.

better person of you." The popular notion that physical or mental pain may be strengthening and character-building is quite conspicuous in cultural truisms about a variety of areas, from sports to the painful process of emotional maturation. We tend to believe that those who have suffered most—survivors of death camps, for instance—are elevated to a plane not achieved by those who have led untroubled lives. While at first glance, then, the contention that suffering is valuable may seem to be false and even scandalous, we find some support for this view in popular ideas, and we may suspect that the issue here is not confined to religious questions alone.

This dispute may center in part on an empirical question: what are the effects of suffering—physical or mental—on the character of an individual? But combined with this question is that of whether the effects of suffering on an individual are ones we should *value*. For instance, John MacQuarrie, stating a contemporary Anglican position, claims that at least some suffering has a "morally educative character." [89] Teilhard de Chardin gives a religious view of what we might call the purifying and perfecting effects of suffering on society as a whole:

> *Without Christ, suffering and sin would be the earth's 'slagheap.' The waste-products of the world's activities would pile up into a mountain of laborious effort, efforts that failed, efforts that had been 'suppressed.' Through the virtue of the cross this great mass of debris has become a store of treasure: man has understood that the most effective means of progress is to make use of suffering, ghastly and revolting though it be.* [90]

MacQuarrie suggests that the capacity of an individual for "depth of sympathy" and "love" is a product of suffering, and that the individual who has not known suffering would be incapable of these fundamental human attitudes. [91] Flexibility, humility, self-reliance, and a host of other virtues are also sometimes named as the products of suffering. Whether or not we have empirical evidence to confirm such claims, it cannot be denied that this notion is a strong component of contemporary popular belief.

But one may ask whether *all* suffering can be of morally educative character, and whether all suffering "regenerates the soul." Some contemporary thinkers who deal with this issue distinguish, though not always explicitly, between "productive" or "constructive" suffering, and that which is unproductive or even destructive. Many writers on euthanasia hold that suffering of the destructive variety may be legitimately avoided by (voluntary) euthanasia, since such suffering can have "no beneficial result." [92] Presumably, suicide to avoid this sort of suffering would be permitted. On the other hand, it would be cowardly or morally wrong for an individual to kill himself in order to avoid suffering if that suffering could be "regenerative," on the grounds that even though it may mean undergoing considerable pain, the individual has a moral duty to grow and develop where he can. The

[89] John MacQuarrie, *Dictionary of Christian Ethics* (Philadelphia, Pa.: The Westminster Press, 1967), p. 335, entry "Suffering."

[90] Pierre Teilhard de Chardin, *Writings in Time of War,* tr. Rene Hague (New York: Harper and Row, 1968), pp. 67–68.

[91] MacQuarrie, *Dictionary of Christian Ethics* (*op. cit.* I/89), p. 335.

[92] Matthews, "Voluntary Euthanasia: The Ethical Aspect," (*op. cit.* I/87), p. 26.

only suffering which one may without cowardice avoid by suicide is that from which no conceivable benefit can come.

If one accepts the premise that suffering is sometimes of value, but recognizes the distinction between constructive and destructive suffering, there will still be problems. It may not be possible for either an observer or the individual himself to tell in advance whether future suffering will be of the constructive or destructive sort. This is particularly difficult in circumstances where the suffering can be expected to be long-term or permanent and comparatively severe, that is, in just the cases where suicide might most likely be considered. Those who are religiously convinced, however, are likely to reject this sort of distinction, since on the central Christian model *all* suffering of the innocent—even that which appears entirely fruitless—can lead to ultimate spiritual reward.

The Religious Invitation to Suicide

The theologically-based arguments we have been considering are generally advanced to demonstrate the moral impermissibility of suicide, and although they do not always succeed, it has been widely assumed that the religious arguments are uniformly directed against suicide. But some theologies, particularly Christianity, lend themselves to arguments in favor of suicide; it is these that we now wish to examine. For the most part, these considerations have not been stated explicitly anywhere in historical or contemporary religious literature, and certainly not as explicit arguments in favor of suicide; nevertheless, they are crucial to a full understanding of the religious view of suicide.

Suicide as Reunion with the Deceased

Most western as well as some eastern theologies promise that life after death will involve reunion with one's already deceased relatives, lovers, associates, and friends. In classical Greek culture, this promise was recognized as a strong motivation for suicide; in the *Phaedo,* for instance, Plato remarks:

Surely there are many who have chosen of their own free will to follow dead lovers and wives and sons to the next world, in the hope of seeing and meeting there the persons whom they loved.[93]

The promise of reunion with the dead is an equally strong motivation in many other cultures as well. In *junshi,* one of the three traditional forms of Japanese suicide, a subordinate kills himself upon the death of his master or lord in order to follow him into the next world; the act is viewed as one of ultimate loyalty.[94] In the now

---

[93]Plato, *Phaedo* 68A (*op. cit.* I/11), p. 50.

[94]According to Tasuku Harada's entry "Suicide (Japanese)," *The Encyclopaedia of Religion and Ethics* (*op. cit.* I/1), XII, 35–37, in ancient Japanese society *junshi* was an act of loyalty required by custom, until the emperor Juinin (29 B.C.–70 A.D.) ordered the substitution of clay images for the bodies of attendants and animals. The custom was revived during the feudal period in Japan and forbidden again in 1744; however, occasional modern examples still occur, such as the suicide by *harakiri* of General Nogi

virtually abolished Hindu custom of suttee (also said to have been practiced in very early Greece and the Nordic countries), the newly widowed wife throws herself upon her husband's funeral pyre. The primary motivation may be the feeling that life has no point without the husband, but voluntary suttee is also viewed in part as an act of loyalty on the wife's part in following her husband into the next world.[95] Christian theology, too, tends to promise reunion with loved ones in the afterlife, though exact description of the kind of personal intercourse expected in the afterlife varies considerably among different denominations.

Even if one believes in this kind of afterlife activity, it still does not generate a case in favor of suicide if one's ties and obligations to persons still alive are as strong as to those in the next world. However, if the individual who is the object of one's primary personal loyalty dies, the case may be reversed; it is precisely this that occurs in *junshi* and in *suttee*. Some suicides for love are of the same order: Homer regards it as a mark of Andromache's great nobility that she was willing to sacrifice her own life to join the dead Hector. A variation of this theme occurs in the classic Japanese suicide form known as *shinju* (or *aitaishi*), where lovers who are not permitted union in this world kill themselves together—usually by drowning, tied together by a rope—in order to bring about their union in the next.

Such considerations, of course, do not form an explicit theological argument in favor of suicide in any religious tradition. But they do, I think, show the way in which a theology which offers personal reunion in an afterlife tends, however subtly, to invite suicide.

Suicide as Release of the Soul

A similar, though perhaps more abstract, invitation to suicide occurs in those theologies which view death as the moment of release of the soul. We've already seen that Plato, drawing on Pythagorean and Orphic teachings, conceives of life as a condition of penal imprisonment of the soul within the body. As long as the soul remains imprisoned within the body, it is subject to the body's limitations, and is dependent for knowledge upon the body's sensory faculties: sight, hearing, touch, and so forth. But the senses are untrustworthy and misleading, according to Plato; knowledge gained through them can never be certain. It is only when the soul is freed from these limitations imposed by the body that true knowledge can be attained. Socrates says:

We are in fact convinced that if we are ever to have pure knowledge of anything, we must get rid of the body and contemplate things by themselves with the soul by itself. It

---

and his wife at the time of the funeral of the emperor Meiji in September 1921. For a classification of types of suicide in Japanese culture, see Mamoru Iga and Kichinosuke Tatai, "Characteristics of Suicides and Attitudes Toward Suicide in Japan," in Norman L. Farberow, ed., *Suicide in Different Cultures* (Baltimore: University Park Press, 1975), pp. 255–80.

[95]See Upendra Thakur, *The History of Suicide in India* (Delhi: Munshi Ram Manohar Lal, 1963), for a discussion of many types of suicide in Indian culture, and A. Venkoba Rao, "Suicide in India," in Farberow, *Suicide in Different Cultures*, (*op. cit.* I/94), pp. 231–38, esp. 233ff. on *sati*. In Hinduism, the "next world" referred to is not the next incarnation, but Hinduism's dimly defined interval between this incarnation and the next. Of course, suttee can be explained on other grounds; as Venkoba Rao points out (p. 233), in at least some areas suttee was a matter of law intended to prevent the wife from poisoning her husband, since if the poisoning were successful she would be required to die with him.

seems, to judge from the argument, that the wisdom which we desire and upon which we profess to have set our hearts will be attainable only when we are dead, and not in our lifetime.[96]

To get rid of the body is to die. But if one's goal can be attained only in death, the question arises—and it is an acute one for Socrates—why not hasten that death by suicide?[97]

Plato attempts to resolve the conflict by arguing that suicide is not permitted unless one is compelled to do so by intolerable disgrace or unavoidable calamity, or is ordered to execute oneself by the state.[98] Suicide in sheer eagerness to rid oneself of the troublesome body, or in impatience to reach the afterlife, is condemned. (Plato's restrictions apparently failed to convince the young Greek philosopher Cleombrotus, who, after reading the *Phaedo's* account of the liberation of the soul in death, threw himself from the city wall into the sea.[99]) While Christian theology does not accept the Platonic metaphysics or epistemology, it does preserve the notion of death as a separation of the soul from the body (though a resurrected form of that body may later be restored). This basic dichotomy, between a world in which the soul is conjoined to a body and an afterworld in which it is not, supplies one of the root views of Christianity. The more flamboyant forms of Christianity might put it this way: in this carnal, corrupt world, the soul is shackled to the lusts of an insatiate body; in contrast, the next world promises luminous, clarified existence, in which the soul, cleansed and purified of its contaminating association with the body, is finally free. While this view is not orthodox, and may conflict with other basic views common to Christianity, particularly those which celebrate the fruitfulness of the world and the goodness of its creator's work, it may be quite a strong leaning, particularly in monastic and popular belief.

Again, this attitude does not give rise to a formal argument in favor of suicide, but it does, as does the notion of personal reunion with loved ones in an afterlife, subtly recommend it.

Suicide as Self-sacrifice

A third religiously-based inducement towards bringing about one's own death, particularly evident in Christianity and in Buddhism, is the importance given to self-sacrifice in the interests of other persons or groups. Self-sacrifice for others may take a variety of forms; so strongly is it emphasized in these two cultures that it is sometimes held laudable even when its object appears insignificant. Mahayana Buddhism, for example, preserves the story of the future Sakyamuni, who sacrificed his body to feed a starving tigress,[100] though in both traditions self-sacrifice is usually practiced for the protection or benefit of other human beings, not animals.

[96]Plato, *Phaedo* 66E (*op. cit.* I/11), p. 49.

[97]This issue is discussed in my "Philosophers' Death and Intolerable Life: Plato on Suicide" (*op. cit.* i/59).

[98]Plato, *Laws* IX, 873C (*op. cit.* I/11), p. 1473.

[99]Cicero, *Tusculan Disputations* I.34.84, quoting Callimachus. The story of Cleombrotus is also discussed by Augustine in *City of God,* (*op. cit.* I/19), Book I, Chapter 22.

[100]L. De La Vallée Poussin, entry "Suicide (Buddhist)," in *The Encyclopaedia of Religion and Ethics* (*op. cit.* I/1), XII, 26. The reference cited is to the *Jatakamala,* i.

Self-sacrifice for the spiritual benefit of another person, Catholicism has traditionally taught, is highly praiseworthy. Christ and Buddha, in their respective traditions, are exemplary of self-sacrifice, and in each tradition the believer is encouraged to emulate them. Self-sacrifice for others also occurs in situations which are not specifically religious; perhaps the best-known of these in recent western experience is the self-sacrifice of Captain Oates, an ailing member of an antarctic exploration party under Admiral Scott, who walked out into a blizzard to die rather than slow the progress and thus imperil the safety of the rest of the party.[101] Acts of self-sacrifice occur often in military, rescue, and a variety of other secular situations.

Christianity has strongly encouraged self-sacrifice, though it has continued to forbid suicide. Traditionally, it has distinguished between these two forms of self-killing by employing the principle of *double effect,* according to which the primary intention under which an act is performed is to be distinguished from secondary, foreseen but unintended consequences, and the moral status of a given action is judged by its primary intent. According to the principle of double effect, an action is permitted if (1) the action itself is morally good or neutral; (2) the evil effect is not directly intended, although perhaps foreseen; (3) the good effect follows directly from the action and not from the foreseen evil effect; and (4) there is grave reason for allowing the evil to occur.[102] Under this doctrine, it is permitted (to use the traditional examples) for a physician to enter a plague-infected area to treat victims, or a priest to enter a minefield in order to bring the sacraments to a dying soldier, even though both the physician and the priest may die; such cases will generally be called "self-sacrifice" or "heroism," and the term "suicide" is not used. In each case the primary intention is to bring aid to the needy, though in each case the agent also foresees the possibility of death. It would not be permitted, however, to kill oneself in order to provide donor organs for a dying relative; here the act performed, termed "suicide," is regarded as in itself evil, and is not permissible regardless of the good consequences which may flow from it.

In recent years there has been considerable debate, particularly among non-Catholic writers, as to whether the principle of double effect in fact effectively distinguishes between morally good and morally evil actions, not only in cases of self-killing and exposure to death, but in other areas such as abortion.[103] There is no doubt that the principle has been applied in some very strained ways. A particularly glaring example is the traditional justification of suicide by women to protect their virginity: it has been said that if a virgin leaps to her death from a building to escape an attacker, no evil act is involved, since she merely "wishes the jump, and puts up with the fall."[104] Robert Martin concedes that the principle of double effect distinguishes effectively between kinds of cases we tend to consider permissible and those

---

[101]For a brief account of Captain Oates' self-sacrifice, see R. F. Holland, "Suicide," (*op. cit.* I/45) p. 394. Holland quotes from Vol. I, p. 462 of *Scott's Last Expedition* (London, 1935).

[102]An accessible statement and useful discussion of the principle of double effect in bioethical contexts may be found in Tom L. Beauchamp and James F. Childress, *Principles of Biomedical Ethics* (New York: Oxford University Press, 1979), pp. 102–5. Their footnote 10, on p. 131, provides further references to the literature on double effect.

[103]See esp. Philippa Foot, "The Problem of Abortion and the Doctrine of the Double Effect," *Oxford Review* no. 5 (1967), reprinted in James Rachels, *Moral Problems* (*op. cit.* I/45) pp. 59–70.

[104]Henry Davis, S. J., *Moral and Pastoral Theology* (*op. cit.* I/75), 2, 116.

we do not, but argues that the principle itself is unsatisfactory. He says that although the principle holds that no morally praiseworthy action involves the accomplishment of a worthy goal by means which are intrinsically evil, nevertheless in punishment we routinely subject persons to suffering in order to bring about repentance or rehabilitation.[105]

One might want to challenge the assumption that suicide is intrinsically evil; thus it would not need to be excused by the doctrine of double effect. Alternatively, one might want to point out that the distinction between self-sacrifice and suicide under the doctrine of the double effect depends on the motivation for a given act. Much contemporary psychology suggests, however, that the true motive for a given action is not always evident, either to the agent who performs the action or to outside observers. For instance, although one may believe himself to be submitting to death in order to prove the strength of his religious faith or bring aid to another, his real (though not fully conscious) reasons for doing so may be quite different. As soon as we admit the possibility of actions which are performed under intentions not apparent or acknowledged by the agent, the distinction drawn between martyrdom and suicide is blurred. This would apply to any moral theory which considers intentions, but is particularly important in evaluating a highly stressful, often ambivalent act like suicide.

Durkheim, Brandt, and many other recent and contemporary writers define "suicide" without reference to the intentions under which the death-producing act is performed; it is sufficient, according to such definitions, that the individual know that the act he is performing will directly or indirectly bring about his death. Durkheim introduces this view:

> The soldier facing certain death to save his regiment does not wish to die, and yet is he not as much the author of his own death as the manufacturer or merchant who kills himself to avoid bankruptcy? This holds true for the martyr dying for his faith, the mother sacrificing herself for her child, etc. Whether death is accepted merely as an unfortunate consequence, but inevitable given the purpose, or is actually itself sought and desired, in either case the person renounces existence, and the various methods of doing so can be only varieties of a single class.[106]

This may seem to be merely a trick of redefinition, but it underscores the crucial point here: it allows us to see the way in which Christianity has actively encouraged its believers to choose death. Christianity does not call such choices suicide, but, rather, heroism and self-sacrifice; nevertheless, death is part of what is knowingly chosen, and Christianity celebrates that choice.

Suicide as Martyrdom and the Avoidance of Sin

One of the strongest pulls towards self-imposed death originates in the early Christian church's celebration of those who suffer, accept, or willingly embrace a violent and painful death at the hands of religious persecutors; it would be difficult

---

[105]Robert Martin, "Suicide and Self-Sacrifice," in Battin and Mayo, eds., *Suicide: The Philosophical Issues* (*op. cit.* i/10), pp. 48–68.

[106]Durkheim, *Suicide* (*op. cit.* :/20), p. 43.

to overestimate the importance of these persecutions in shaping the eventual Christian view of suicide. Martyrdom was prevalent in the early years of the Church; although reliable data is not available, contemporary estimates of the total number of victims in the years from the onset of persecution under Nero in A.D. 64 until the conversion of Constantine in 313, range from 10,000 to 100,000. The frequency of martyrdom may be strongly overestimated by some of the more fervent writers, but these accounts, even if exaggerated, have been influential in shaping Christianity's attitudes towards suicide. For instance, Eusebius writes:

> Why should I now make mention by name of the rest or number the multitude of the men or picture the various sufferings of the wonderful martyrs, sometimes slaughtered with the axe, as happened to those in Arabia, sometimes having their legs broken, as fell to the lot of those in Cappadocia, and on some occasions being raised on high by the feet with heads down and, when a slow fire was lit underneath them, choking to death by the smoke sent out from the burning wood, as was visited upon them in Mesopotamia, sometimes having their noses and ears and hands mutilated, and the other limbs and parts of the body cut to pieces, as took place in Alexandria?
> Why should we rekindle the memory of those in Antioch who were roasted on hot grates, not unto death but with a view to a lingering punishment, and of others who let their right hand down into the very fire sooner than touch the abominable sacrifice? Some of these, avoiding their trial, before they were captured and had come into the hands of the plotters, threw themselves down from high buildings, considering death as booty taken from the wickedness of evil men.[107]

Whatever the actual extent of martyrdom, it is clear that the Christians played an active role in the persecutions. Martyrdom was heavily encouraged. Confessors—those subjected to imprisonment and torture—attracted widespread support among the Christian community; they were frequently brought food and other articles while in prison and were the focus of extensive prayer. Some early Christian writers condemned the practice of offering support to jailed confessors, claiming that it undermined the hardships which these individuals had elected; nevertheless, these practices continued, and the confessors became the Christ-like heroes of their communities. This served, of course, to increase the eagerness of others for a similar role. The theological writers of the third century began to assert that those who actually died for the faith—not merely confessors, but martyrs proper—were assured of immediate salvation. They believed that the baptism of blood could completely remit sin, and thus render the sufferer worthy of immediate admission to Paradise. This, too, served to encourage willing subjection to the persecutions.

There was yet another ingredient in the early Christian enthusiasm for death which invited not merely submission to persecution but an active role in one's own death. The body was often regarded as the locus of sin. This is not a new idea; it occurs in many eastern cultures, though it probably enters Christianity through Greek culture. Plato, as we have seen, had described the body's demands for food, drink, sex, and other physical pleasures as an obstacle to the soul's achievement of genuine knowledge; his view of the body as impediment or obstacle is adopted by many early Christian thinkers. In St. Paul, it is transformed into the notion that the body is an impediment to true spiritual life.

[107]Eusebius, *Ecclesiastical History,* Book 8, Chapter 12. Tr. Roy J. Deferrari, (New York: Fathers of the Church, Inc., 1955), 29, 184–85.

For those who live according to the flesh set their minds on the things of the flesh, but those who live according to the spirit set their minds on the things of the spirit. To set the mind on the flesh is death, but to set the mind on the spirit is life and death. For the mind that is set on the flesh is hostile to God; it does not submit to God's law; indeed, it cannot; and those who are in the flesh cannot please God.[108]

But if the body inevitably leads one to sin, and if sin is unavoidable as long as one is in the body, then it is clear that one's chances of leading a sinless life improve if one can be released from that body. Thus, release from the body is desired not only for its own sake, but for an additional reason. To die and thereby to avoid this sinful world altogether is one's best hope of salvation. We see here the characteristic Christian contempt of this worldly existence: what one longs for is not an extension of one's sinful existence in this corrupt world, but attainment of the blessed life beyond. Suicide, then, is clearly the reasonable and religious choice: by killing oneself to avoid the sins that one will inevitably commit in this world, one secures one's hopes of heaven. Death is not an evil; it is merely a gateway, as it were, to the world beyond, and it is in one's best interests to pass through that gate as soon as possible.

These beliefs invite suicide in very specific circumstances: for maximum effectiveness, one is to end one's life immediately after confession and absolution, at that moment when one has been forgiven for all previous sin, and before any new misdeeds can be committed. St. Augustine sees clearly what the practical consequences of this religious reasoning would be; ironically, he says:

> ... we reach the point when people are to be encouraged to kill themselves for preference, immediately they have received forgiveness of all sins by washing in the waters of holy regeneration. For that would be the time to forestall all future sins—the moment when all past sins have been erased. If self-inflicted death is permitted, surely this is the best possible moment for it! When a person has been thus set free why should he expose himself again to all the perils of this life, when it is so easily allowed him to avoid them by doing away with himself?[109]

This attitude, together with the growing enthusiasm for martyrdom, made voluntary death a crucial issue for the early church: can one *seek* death or martyrdom, whether to prove one's faith or to avoid sin, in order to achieve salvation? Some early writers actively encouraged the seeking of martyrdom: Tertullian, for instance, applauds a group of North African Christians for voluntarily surrendering themselves to the Roman governor, and counsels confessors and prospective martyrs:

> ... if you have missed some of the enjoyments of life, remember it is the way of business to suffer some losses in order to make larger profits.[110]

---

[108]*Romans* 8:5–8.

[109]Augustine, *City of God* (*op. cit.* I/19), I, 27.

[110]Tertullian, Letter "To the Martyrs," in *Disciplinary, Moral and Ascetical Works*, tr. Rudolph Arbesmann (New York: Fathers of the Church, Inc., 1959), Vol. 40, p. 20.

Valerian, similarly, exhorts his readers to martyrdom on the basis of the same trade-off analogy: "The wise man will hasten eagerly to martyrdom, since he sees that giving up present life is part of the gaining of [eternal] life."[111]

Some writers did take a stand against self-initiated martyrdom; Gregory of Nazianzus, for instance, says that it is "mere rashness to seek death, though cowardly to refuse it."[112] But many applauded voluntary death, especially as a means of preserving one's virtue and faith. Of particular importance was the issue of whether Christian women whose virginity or chastity was threatened (like St. Pelagia, mentioned earlier) might kill themselves in order to avoid violation. While some thought not, Tertullian, Eusebius, and Jerome approved. Eusebius narrates as an example of Christian virtue, the following story:

> And a certain holy and marvelous person in virtue of soul, but a woman in body, and otherwise celebrated among all those at Antioch for wealth and birth and good repute, who had brought up two unmarried daughters in the precepts of religion, pre-eminent for beauty and bloom of body, when the great envy that was stirred up over them endeavored in every way to track them to where they were concealed, then on learning that they were staying in a foreign country deliberately called them to Antioch and they presently fell within the trap of the soldiers, on seeing herself and her daughters in difficulty, and giving consideration to the terrible things that will arise from human beings, and the most terrible and unbearable of all, threat of fornication, exhorting both herself and her girls that they should not submit to listening to this even with the tips of their ears, but saying that the surrendering of their souls to the slavery of demons was worse than all deaths and every destruction, submitted that taking refuge with the Lord was the one release from all these troubles, and then when they had agreed with her opinion and had arranged their garments suitably about their bodies, as they came to the very middle of their journey, they requested of the guards a little time for retirement, and cast themselves in a river that was flowing by.[113]

Numerous other virgin martyrs were venerated for making similar choices.

Not only did the martyr cults flourish, but sects of Christians and deviant Christians openly advocating self-initiated death arose. The Donatists, Augustine writes,[114] "seek to frighten us with their acts of self-destruction"; the Circumcellions, a still more extreme group within Donatism, openly advocated and practiced suicide in the effort to achieve martyrdom. They were immediately labeled heretics, but that apparently did not diminish their zeal. They have been described in this way:

[111]Valerian, Homily 15, "The Excellence of Martyrdom," in *Saint Peter Chrysologus, Selected Sermons, and Saint Valerian, Homilies,* Tr. George E. Ganss (New York: Fathers of the Church, 1953), 17, 397–403; quotation p. 398.

[112]Gregory of Nazianzus, *Orationes* xlii, 5, 6, cited by Maurice H. Hassatt, entry "Martyr," *Catholic Encyclopaedia* (New York: The Gilmary Society; Robert Appleton Co., 1910, The Encyclopaedia Press, 1913), 9, 736–40.

[113]Eusebius, *Ecclesiastical History* (*op. cit.* I/107), Chapter 12, pp. 185–86.

[114]Augustine, Letter 204, to Dulcitius, in *Letters,* Vol. V, tr. Sister Wilfrid Parsons (New York: Fathers of the Church, Inc., 1956), 5, 3.

Warned by a dream or revelation that his time was at hand, a Circumcellion would go forth and stop a traveller, or better still, more reminiscent of the heroic age of Christianity, a magistrate. The unfortunate would be given the choice of killing or being killed. Others would rush in on a pagan festival and offer themselves for human sacrifice. These became martyrs automatically... The alternative was mass suicide. Crowds would fling themselves over precipices or drown in the Chotts, or even burn themselves alive...[115]

Self-elected death as a way of avoiding inevitable sin, as a way of preserving oneself from sexual violation, and as a way of achieving the immediate salvation of a martyr was epidemic in the Christian community, most particularly in North Africa. It took place individually, but it also took place in group or mass suicides, some of quite large scale. It is against this situation that Augustine takes the stand which has become the central statement of Christianity on the issue of suicide: suicide is prohibited by the commandment "Thou shalt not kill," and except when expressly commanded by God, wholly and seriously wrong. So great a sin is suicide, that no other sin—whether fornication, injury to another, or apostasy—may be avoided by it; no salvation can be attained by this means.

Although there is little reason to think that Augustine's position is authentically Christian,[116] and although it clearly was a response to pressing practical circumstances, it nevertheless rapidly took hold and within an extremely short time had become universally accepted as fundamental Christian law.

Martyrdom, like self-sacrifice, it may be argued, is not the same as suicide, and the early Christian encouragement of martyrdom should not be interpreted as an enticement towards suicide itself. But there is clear historical evidence that the early church's call to martyrdom was in fact interpreted as an invitation to deliberate self-killing by many (for example, the Circumcellions); it was the early church's enormous enthusiasm for martyrdom which obligated Augustine to formulate his position against suicide. Of course, the fact that Augustine's condemnation of suicide was necessitated by historical circumstances does not entail that it is wrong.[117]

Suicide and the Attainment of the Highest Spiritual State

Finally, in what is perhaps the most powerful of the Christian inducements to suicide, self-willed departure from this life may be viewed as a way of attaining the highest spiritual state, usually termed salvation or union with God. This notion is extremely strong in a number of eastern religious traditions as well. For instance, the Hindu *Saiva Puranas* advocate suicide by fire or by falling from a mountain cliff, in order to obtain a post-death existence of unalloyed sensual pleasure;[118] the Dharmasutras expressly state that the world of *Brahman* is obtained by self-immolation

[115]W. C. Frend, *The Donatist Church* (Oxford, Clarendon, 1952), p. 175.

[116]See A. Bayet, *Le Suicide et la Morale* (Paris: Alcan, 1922).

[117]Baelz, "Voluntary Euthanasia: Some Theological Reflections," (*op. cit.* I/48), p. 240.

[118]See Thakur, *The History of Suicide in India* (*op. cit.* I/95), in the section on "Religious Suicides," pp. 77–111, for this and other examples of Hindu, Buddhist, and Jain religious suicide.

in fire.[119] Release from the world of illusion and the eternal cycle of rebirth is said to be attainable by various means, including drowning, self-immolation, starvation, self-dismemberment, or falling from a cliff, often at specific holy sites.[120] Although these religious traditions also contain prohibitions of suicide, and although in particular the Buddha appears to have been opposed to suicide, religious suicide in order to attain the highest religious state has been widely recommended and practiced in Hinduism and Buddhism.

In Christianity, an explicit longing for death in order to achieve the highest spiritual condition is expressed by a great many thinkers; it is also a powerful element in the motivation for martyrdom. John Donne, as has been mentioned, claims that we all have a religiously fortified "natural desire of dying," and he confesses to his own "sickly inclination" to commit suicide.[121] St. Paul had revealed his own desire for death in his letter to the Philippians:

> *I am torn two ways: what I should like is to depart and be with Christ; that is better by far; but for your [the Church's] sake there is greater need for me to stay on in the body.*[122]

Where the desire for death is strongest, it is also held most praiseworthy. It is seen as a triumph over the pleasures of the flesh and entanglements of this world, and as devout commitment to the ultimate spiritual experience of the next. The sheer immediacy of one's need for union with God is a sign of the highest spiritual elevation, and it is the individual who has achieved the greatest degree of spiritual enlightment who prays most earnestly for death. As the Christian mystic Angela of Foligno confesses, after experiencing a vision of God:

> *So I was left with the certainty that it was God who had spoken with me; and because of this sweetness and the grief of his departure did I cry aloud, desiring to die. And seeing that I did not die, the grief of being separated from Him was so great that all the joints of my limbs did fall asunder . . .*
> *I longed for death that I might attain unto that delight of which I now felt something, and because of this did I wish to depart from this world. Life was a greater grief unto me than had been the deaths of my mother and my children, more heavy than any other grief of which I can bethink me.*[123]

The lure exerted by the promise of reunion with the deceased, release of the soul, the rewards of martyrdom, and the attainment of the highest spiritual states, including union with God, all occur in Christianity. Indeed, this sort of lure occurs in any theology which deems earthly life inferior to an afterlife. Thus the question of the permissibility of suicide arises, though often only inchoately, for any sincere

[119]A. Berriedale Keith, entry "Suicide (Hindu)," in *The Encyclopaedia of Religion and Ethics (op. cit.* I/1), XII, 33–35.

[120]Thakur, *History of Suicide in India (op. cit.* I/95), p. 79. Also see Venkoba Rao, "Suicide in India," *(op. cit.* I/95), pp. 231–32.

[121]Donne, *Biathanatos, (op. cit.* I/24), Preface.

[122]Philippians 1:23.

[123]Angela of Foligno, *The Book of Divine Consolation of the Blessed Angela of Foligno,* tr. Mary G. Steegman (New York: Cooper Square Publishers, 1966), Treatise III, "Of the Many Visions and Consolations Received by the Blessed Angela of Foligno," pp. 167–68.

believer in a religious tradition of this sort, whether that individual's present life is a happy one or filled with suffering. Religious suicide is not always a matter of despair; it is often a matter of zeal. The general problem presented by the promise of a better afterlife may be strongest in Christianity, since the afterlife of spiritual bliss depicted by Christianity is a particularly powerful attraction.

The religious invitation to suicide is strong in other cultures, too, but instead of prohibiting suicide entirely, most other religious cultures have continued to permit some religiously motivated suicide. Usually, however, religious suicide is channeled into controlled institutional practices. Examples of this include the ritual deaths of African tribal kings, whose fixed term of office was terminated in compulsory but willingly performed self-execution,[124] and the Brahmin practice of retiring into the forest to complete one's life in ascetic rituals culminating in death.[125] However, these religiously based practices serve to regulate not only religiously motivated suicide but also suicides for a variety of other reasons, including ill health, grief, social or political disgrace, and old age. In India, for instance, it was common for persons afflicted with leprosy or other incurable diseases to bury or drown themselves with appropriate religious ceremony;[126] this practice was believed to make them acceptable to the deities, but also served to facilitate both sanitation and humane self-euthanasia among the incurably ill. The ill also practiced self-immolation, believing that this purification guaranteed transmigration into a healthy body.[127] *Suttee*, widely practiced, was the institutional form of suicide associated with bereavement and the potential economic dependence of women. Japanese *seppuku*, the method of punishment frequently required of wrongdoers from the nobility and military classes,[128] was associated with social or political disgrace. In Hindu culture, as in Eskimo, Arab, American Indian, and a great variety of other cultures, the aged committed suicide, sometimes directly and sometimes by acquiescence to abandonment when they were no longer capable of governing a family or contributing to its economic welfare.[129] By and large, widespread efforts to prevent institutionally governed suicides of these sorts developed only after the intrusion of western, Christian-based culture into these societies.

Christianity, however, has not developed institutional practices regulating suicide, either in cases of religious motivation, or where occasioned by illness, old age, bereavement, economic scarcity, or other practical calamity. Of course, institutional suicide is not entirely unknown in western, Christian-based culture: for instance, until recently it was expected that the captain would "go down with his ship." Among Prussian army officers of the nineteenth century, suicide was expected of those unable to pay their gambling debts. There are also reports from

---

[124]Fedden, *Suicide (op. cit.* i/11), p. 23, describes such practices on the Malabar coast, based on accounts in James Frazer's *The Dying God*.

[125]Venkoba Rao, "Suicide in India," (*op. cit.* I/95), p. 232.

[126]Thakur, *History of Suicide in India (op. cit.* I/95) p. 78.

[127]*Ibid.*, p. 78.

[128]Tasuku Harada, entry "Suicide (Japanese)" (*op. cit.* I/94), pp. 35-37. See also Iga and Tatai, "Characteristics of Suicides and Attitudes towards Suicide in Japan," (*op. cit.* I/94).

[129]Simone de Beauvoir's *The Coming of Age*, tr. Patrick O'Brian (New York: G. P. Putnam's Sons, 1972) provides a readable survey of senicide and self-senicide practices in a wide variety of cultures; see esp. Part I, Chapter 2: "The ethnological data."

seventeenth century Brittany of a religious practice known as the "Holy Stone," whereby, at the request of the victim, the priest would bring down a large stone upon the head of someone suffering from a painful and incurable disease.[130] These practices have been of extremely limited scope, however. By and large, institutional suicide, other than that associated with self-sacrifice and martyrdom, has been unknown in the Christian west. Thus the issue of whether or not suicide is permissible in the kinds of personal and social circumstances frequently governed by institutional suicide in other cultures has remained acute in Christianity, and is made more acute by the fact that the central, scriptural texts and early history of Christianity do not contain any explicit prohibition of suicide.

I think this is why we find so many of the religious arguments against suicide unconvincing, even if one accepts the theological premises on which they rest. One is struck by their heuristic character and the shallowness of the surface analogies upon which many of them rest. One also sees that these arguments do not account for many of the circumstances in which the question of suicide is most likely to arise. Schopenhauer, observing that there is no prohibition or positive disapproval of suicide in the scriptures of the Judaeo-Christian tradition, remarks that therefore

> . . . religious teachers are forced to base their condemnation of suicide on philosophical grounds of their own invention. These are so very bad that writers of this kind endeavor to make up for the weakness of their arguments by the strong terms in which they express their abhorrence of the practice . . .[131]

Schopenhauer also remarks that if there are any moral arguments against suicide, "they lie very deep and are not touched by ordinary ethics";[132] we might say that if there are any effective religious arguments against suicide, they too are deep, and have not yet been touched by the sort of argument traditionally offered within Christian religion.

We have considered here the central religious arguments against suicide; a great number of others have been advanced as well. Suicide, some Epicureans and Stoics claimed, is wrong because it involves the destruction of the divine spark or soul. Plotinus held that suicide was a perturbation or pollution of the soul, since its separation from the body is the product of passion.[133] The Council of Arles (A.D. 542) pronounced suicide to be "diabolically inspired"; this view is echoed by Luther, who held suicide to be a work of the devil.[134] Blackstone, commenting on eighteenth-century English law, remarked that the suicide "rushes into God's presence uninvited."[135] In addition to the arguments already considered here, Thomas

---

[130]Fletcher, *Morals and Medicine*, (*op. cit.* I/18) p. 180.

[131]Arthur Schopenhauer, "On Suicide," in *Studies in Pessimism*, tr. T. Bailey Saunders, *Complete Essays of Schopenhauer* (New York: Wiley Book Co., 1942), p. 25.

[132]Arthur Schopenhauer, *Foundation of Morals*, Section/Paragraph 5.

[133]Plotinus, *Enneads*, tr. A. H. Armstrong (Cambridge: Harvard University Press, 1966), Ennead I, ix, pp. 322–25.

[134]Martin Luther, *The Table Talk or Familiar Discourse of Martin Luther*, trans. William Hazlitt (London: David Bogue, 1848), DLXXXIX, p. 254. The saying attributed to Luther is: "It is very certain that, as to all persons who have hanged themselves, or killed themselves in any other way, 'tis the devil who has put the cord round their necks, or the knife to their throats."

[135]Blackstone, *Commentaries on the Laws of England* (*op. cit.* I/55), Book IV, p. 189.

Aquinas also saw suicide as a "deliberate choice of evil," and a violation of the charity one owes oneself.[136] Because death is "the wages of sin," it has been argued, it is something we ought not deliberately bring about;[137] death is a punishment, and should not be self-inflicted. Suicide is a failure of trust, say others. And it has often been said that God has "appointed" or "fixed" or "allotted" a duration of time that each individual shall spend on earth, so that to commit suicide is to tamper with this plan. Some of these arguments may overlap with those we've already examined; none of them, I think, will survive analysis any more successfully than those we have already examined, and it is tempting to discard them all as expedients necessary to counteract the strong lure of the tacit Christian invitation to suicide. Nevertheless, the reader is invited to examine these arguments for himself, or to add still others to the list; there may be a deeper, more profound religious argument against suicide we have not yet reached. Or the reader may prefer to adopt the attitude of the seventeenth-century cardinal John De Lugo, who recognizes the arguments to be weak and nevertheless asserts their conclusion to be true:

> For though its [suicide's] turpitude is immediately apparent, it is not easy to find the foundation for this judgment. Hence (a thing that happens in many other questions), the conclusion is more certain than the reasons adduced by various authors for its proof.[138]

This is hardly, however, a philosopher's stance.

[136]Thomas Aquinas, Summa Theologiae (op. cit. I/35), 2a2ae64.5.

[137]The Church Assembly Board for Social Responsibility, Ought Suicide To Be a Crime? (op. cit. I/3), discusses this view on p. 26, but does not adopt it.

[138]John De Lugo, De Justitia et Jure, Disp. X, Sec. I, 2. (Lugduni: Sumpt. Lavrentii Arnaud, & Petri Borde, 1670), p. 237.

CHAPTER 2

The Social Arguments Concerning Suicide

A second major group of arguments is of a secular nature and does not rely on theological assumptions such as the existence of God. These arguments consider the moral permissibility of suicide in terms of the suicide's effect on other persons and groups, and take stances both against suicide and in favor of it.

To say that the social arguments do not rely on theological assumptions is not to say that they can be examined without assumptions of any sort. For instance, we will consider the argument that suicide is wrong because it injures the individual's family and friends; indeed, in many cases the injury is quite severe. But this involves an assumption that considerations of the impact of suicide upon other individuals or upon society as a whole are to be taken into account in assessing the moral status of suicide. One might, however, argue an extreme individualism and maintain that whatever the effect upon family, friends, cr society, the decision whether to continue to live or not is ultimately wholly private. Paul-Louis Landsberg, for instance, writes:

> *It is purely and simply anti-personalist to try to decide such an intimately personal question as to whether or not I have the right to kill myself, by reference to society. Suppose I die a little sooner or a little later, what has that to do with a society to which, in any case, I belong for so short a space?*[1]

This, however, is to deny the assumption underlying all the social arguments concerning suicide, both for and against: that the consequences of suicide for persons other than the one who kills himself are relevant in assessing the act's moral status.

For assessing the social arguments, this assumption is as crucial as was the assumption of the existence of God for assessing religious arguments. But there is this difference: Landsberg's view excepted, the social-effects assumption is already very much a part of both popular and professional thinking about suicide. It is very

---

[1]Landsberg, *The Moral Problem of Suicide (op. cit.* I/81), p. 84.

widely assumed that suicide, as a deliberate and voluntary choice, is morally wrong if it has severely damaging effects upon family or other members of the society. We do not intend to dispute this assumption here, but only to recognize that it is an assumption.

Suicide as an Injury to the Community

Aristotle is widely acknowledged as the originator of the view that suicide damages society. In the *Nicomachean Ethics,* he claims that the individual who destroys himself is "treating the state unjustly," and that therefore criminal sanctions against the suicide are appropriate.

> ... he who through anger voluntarily stabs himself does this contrary to the right rule of life, and this the law does not allow; therefore he is acting unjustly. But towards whom? Surely towards the state, not towards himself. For he suffers voluntarily, but no one is voluntarily treated unjustly. This is also the reason why the state punishes; a certain loss of civil rights attaches to the man who destroys himself, on the ground that he is treating the state unjustly.[2]

Inspection of the context surrounding this passage will reveal that Aristotle makes his remark on suicide parenthetically, as an illustration of his theory of just and unjust behavior. Nevertheless, the notion he puts forward of suicide as an "injury to the state" is accepted by a great many later writers on suicide. For Thomas Aquinas, it is another of the three principal reasons why suicide is wrong:

> Second, every part belongs to the whole in virtue of what it is. But every man is part of the community, so that he belongs to the community in virtue of what he is. Suicide therefore involves damaging the community, as Aristotle makes clear.[3]

By late medieval times, we find this argument incorporated into English law, and expressed in the metaphorical notion of "injury to the king." The judge deciding the case *Hales* v. *Petit* (1537–38) remarks:

> [*Suicide is an offense*] ... against the King in that hereby he has lost a subject, and he being the head has lost one of his mystical members.[4]

This notion is taken to supply the theoretical basis upon which legal sanctions and punishment can be imposed: since suicide damages the state, suicide prohibitions, and punishments for attempted, assisted, and even completed suicide, are justified.

Yet it is not immediately clear just how the suicide injures the community of which he is part. In this section, we shall explore a number of possibilities, among them: (1) that suicide damages society by causing suffering for particular other individuals, especially family members; (2) that suicide sets a bad model, and

[2]Aristotle, *Nicomachean Ethics* 1138a (*op. cit.* I/76).

[3]Thomas Aquinas, *Summa Theologiae* 2a2ae64.5 (*op. cit.* I/35).

[4]*Hales* v. *Petit,* Michaelmas Term 4 & 5 Elizabeth in C. B., 1 Plowden 261.

causes additional suicides; (3) that suicide damages society by depriving it of the labor or other contribution of the individual; (4) that suicide is an affront to society; and (5) that suicide undermines the justice system of society, thus promoting disobedience, disorder, and lawlessness. In all of these arguments, suicide is said to be wrong because it is an injury to society, and all of them might be considered support for the original Aristotelian claim.

Suicide as an Injury to Family and Friends

The suicide of an individual may have serious and painful effects on his immediate family and friends. It causes grief and emotional pain; it may also cause other distress, such as the economic deprivation incurred if the victim was the central supporter of the family. It may deprive children of a parent, a spouse of conjugal companionship, and friends, acquaintances, and fellow-workers of the benefits and pleasures of association with the victim. Some of these effects may be more severe and more damaging than others, but in general, suicide can cause deep grief and deprivation to family and friends.

This is a familiar argument against suicide, one which we give great weight. Fedden, for instance, though an advocate of suicide under many circumstances, says in his history of suicide that it is the "selfishness of suicide from the point of view of the survivors" which is the "true and valid criticism applicable to most suicides."[5] Lebacqz and Engelhardt, remarking that harm to family and friends is one of the strongest arguments against suicide, argue that duties to other persons, particularly where there are no countervailing considerations (such as incapacitating illness) which make it impossible to discharge those duties, are usually sufficient to override one's right to suicide.[6] The central reason why one ought not commit suicide is that it will bring injury to others.

Curiously, this argument occurs only remarkably late in the history of thinking about suicide, and does not find explicit formulation until a good deal later than most of the other social, religious, and philosophical arguments against suicide. It is true that Seneca refrained from suicide during an episode of chronic catarrh in order not to cause grief to his father:

> *Reduced to a state of complete emaciation, I had arrived at a point where the catarrhal discharges were virtually carrying me away with them altogether. On many an occasion I felt an urge to cut my life short there and then, and was only held back by the thought of my father, who had been the kindest of fathers to me and was then in his old age. Having in mind not how bravely I was capable of dying but how far from bravely he was capable of bearing the loss, I commanded myself to live.*[7]

[5]Fedden, *Suicide (op. cit.* i/11), p. 209.

[6]Karen Lebacqz and H. Tristram Engelhardt, Jr., "Suicide," in Dennis J. Horan and David Mall, eds., *Death, Dying and Euthanasia* (Washington, D.C.: University Publications of America, 1977), pp. 695–96, also 669. An excerpt is reprinted as "Suicide and Covenant" in Battin and Mayo, eds., *Suicide: The Philosophical Issues (op. cit.* i/10), pp. 84–89.

[7]Seneca, *Letters from a Stoic (Epistulae Morales)*, tr. Robin Campbell (Baltimore, Md.: Penguin Books, 1969), Letter 78, p. 131.

But Seneca's reasoning here is atypical of the early discussions of suicide, and in classical Greek and Roman literature the expected grief of family or friends is only very rarely cited as a consideration against suicide. This is true of medieval literature as well, and it is only at the time of the pro-suicide arguments of the Enlightenment and eighteenth century that the immediate social results, and particularly the sorrow suicide may cause to immediate family and friends, begin to be earnestly considered.[8]

The general argument that suicide causes injury to one's family or friends is disputed in several classic ways. Some authors have claimed that although suicide may cause grief and harm to one's family or friends, it is no worse than desertion, and thus not an evil of greater degree. Others have pointed out that although suicide does often cause such harm, some people have no family or friends who would be affected by their suicide. Finally, it is often suggested that the harm is essentially transitory; Landsberg remarks that "everyone dies sooner or later, and society and the family get over it."[9] The general answer to this first social argument against suicide, then, is that although in some cases suicide may cause harm to other persons such as family or friends, in some cases it does not, and that typically the harm—if it occurs at all—is temporary. Thus, although suicide may produce some pain for family and friends in particular cases, it cannot on this basis be declared generally wrong.

But this, I think, is to treat somewhat cavalierly a point which should be treated with extreme gravity and circumspection. The suicide of an individual can cause more than a simple episode of grief or a limited period of pain in the people he leaves behind; it can ruin their lives.[10] Of course, even death from accidental or natural causes can produce severe grief reactions in a survivor: it creates anxiety in the survivor about his own mortality; it produces feelings of isolation and loneliness, which are increasingly sharp in proportion to the centrality of the victim in the survivor's life; and it may produce rage and feelings of abandonment in the survivor, who sees himself as deserted.[11] But when the death is due to suicide, the normal grief reaction becomes much more complex.[12] Most importantly, the fact of suicide adds to the ordinary grief a new component of guilt: since suicide is an act often resulting from extreme unhappiness and stress, the survivor will tend to see himself as having had a central role in producing that unhappiness and stress. "What did I do wrong?" or "Why did I make him do it?" are perhaps the simplest expressions of the grief/guilt constellation which death by suicide engenders in survivors; its manifestions can be considerably more complex. The guilt response may be based on a faulty picture of one's own role and importance in the victim's

[8]Fedden, *Suicide (op. cit.* i/11), pp. 209–10.

[9]Landsberg, *The Moral Problem of Suicide (op. cit.* I/81), p. 85.

[10]There is a large amount of sociological and psychological literature on the impact of suicide on survivors. See, for instance, Albert C. Cain, ed., *Survivors of Suicide* (Springfield, Ill.: Charles C. Thomas, 1972). Francine Klagsbrun's *Too Young to Die* (Boston: Houghton Mifflin, 1976) contains a readable and nontechnical chapter, "Friends and Relatives," pp. 103–117, on the effect of suicide on others.

[11]See Bernice Augenbraun and Charles Neuringer, "Helping Survivors with the Impact of a Suicide," in Cain, ed., *Survivors of Suicide (op. cit.* II/10), pp. 178–79.

[12]See Albert C. Cain and Irene Fast, "The Legacy of Suicide: Observations on the Pathogenic Impact of Suicide upon Marital Partners," in Cain, ed., *Survivors of Suicide (op. cit.* II/10), p. 149.

life, or it may accurately betray one's own causal role in producing the suicide. Either way, this guilt is often ruinous and absolute, as in the case of a parent whose only child has killed himself, or the spouse of a suicided mate. Counseling of the survivors may help, but even with counseling the psychological damage to the survivor may be extensive and sometimes permanent.

Nor are the effects entirely psychological. There are many other forms of damage which suicide may render to the survivors: for instance, legal, financial, and insurance-associated[13] difficulties, as well as readjustment and job-related difficulties rooted in ostracism by one's social or religious group. This ostracism, which may have both psychological and economic effects, is itself exacerbated by the tacit but pervasive assumption that family members and other close associates must have had some covert causal role in the victim's suicide. They may be thought to have responsibility for the suicide by indirect or coercive suggestion, by insensitivity to warnings, or by simply having made the victim's life so miserable that he saw no other choice. Whether justified or not, the ostracism of a suicide survivor often constitutes a severe hardship; coupled with genuine grief and with practical difficulties, it can be ruinous. It is almost impossible to overestimate the impact suicide can have on other, especially closely related, individuals.

Nevertheless, even the likelihood of ruinous impact does not argue adequately against the moral permissibility of suicide in general. The severe grief/guilt constellation among survivors occurs only in a society in which suicide is believed wrong, and most strongly in a society in which not only the practice but the discussion of suicide is under heavy taboo. This is certainly true of our own, present society; but it is not true of all. In Stoic Rome, for instance, suicide was thought to be a noble kind of death, the free choice of an enlightened human being; it occasioned grief but no guilt; ideally, it brought admiration. In our society, the suicide of a child is almost certain to cause severe grief and guilt to the surviving parents, but this is not always the case in suicide-permissive societies. Consider, for instance, Seneca's description of the suicide of a Spartan youth, and the reactions he indicates a parent should have:

> History relates the story of the famous Spartan, a mere boy who, when he was taken prisoner, kept shouting in his native Doric, "I shall not be a slave!" He was as good as his word. The first time he was ordered to perform a slave's task, some humiliating household job (his actual orders were to fetch a disgusting chamber pot), he dashed

---

[13]Insurance-associated difficulties are of two kinds. Contrary to popular belief, suicide does not automatically invalidate one's life insurance; ordinary life policies usually exclude the risk of suicide for a specified period only (typically two years) from the date of issue of the policy. If the insured commits suicide within the exclusion period, the insurance company's only liability is for return of premiums paid; after the exclusion period the company pays the full face amount of the policy, whether the death is by suicide or not. However, double-indemnity policies, which pay double the face amount if death is due to accident, pay only the single amount if death is by suicide, at least if the suicide is intentional and deliberate; death by suicide while insane may, however, be construed as accidental death. For a summary of life insurance regulations in suicide, see William F. Meyer, *Life and Health Insurance Law, A Summary* (International Claim Association, 1976), esp. Section 13:3–13:5, pp. 225–28 and Section 21:8, pp. 447–48.

The second form of insurance-associated difficulty in suicide involves medical insurance. Many health-care plans do not cover medical expenses resulting from attempted but incomplete suicide, or those incurred where there is a substantial period of time elapsed between the initiation of the attempt and death. Health insurance plans vary widely in this respect. As of 1978, Blue Cross/Blue Shield had no uniform policy regarding payment for treatment in cases of attempted suicide; some plans pay full benefits while other exclude suicide cases. Health maintenance organizations are not required by law to

his head against a wall and cracked his skull open. Freedom is as near as that—is anyone really still a slave? Would you not rather your own son died like that than lived by reason of spinelessness to an advanced age?[14]

Perhaps now we can explain the relatively late occurrence in the western tradition of an explicit argument against suicide on the basis that it causes harm to family and friends. As we've seen, in the earlier periods of western history, in both Greece and apparently also in the early Hebrew communities, suicide was not thought intrinsically wrong. Consequently, the particular grief/guilt constellation so damaging to suicide survivors in our society most probably did not occur, or did not occur to such a degree. What did occur was normal, genuine grief over a death. This occurred in even the most noble suicides: Lucretia's father and husband, for instance, are reported by Livy to have been ''overwhelmed with grief,'' but there is no evidence in Livy's description that they are subject to the grief/guilt constellation characteristic of contemporary reactions to suicide, which arises from association with, and alleged complicity in, something believed to be seriously wrong.[15] The severity of the psychological damage which suicides in our present society produce in the survivors is not to be underrated; on the contrary, we tend to treat it much too lightly. But that such damage occurs does not show that suicide is in itself morally wrong; what we see, rather, is that the damage may be very largely the product of our own society's pervasive belief that suicide is seriously wrong.

This suggests that a present-day suicide could do a great deal to minimize the impact of his death upon others. A prospective suicide, for instance, might be encouraged to explain in advance to those around him his reasons for choosing to end his life, and particularly to attempt to show family and friends that they are not the reason for this choice.[16] Perhaps this sounds unlikely in the cases of suicides caused by revenge, isolation, or an inability to communicate; no doubt it is. But it is not at all unreasonable or impossible in certain cases: for instance, euthanatic suicides in debilitating or terminal illness, and, generally, ''rational suicides'' of the sort we shall later discuss.

Of course, suicide is not infrequently performed precisely with the intention (not always consciously recognized) of injuring someone else; these are the ''I'll get even with you, you bastard, just see how bad you feel'' sorts of cases. (For this reason, appeals to effects of a suicide on others are considered tactically unwise in suicide-prevention counseling; often, these effects are just what the individual wants.) These ''get-even'' suicides are often extraordinarily effective in accomplishing their aim; the individual against whom such an action is directed does indeed

---

cover treatment for injury in attempted suicide, and many do not. It should be pointed out that while the costs of treatment and/or resuscitation may be small for some forms of attempted suicide, e. g. sublethal overdoses, in other cases they may be severe, as in self-blinding by gunshot wound, multiple fractures and internal injuries in jumping, etc., and that these expenses can cause severe hardship for the individual and his or her family members even if the attempt is not fatal.

Also see Chapter Six, footnote 28.

[14]Seneca, *Letters (op. cit.* II/7), Letter 77, p. 128.

[15]Livy, *The Early History of Rome,* I. 57-60, on the rape of Lucretia. (Tr. Aubrey de Selincourt, Harmondsworth: Penguin, 1960).

[16]Doris Portwood stresses this possibility in her *Commonsense Suicide: The Final Right* (New York: Dodd, Mead, 1978).

feel bad. No doubt we would agree that such suicides are wrong. But what is wrong with them is not the act of suicide as such, but the intentional injury of someone else in as serious a way as possible.[17]

We see, then, that no general argument against suicide can be based on the claim that it is invariably injurious to family and friends. There may be strong arguments against the moral permissibility of a specific suicide—when a severe grief/guilt reaction or social ostracism for the survivors can be accurately predicted, for instance—but in many cases, especially in societies other than the present one, there may be ways of avoiding such consequences. Where they can be avoided, they provide no argument against suicide. In a particular case, the problem may seem to be one of weighing the disadvantageous consequences to others against the advantages to the individual who chooses to end his life. That the self-death of an elderly, failing parent will cause distress to adult children whose religious beliefs prohibit suicide does not entail that the parent must refrain from ending his life; we would require some further evidence that the harm to the child would outweigh the benefit to the parent. On the other hand, where a young and physically healthy parent contemplates essentially frivolous suicide, we may be quite ready to say that his obligations to small, dependent children outweigh any right he may have to do so.

Suicide as the Deprivation of an Individual's Contribution to Society

Although not every suicide causes harm to particular individuals among family, friends, or immediate associates, it may still be the case that suicide does harm the society as a whole. Among the oldest arguments of this sort—arising not only from Aristotle but from Plato before him—is that which considers the suicide to be depriving the community, state, or social group of his labor or other contribution to its welfare.[18] This general argument takes three major forms: the simple "deprivation of labor" argument, a second argument concerning the deprivation of special talents or contributions, and a third issue concerning "deprivation of good"; it also leads to the problem of universalization, or the question "what if everybody did it?"

DEPRIVATION OF LABOR.   Society, it is often assumed, cannot survive without the efforts and contributions of its members; and since society is a benefit to all, it must be preserved. Each member of society, then, by virtue of his membership in society, has an obligation to contribute his labor or other services to promote the welfare of society. Suicide is wrong because it permanently deprives society of these contributions.

This argument, however, is open to a variety of objections. Some of the oldest objections point out that we already condone certain practices which deprive the

---

[17]The trend is to eliminate criminal sanctions against suicide; this has happened in England, and in most of the states of the U.S. But were the difficulties of establishing intent, especially subconscious intent, not so great, it might well be recommended that suicide with deliberate intent to injure another remain a criminal offense, punishable in those cases in which the attempter survives. The attempters do survive in a great many such cases, since their actual aim is not so much to kill themselves but to injure or hurt another; here moral and perhaps even legal sanctions may be warranted, as part of a general sanction against intentional serious injury to others.

[18]See my "Philosophers' Death and Intolerable Life: Plato on Suicide," (*op. cit.* i/59), for an account of Plato's argument concerning suicide and society.

society of an individual's labor or contribution. The monk or hermit, John Donne suggested, also "steals himself away from the state," and yet these practices are not condemned.[19] Beccaria, a century and a half later, compared suicide with emigration, but held:

> *He who kills himself does a less injury to society, than he who quits his country for ever; for the other leaves his property behind him, but this carries with him at least a part of his substance.*[20]

A second kind of objection observes that the claim that a suicide damages his society by depriving it of his labor rests on a highly idealized model of society.[21] We can, of course, construct a hypothetical society in which the suicide of one member does damage the whole: for instance, in an entirely isolated unit consisting of a farmer, who sows and harvests grain, a miller, who converts the grain into edible foodstuffs, and a blacksmith, who provides the tools which make both farming and milling possible, the suicide of any one of the three will cause the other two to starve. But we do not live in this sort of highly mutually interdependent society, Furthermore, in a society in which unemployment is a substantial and continuing fact of the economy, the deprivation of an individual's labor or services will not injure the society as a whole. If he is unemployed, there is no loss in labor due to suicide; if employed, he will be replaced by another individual who is not now contributing. High mutual interdependence and consequent indispensability of individuals may be a feature of certain primitive or marginal societies, communal groups, or isolated clans, in which the labor and talents of each member are crucial for the survival of the group; it may also be true for artificially isolated contemporary social groups—say, exploration teams—in which each member has a fixed and essential task, and in which no hope of replacement or redistribution of tasks is possible for the duration of the isolated period. However, this is not the case for contemporary society as a whole, and the claim that suicide "deprives society of one's labor" provides no argument against suicide in most cases.

DEPRIVATION OF SPECIAL TALENTS. Even in a society which is not highly mutually interdependent, some individuals' contributions of labor or services to the

---

[19]Donne, *Biathanatos* (*op. cit.* I/24), II. V. 1:3143–49. *Biathanatos* was written in 1608, but published posthumously in 1647.

[20]Cesare Beccaria (1738–1794), *An Essay on Crimes and Punishments,* with a commentary by M. De Voltaire (Albany: W. C. Little, 1872), pp. 121–22 (also available from Bobbs-Merrill, 1963). Thomas Szasz uses this argument in a contemporary argument against psychiatric invasion in suicide: "In the final analysis, the would-be suicide is like the would-be emigrant: both want to leave where they are and move elsewhere. The suicide wants to leave life and embrace death. The emigrant wants to leave his homeland and settle in another country." ("The Ethics of Suicide," (*op. cit.* i/10, p. 196.)

[21]Plato's tacit argument against suicide appears to rest on just such a model, the ideal society in which "there is a work assigned to each man in the city which he must perform" (*Republic* III 406C, *op. cit.* I/11), p. 651; suicide is default on this task. Plato does not actually advance this consideration as an explicit argument against suicide anywhere in his writings, but it is clearly the basis of his carefully restrictive attitude. See, for instance, his discussion in the third book of the *Republic* of why the chronically ill or disabled patient ought to refuse medical treatment (and, if he cannot return to work, die); if he is unable to perform his task he is of "no use either to himself or to the state," but if he can continue to perform his task, he is obligated to do so. See my paper "Philosophers' Death and Intolerable Life: Plato on Suicide," (*op. cit.* i/59), and the references given there, for a fuller discussion of Plato's view.

society may be unique and nonreplaceable, or may involve skills that are in shortage or for which substitutions cannot easily be made: one might mention the physician in a small town, the highly talented musician or artist, the key scientist, diplomat, and so forth. In this case, because the labor of individuals with unique gifts or crucial skills cannot be replaced, the suicide of such individuals would deprive society of a considerable need and good.

According to this argument the common laborer and the unemployed worker may take their lives if they choose, though the talented and skilled elite are not to do so. Since members of this elite constitute only a small proportion of the population, and since those whose skills and talents are genuinely irreplaceable form an even smaller group, this argument against suicide would apply to only a very small number of individuals among the total. Then, too, it would not apply to those whose talents have been diminished by various circumstances, say, deafness in a musician, disabling injury in an athlete, approaching senility or insanity in a diplomat.

Nevertheless, it is still not clear that the deprivation-of-special-talents argument succeeds as an argument against suicide even for those who have irreplaceable special talents and whose talents and skills remain intact. The argument against suicide is really an argument against failure to exercise those talents; consequently, it will be applicable not only to suicide but also to other actions which would deprive society of these special services or labor. But it is not evident that we consider this position correct with respect to other actions; for instance, we do not prevent the physician from leaving practice to join a monastery, and we do not force musicians or dancers or actors to continue to perform. There are no legal sanctions which oblige specially talented individuals to continue to practice their skills, though social sanctions may in fact sometimes be in force. This may be truer for some sorts of skills and talents than others—for instance, the social sanctions against a physician or cancer researcher discontinuing practice may be much stronger than those against a ballet dancer or a chess master, though the skills of each may be scarce or irreplaceable. To be consistent, we should consider the suicide of a skilled physician more wrong than that of a master chessplayer;[22] the suicide of a car-wash attendant not wrong at all. The special talents argument presents only a very weak case against suicide, prohibiting it in only those individuals whose contributions are highly valued and unique.

THE RECIPROCITY ARGUMENT.   The argument that suicide is wrong because it deprives the society of ordinary or specially skilled labor may also involve an assumption of reciprocity. This concept assumes membership in society to be essentially reciprocal; each individual member of the society contributes his labor or services in exchange for goods, services, and protection rendered by society. It is this basis upon which hippies, welfare recipients, and dropouts are sometimes labeled "drains" or "sponges" on society. Socrates gives a similar reason in the *Crito* for not escaping from prison in order to avoid execution: since the society provides him with education, nurturance, legal protection, and many other goods, it is his duty to contribute to its welfare by not disrupting its laws.[23]

But while the argument may have some bearing on hippies, welfare recipients, and Socrates, it is not an argument against suicide. The reason is quite simple: at the moment one ends one's life, one ceases to draw goods, services,

---

[22]Interestingly, physicians as a group display one of the highest rates of suicide in the United States.

[23]Plato, *Crito;* see esp. 49E–53A (*op. cit.* I/11), pp. 35–38.

protection, and other benefits from the society, and so is no longer obliged to reciprocate. David Hume puts the point this way:

> All our obligations to do good to society seem to imply something reciprocal. I receive the benefits of society and therefore ought to promote its interests, but when I withdraw myself altogether from society, can I be bound any longer?[24]

Similarly, reflecting eighteenth-century contract theories of political organization, Montesquieu had asked in the *Persian Letters:* "Society is based on mutual advantage, but when I find it onerous what is to prevent me renouncing it?"[25] Baron d'Holbach, also writing within eighteenth-century contract theory, expands this notion still further: when the state fails to provide continuing benefits for an individual and does not serve to improve the quality of his life, the individual has no further obligation to the society, and may quit it when he wishes.

> If the covenant which unites man to society be considered, it will be obvious that every contract is conditional, must be reciprocal; that is to say, supposes mutual advantages between the contracting parties. The citizen cannot be bound to his country, to his associates, but by the bonds of happiness. Are these bonds cut asunder? He is restored to liberty. Society, or those who represent it, do they use him with harshness, do they treat him with injustice, do they render his existence painful? Does disgrace hold him out to the finger of scorn; does indigence menace him, in an obdurate world? Perfidious friends, do they forsake him in adversity? An unfaithful wife, does she outrage his heart? Rebellious, ungrateful children, do they afflict his old age? Has he placed his happiness exclusively on some object which it is impossible for him to procure? Chagrin, remorse, melancholy, despair, have they disfigured to him the spectacle of the universe? In short, for whatever cause it may be, if he is not able to support his evils, let him quit a world which from thenceforth is for him only a frightful desert . . . [26]

This, of course, is not yet a general argument favoring suicide; it would license suicide only when the society can be said to have defaulted upon its obligations to the individual. What these obligations are, and how default is to be determined, would of course be part of a larger political theory.

The reciprocity argument is sometimes used to promote a special-talents argument against suicide. For instance, the trained physician, unlike ordinary laborers, may be said to have an obligation to continue to practice, and hence refrain from suicide, because he has already benefited from an elaborate, expensive and scarce education. Here, the benefits are received in advance, and take the form of education received largely at society's expense; it is now the beneficiary's duty to reciprocate by practicing those special skills in which he has been trained. Similar arguments concern the "brain drain" problem of various nations, and whether individuals who have received training using the resources of one nation have an obligation to render their services to that nation. That our conclusions with regard to

[24]David Hume, "Essay on Suicide," (*op. cit.* I/49), p. 566.

[25]Montesquieu [Charles Louis de Secondat, baron de La Brède et de Montesquieu], *Persian Letters,* Letter 76. Tr. C. J. Betts (Harmondsworth: Penguin, 1973), p. 153.

[26]Paul Henri Thiry, baron d'Holbach, *The System of Nature, or Laws of the Moral and Physical World,* with notes by Diderot. Tr. H. D. Robinson (originally published 1868) (New York: Burt Franklin, 1970), Vol. 1, pp. 136–37.

the brain-drain issue are far from settled, however, suggests that our conclusions with regard to suicide among such individuals would be similarly unsettled, and that we have no firm conviction whether or not the specially talented have an obligation to exercise their skills.

DEPRIVATION OF GOOD. Closely related to the deprivation of labor, special-talents, and reciprocity arguments, although probably stemming more from the religious natural-law tradition's conception of the natural end of man than from the eighteenth-century contract theories, is what might be called the ''deprivation-of-good'' argument against suicide. We have described it in its religious form; it recurs here in a secular version. The argument is simply this: one ought not commit suicide if one can, alternatively, do good; suicide is wrong because it deprives society of whatever good an individual might do. ''Doing good'' is not to be confused with the contribution of economically valued labor or services; it is a moral activity, though it may take practical forms. Nor is doing good merely the absence of doing harm. Rather, doing good is a positive duty for every individual, and there is no limit on the amount of good-doing from which society may benefit.

No doubt the most eloquent spokesman for the deprivation-of-good argument against suicide has been Charlotte Perkins Gilman, the labor and women's-rights activist of the early part of the twentieth century. She writes:

> *A last duty. Human life consists in mutual service. No grief, no pain, misfortune or "broken heart" is excuse for cutting off one's life while any power of service remains.*[27]

Gilman offers no support for the central premise in this argument, that ''human life consists in mutual service.'' Whether such a premise is provided by utilitarian or by other ethical theories is, of course, a much-debated issue: do we have an obligation to do good, or simply to refrain from harm?

But there is a second question here: even if we could establish that human beings have a positive obligation to do good, would this serve as the basis of a general argument against suicide? For Gilman, it does not. The words begun above are taken from her suicide note, written as she was afflicted with terminal cancer. They continue:

> *. . . But when all usefulness is over, when one is assured of an imminent and unavoidable death, it is the simplest of human rights to choose a quick and easy death in place of a slow and horrible one. Public opinion is changing on this subject. The time is approaching when we shall consider it abhorrent to our civilization to allow a human being to lie in prolonged agony which we should mercifully end in any other creature. Believing this choice to be of social service in promoting wiser views on this question, I have preferred chloroform to cancer.*

Gilman assumes that her ''usefulness'' or power of doing good will be lost to medical dependency, pain, and the disruption of social relationships that terminal illness often produces, and that consequently the obligation to do good is no bar to suicide in these circumstances. Is her view correct? Popular medical literature is filled with tales of heroic individuals who have done astonishing good from their iron lungs or their respirators or their quadriplegic wheelchairs, and of people who

---

[27]Charlotte Perkins Gilman, in R. Howard, ''Taking Life Legally,'' *Magazine Digest* XC (1947), p. 33, quoted in Joseph Sullivan, *Catholic Teaching on the Morality of Euthanasia* (*op. cit.* I/28), pp. 15–16.

even in the intense suffering of their dying moments have served as an inspiration to others; this might suggest that Gilman's view that suicide is morally permitted in the face of oncoming death, since one can no longer do good, is wrong. But it is not clear that the deprivation-of-good argument, even if such tales are accepted, will speak against the permissibility of suicide even where the individual could continue to do good. The deprivation-of-good argument does not consider the degree to which satisfaction of the individual's own interests may be outweighed by the obligation to do good. The principle that individuals have an obligation to do good is not one of utter self-sacrifice, and we might find it morally odd to *insist* that persons do good at the cost of severe harm to themselves. Someone whose life has already reached such excesses of misery that he is considering ending it would hardly be obligated to continue that misery-filled life in order to do good for others—especially when doing good for others carries no guarantee of improving one's own condition and may even worsen it. Of course, different ethical theories will weigh this balance in different ways; the utilitarian, for instance, may believe that the individual is obligated to continue to live and do good despite his suffering when the amount of good he can do is very large; other theories may resolve this issue in quite different ways. But this is the issue which must be resolved before we can determine whether the deprivation-of-good argument is successful against suicide in the very kinds of cases in which suicide is most likely to be contemplated—namely, those in which human misery is greatest.

A variant of the argument from doing good maintains that the collective presence of disabled or defective individuals contributes good to society even though the individuals themselves do not perform good acts or actively do good in any other way. Here, the good contributed by such individuals inheres in the responses of others to them, not in any actions of their own, and it is this good which precludes their suicides. For instance, the violinist who contracts a degenerative disease and loses the use of his hands, although he can no longer contribute his violin-playing services to society and directly performs no morally good acts, nevertheless continues to do good by becoming the object of the moral intentions of others. The victim need take no active role, but functions as a kind of whetstone upon which those not afflicted may sharpen their moral feelings. Since the exercise of moral feelings is a good which the afflicted person makes possible, he ought not end this opportunity by suicide. David Novak, discussing Thomas Aquinas, expresses such a view; it is prevalent in a wide variety of religious and nonreligious sources. Novak writes:

> . . . one can see a need for even the helpless and infirm. Their very presence enables us to practice the human virtues of benevolence and generosity.[28]

Of all the social arguments against suicide, this may be one of the most disturbing. It may be true that contact with debilitated, disabled, deformed, or otherwise distressed persons does intensify our moral feelings and give rise to greater sympathy, benevolence, and caring for other persons in general. Such persons may serve as inspiring models, and make us more courageous in enduring our own afflictions. But to claim that those persons have an *obligation* to live (and suffer) in order to make normal individuals more humane or courageous is ethically question-

[28]David Novak, *Suicide and Morality. The Theories of Plato, Aquinas and Kant and their Relevance for Suicidology.* (New York: Scholars Studies Press, Inc., 1975), p. 66.

able at best. One might also see it as a barbaric holdover of earlier European practices, according to which caged lunatics were placed on public display, criminals put in public stocks, and physically anomalous persons were displayed in circuses, presumably for the moral edification as well as entertainment of individuals not so afflicted. It is not at all obvious that we should sanction an argument which, in essence, argues that the helpless and infirm have an obligation to submit to similar treatment—to refrain from suicide and remain alive as objects for our pity and moral elevation.

Another version of the argument from doing good claims that the helpless and infirm may also render good to society as subjects for medical, psychological, or other experimentation. This, it is argued, will make improved life conditions possible for other members of society. But this is a service which can be performed only by the helpless and infirm, since it is only they who have the illnesses or conditions upon which experimentation can be conducted. Since this is a service of extreme utility to the society at large, they ought not commit suicide. Joseph Fletcher, for instance, discussing this issue in the context of voluntary euthanasia, writes:

> One of the most significant services open to terminal patients is willingness to submit to drugs and cures and narcotics of an experimental kind, aimed at eliminating the very pain and demoralization which is a major justification for euthanasia.[29]

It is indeed a significant service. But whether those who are candidates for experimentation have an obligation to perform, or to remain alive in order to do so, is not at all obvious, any more than that those who are ill or disabled ought to remain alive in order to serve as a moral whetstone for others.

THE PROBLEM OF UNIVERSAL SUICIDE. Of course, if large numbers of individuals—even ordinary individuals without special talents—were to withdraw their labor, services, or good-doing from society by suicide, the function of the whole might be seriously impaired. This would certainly constitute an "injury to society." While the possibility of widespread suicide may seem remote, there is some historical evidence that it has been considered a threat at various times. For instance, the Roman legal sanctions against suicide, which applied only to slaves and to soldiers on duty, were apparently designed to prevent widespread suicide among groups whose labor was considered critical. John Donne implies that strong suicide prohibitions serve to ensure the availability of the laboring class:

> ... yet the number of wretched men exceeds the happy (for every laborer is miserable and beastlike, in respect of the idle, abounding men). It was therefore thought necessary, by laws and by opinion of religion ... to take from these weary and macerated wretches their ordinary and open escape and ease, voluntary death.[30]

Not only do these views suggest the possibility of widespread suicide, but various historical periods offer actual instances of it as well. In Russia in 1666, the year in which Russian zealots expected the appearance of the Antichrist, suicide was epidemic: whole communities starved themselves to death, though this choice of

[29]Fletcher, *Morals and Medicine* (*op. cit.* I/18), p. 202.

[30]Donne, *Biathanatos* (*op. cit.* I/24), II. iii. 1, 2723–29. I have been unable to discover, however, any Marxist thinker who pursues this argument.

means later gave way to death by fire.[31] Mass suicides of armies and of entire populations facing capture were apparently not uncommon in earlier periods of western history; perhaps the best-known mass suicide of this type was that at Masada, though similar incidents are recorded by Xenophon,[32] Lucan,[33] and Plutarch.[34] Accounts of the taking of Saipan include descriptions of a Japanese officer cutting off the heads of his kneeling men with a Samurai sword, crowds of civilians and soldiers walking off cliffs or wading into the ocean, and a hundred Japanese soldiers at Marpi Point who bowed to the U.S. Marines from the cliff-tops, spread a large Japanese flag on the rocks, and then blew themselves up with grenades.[35] As we have pointed out in Chapter One, the early Christian community appeared to be on the verge of complete self-decimation in voluntary martyrdom and suicide until Augustine took a firm position against such practices. Other mass suicides, including that at Jonestown in 1978, have all but succeeded in annihilating particular cultural or religious groups.

Although these practices have not spread beyond the immediate membership of the cultural or religious group involved, the possibility of extremely widespread or universal suicide may not be entirely discounted. John Donne, as we have seen, believed that there is in all of us a "natural desire of dying," which, if not checked by religious and legal prohibitions, might destroy human society. But even an assumption like Donne's that the possibility of mass self-extinction is undesirable and hence is grounds for a general policy against suicide is open to philosophic question. One could argue that not even widespread suicide constitutes an injury to society. Indeed, some thinkers appear to welcome the prospect of widespread suicide. Though little is known of his exact views, Hegesias the Cyrenaic is said to have preached a doctrine recommending suicide so effectively that Ptolemy II was forced to put a stop to his teachings.[36] Schopenhauer advocates the overcoming of the will to live, though this, he says, cannot be accomplished by ordinary suicide, and only rarely through self-starvation.[37] Eduard von Hartmann argues that instead of private, individual suicide, all mankind—having continued to suffer and to achieve a common awareness that life is essentially evil and futile—must join together and, in a common act of will, decree their own extinction; this is universal,

---

[31]Rose, "Suicide (Introductory)," (*op. cit.* I/9), p. 22, quoting I. Stchoukine, *Le Suicide collectif dans le Raskol russe,* Paris 1903.

[32]Xenophon, *Anabasis,* Book IV:7. Available in translation as *The March Up Country,* tr. W. H. D. Rouse (Ann Arbor: The University of Michigan Press, 1958). The Greeks stormed a small fortified settlement located on a high rock; as the inhabitants saw that they were about to be defeated, the women threw their children and themselves down from the rock; the men did the same.

[33]Lucan, *Pharsalia; Dramatic Episodes of the Civil Wars,* Book IV, 400–580, on the mass suicide of Vulteius' Gauls. Tr. Robert Graves (Baltimore: Penguin Books, 1957), pp. 96–100.

[34]Plutarch, describing mass suicide among the conquered after the Romans under Marius had defeated the Cimbres near Vercella. Cited by Joost A. M. Meerloo, *Suicide and Mass Suicide* (New York and London: Grune & Stratton, 1962), p. 68.

[35]*Ibid,* p. 67.

[36]Cicero, *Tusculan Disputations,* I.34, 83–84. Cicero claims that Hegesias taught that it is "no advantage at all for anyone to live," and hence recommended suicide. Tr. J. E. King (Cambridge: Harvard University Press, and London: William Heinemann, Loeb Classical Library 1966), pp. 96–99.

[37]Arthur Schopenhauer, *The World as Will and Idea,* Vol. I, Book 4, Paragraph 69. Tr. R. B. Haldane and J. Kemp (London: Routledge and Kegan Paul, Ltd., 1948), pp. 514–20.

simultaneous suicide, designed to rid the world of an unpleasant and unsuccessful form of life.[38] These views may seem bizarre. But even if one believes that universal suicide would be wrong, this of course does not suffice to show that individual acts of suicide are so.

There is another way in which several contemporary authors have advocated universal, though not simultaneous, suicide: this is by recommending that the *normal* end of human life be voluntary death. According to this view, which we shall discuss more fully in Chapter Four, most lives—except those snuffed out prematurely by accident or disease—would end according to one's own plan at a time of one's own choosing, whether by means directly administered by oneself, or in voluntary euthanasia administered by a friend or physician. Suicide, in the form of a rationally planned death at a mature age, would become the usual and chosen way of dying; as medical prophylaxis and accident prevention improve, other deaths would decrease in relative frequency, and suicide would become indeed nearly universal. The question "what if everybody did it?" should be answered, according to these authors, with a resounding "good!"

Suicide as Lawlessness

Perhaps the least explored social argument against suicide is one which maintains that suicide undermines a society's system of justice and punishment. John Adams, in his "Essay Concerning Self-Murther" (1700), warns that "suicide would destroy the force of human laws";[39] other writers speak of the "lawlessness" or "defiance of the law" involved in suicide. It is true, of course, that suicide and attempted suicide have been against the law during much of western history. Although there were few laws penalizing suicide and attempted suicide in classical Greek and Roman times,[40] and these few were usually restricted to specific groups such as slaves or persons under indictment, by late medieval times suicide and attempted suicide had become a felony throughout England and Europe. Completed suicide was punished by property forfeiture, desecration of the corpse, and burial restrictions; attempted suicide could be punished by death. As we've seen, changes in the felony status of suicide have been fairly recent: although France dropped its criminal sanctions during the Revolution, England decriminalized suicide only in 1961, and suicide has remained a crime even longer in some U.S. states. To assist a suicide, furthermore, remains a crime in all these areas.[41] Thus, one might interpret the claim that suicide is "lawless" to mean simply that suicide, attempted suicide, and assisted suicide are (or until recently have been) against the law. However,

---

[38]Eduard von Hartmann, *Zur Geschichte und Begründung des Pessimismus* (Berlin: Carl Dunker, 1880) and *Ethische Studien* (Leipzig: Hermann Haacke, 1898), described by Choron, *Suicide (op. cit.* i/2), pp. 135–36.

[39]John Adams, *Essay Concerning Self-Murther*, Chapter 3, paragraph 2 (For Thom. Bennet, 1700 [Wing A483]), p. 26.

[40]See R. S. Guernsey, *Suicide: History of the Penal Laws, Relating to it in their Legal, Social, Moral, and Religious Aspects, in Ancient and Modern Times*, Read before the New York Medico-Legal Society Sept. 23, 1875. Revised and Enlarged (New York: L. K. Strouse & Co., 1883). Guernsey, itemizing the various laws governing suicide in Greece and Rome, says, "As a general proposition the law recognized suicide as a right, but slight restrictions arose from time to time." (p. 12).

[41]Leslie Francis, "Assisting Suicide: A Problem for the Criminal Law" (*op. cit.* i/37). Also see Helen Silving, "Suicide and Law" (*op. cit.* i/36).

there are two deeper, more interesting notions inherent in the claim that suicide is "lawless," and it is these which we wish to examine.

UNAUTHORIZED SELF-PUNISHMENT. Not infrequently, individuals commit suicide in order to punish themselves for crimes they have committed or believe they have committed; in these cases, suicide might be described as a kind of self-imposed capital punishment. One argument against suicide holds that this punishment is imposed in unauthorized fashion: regardless of the degree of guilt, the one who has committed the offense ought not to judge or punish himself, since that is the prerogative of duly constituted authorities. Suicide in such circumstances morally involves the lawlessness of an individual's taking the law into his own hands, and undermines society's system of justice and punishment.

This view is evident in Thomas Aquinas: considering whether a public official may, in consequence of crime, kill himself, he says:

A representative of the public authority may legitimately kill a malefactor in virtue of his power to adjudge the case. But nobody is a judge in his own cause. Therefore, no representative of public authority may kill himself in respect of any sin, though he may, of course, hand himself over to the judgement of others.[42]

and, more generally, "nobody but a duly commissioned judicial authority may kill a malefactor."[43] St. Thomas notwithstanding, we do of course permit "killing of malefactors" even when a "duly commissioned judicial authority" is not involved; this occurs in self-defense. Nevertheless, this does not show that we permit unauthorized killing *as punishment,* whether of ourselves or others, and so does not show that suicide as capital-self-punishment is morally permissible.

The argument that one ought not to impose capital punishment upon oneself may be supplemented in several ways. For instance, one may raise an objection to capital punishment in principle, and argue that whether death is self-imposed or imposed by the state, it is equally repugnant. Or one may point out that capital punishment by suicide is potentially unfair: the empirical facts about the kinds of crimes for which suicide is committed suggest that this form of self-punishment is very often overly severe. Individuals, especially those with mental disorders, often impose death upon themselves as "penalties" for "crimes" that are trivial or even nonexistent. Freud, for instance, suggests that much suicide is associated with the fantasy of wishing one's parents dead, even though the fantasy results in no overt act.[44] Some psychoanalytically-oriented clinicians maintain that suicide is self-punishment for a wide variety of fantasied crimes, including fantasies of "phallic erection under improper circumstances," "sexual excitement associated with heavy breathing," and the "male homosexual wish to attack or be attacked by a lethal

---

[42]Thomas Aquinas, *Summa Theologiae (op. cit.* I/35), 2a2ae.64.5, reply objection 2.

[43]*Ibid.,* reply objection 3.

[44]Sigmund Freud, "The Psychogenesis of a Case of Homosexuality in a Woman," III, in *The Standard Edition of . . . Freud (op. cit.* I/68) 18, 161–62. Freud writes: " . . . the girl's action [attempted suicide by throwing herself into a railway cutting] shows us that she had developed in her unconscious strong death-wishes against one or other of her parents . . . For analysis has explained the enigma of suicide in the following way: probably no one finds the mental energy required to kill himself unless, in the first place, in doing so he is at the same time killing an object with whom he has identified himself, and, in the second place, is turning against himself a death-wish which had been directed against someone else." (p. 162).

penis."[45] And even where the "crime" is not merely fantasied, the penalty imposed in suicide may be quite out of proportion to the act involved: in traditional Japanese culture, for instance, *harakiri* is sometimes performed to evade the disgrace of relatively minor infractions of the civil or military codes.

But these arguments cannot serve as the basis for a general objection to suicide. Not all suicide is committed as self-punishment, so not all suicide can be condemned under a principled objection to capital punishment;[46] this objection would not apply, for instance, to self-sacrifice, "get-even," and voluntary euthanasia cases. Nor can the fact that suicide is often imposed in cases where the punishment is not proportionate to the crime provide an argument against suicide in general, because in some few self-punishment cases (a frequently cited example is Judas' suicide after the betrayal of Jesus) the penalty does appear to be appropriate to the crime. In the absence of a principled objection to capital punishment in general, this argument would also not serve against suicide under a hypothetical penal system which offered optional capital punishment as an alternative to long-term or life imprisonment in cases of serious crime.

INCREASED CRIMINAL ACTIVITY.   The second major reading of the notion that suicide is "lawless" holds that suicide, by permitting a way of escape from punishment for those guilty of crimes, contributes to increased criminal activity. If permissive attitudes towards suicide mean that an individual can always escape punishment by killing himself, it is said, he will be more likely to commit serious crime. The most explicit example of this argument is in Kant:

> *Nothing more terrible [than suicide] can be imagined; for if man were on every occasion master of his own life, he would be master of the lives of others; and being ready to sacrifice his life at any and every time rather than be captured, he could perpetrate every conceivable crime and vice.*[47]

Kant continues:

> *Those who advocate suicide and teach that there is authority for it necessarily do much harm in a republic of free men. Let us imagine a state in which men held as a general opinion that they were entitled to commit suicide, and that there was even merit and honor in so doing. How dreadful everyone would find them. For he who does not respect his life even in principle cannot be restrained from the most dreadful vices; he recks neither king nor torments.*[48]

The argument is an uncommon one; it is not an uninteresting or unimportant one, but one which has been given far from adequate attention.

One might try to resolve the issue with empirical data: we should, for instance, expect to find that the rates of serious crime increase where suicide rates are

---

[45]Sidney S. Furst, M.D. and Mortimer Ostow, M.D., "The Psychodynamics of Suicide," in Hankoff and Einsidler, eds., *Suicide: Theory and Clinical Aspects (op. cit.* i/2), pp. 165-78; citations from p. 175.

[46]Suicide may, however, be condemned on the basis of the principle of the sanctity or inviolability of life: this is usually the basis also underlying principled objections to capital punishment. See Chapter Three.

[47]Kant, *Lectures on Ethics (op. cit.* I/37), p. 151.

[48]*Ibid.,* p. 153.

higher. But such a correlation could be explained in many other ways, for instance as a function of the overall disruption and lack of stability of a given group. Some theorists have held views quite the opposite of Kant's: the early sociologist Morselli, for instance, treating suicide as the product of internally directed aggression and murder as the result of externally directed aggression, believed that an increase in suicide would produce a decrease in murder,[49] rather than an increase as Kant might expect. Morselli's thesis, however, is no longer accepted, and a modern version of this thesis, Henry and Short's frustration-aggression model,[50] is also subject to serious empirical objections.

It is true that about one in three murders is followed by suicide, and this might seem to give some weight to Kant's claim. However, the spectre which lurks in Kant's view—the established criminal who is "ready to sacrifice his life at any and every time rather than be captured" and is therefore able to "perpetrate every conceivable crime and vice"—seems not to be the figure these statistics describe. In fact, there is a total absence of the "young thug" among suicides who kill themselves after murder: most of them do not have previous convictions, and they are only very rarely insane. Rather, these suicides after murders are very frequently women, and the victims of the murders are very often their own children.[51] One might wish to suggest that these are "extended suicides," where the suicide takes with her those whom she believes will be severely affected by her death; they do not involve an intent to harm, and are not murders in the usual sense at all. This does not excuse such acts, but it does dispute the Kantian claim that permissive attitudes towards suicide breed "every conceivable crime and vice." Perhaps a thesis put forward in the Church of England's 1959 study of suicide might be closer to the truth. This study observes that suicide is rarely the act of a "criminal type of man," and quotes the view that it is much more often "the first, as it is certainly the last, crime of a good and conscientious citizen."[52]

Of course, mothers who kill their children, whether or not they also kill themselves, hardly fit the notion of the "good and conscientious citizen"; it could also be argued that if such mothers believed or knew they would not be able to kill themselves afterwards, they would never kill their children first. Thus it is the very possibility of suicide which contributes to crime. Perhaps this is so; but it is not, I think, the notion which lies at the core of the Kantian argument, nor does it show that the possibility of suicide would in fact cause crime. Rather, the Kantian notion, I think, is that permissiveness towards suicide foments criminal activity because it permits suicide as an escape from punishment whether it is imposed by judicial authorities or by the malefactor's own conscience; thus, it undermines the principal deterrent to crime.

But even this argument may not succeed against suicide, for the crimes which permissiveness might fail to deter must be weighed against the advantages that permissiveness might also bring. A suicide-permissive culture, on this argument,

[49]Henry Morselli, *Suicide: An essay on comparative moral statistics* (1879); revised and abridged. (New York: D. Appleton & Co., 1882).

[50]Andrew F. Henry and James F. Short, *Suicide and Homicide* (Glencoe, Ill.: The Free Press, 1954). See an appraisal of their frustration-aggression model, and further references, in Jerry Jacobs, *Adolescent Suicide* (New York: Wiley-Interscience, 1971), pp. 6–7.

[51]D. J. West, *Murder Followed by Suicide* (London: William Heinemann, 1965), pp. 142–46.

[52]Church Assembly Board for Social Responsibility, *Ought Suicide To Be a Crime? (op. cit.* I/3), p. 7.

would increase other noncriminal activities which also carry considerable risk of pain—exploits of daring, exploration and rescue missions, missionary and spy work, medical experimentation, and other sorts of activities generally regarded as advantageous to the society—since whatever physical or psychological torment might result from these adventures could always be avoided by death.

Finally, there is some evidence that the kind of lawlessness Kant fears is encouraged by strict sanctions *against* suicide, rather than by permissive attitudes towards it. For instance, there is evidence to suggest that individuals sometimes perpetrate serious crimes in order to have their lives taken from them, since they are culturally prohibited from doing so by suicide. According to sociologist and criminologist Ruth Cavan, for example, in traditional Muslim culture self-murder is very strictly prohibited, but the murder of "infidels" is not. "Running amok," she claims, is a fairly highly institutionalized behavior in which a believer commits a series of murders of nonbelievers, and continues to do so until he himself is killed. Since direct suicide is prohibited, the individual is forced to resort to murder in order to bring about his own death.[53] Such practices may be no more characteristic of contemporary Islam than the killing of infidels is characteristic of post-Crusades Christianity, but they do illustrate a counterargument to the Kantian claim.

Nor can such practices be discounted as medieval. As Joel Feinberg points out, a similar phenomenon may occur—at least in theory—in contemporary American society, where concepts of the inalienability but forfeitability of the right to life may entail the paradox that a man, in order to rid himself of his own life, must take someone else's in order to have his life ended for him:

> There is at least one striking paradox in the traditional view that the right to life can be forfeited (by the condemned murderer where capital punishment is permitted by law) but not voluntarily alienated. The would-be suicide can lose the right to life he no longer wants only by murdering someone else and thereby forfeiting the right that keeps him from his desired death. The inalienability of his right to life permits him to shed that unwanted life only by taking the life of someone else and thereby forfeiting it. Those who believe in the inalienability of the right to life, therefore, might well think twice before endorsing its forfeit-ability.[54]

Feinberg's remarks address the theoretical issues only, but they are nevertheless to be considered seriously in the real world. A French convict guillotined in 1972 claimed he had murdered two hostages in order to be executed: "To kill in order to commit suicide, that's my morality."[55] And Friedrich Hacker, writing in the same country at the same time, found clinical evidence of twenty-eight murderers who killed other people in order to be killed themselves.[56] The same issue was discussed again in the

---

[53]Cavan, *Suicide (op. cit.* I/66), pp. 65–66.

[54]Joel Feinberg, "Voluntary Euthanasia and the Inalienable Right to Life," *Philosophy and Public Affairs* 7, no. 2 (Winter, 1978), 112. An excerpt (not including this quotation) is reprinted as "Suicide and the Inalienable Right to Life" in Battin and Mayo, eds., *Suicide: The Philosophical Issues,* pp. 223–28.

[55]Claude Buffet, executed in December 1972. The quotation is from his letter to the President of France, demanding at once to receive the "grace" of the guillotine; see *Le Monde,* Dec. 15, 1972. Quoted in Baechler, *Suicides (op. cit.* i/32), p. 36, ftn. 12.

[56]Friedrich Hacker, *Aggression-violence dans le Monde moderne* (Paris: Calmann-Lévy, 1972), p. 146, as quoted in Baechler, *Suicides (op. cit.* i/32) p. 36, ftn. 12.

United States only a few years later, with the execution of Gary Gilmore. How frequent such occurrences are is not the issue; what is at issue is the possibility that suicide prohibitions, contra Kant, may themselves be instrumental in producing crime.

The first part of this chapter has attempted to summarize the major social arguments against suicide. There are still others, most of them related to the views we have discussed. Arthur Dyck, for instance, says that suicide is psychologically damaging to the family and friends of the victim because it leaves them no time to confess their own shortcomings to the victim or to make up for their past errors or unkindnesses.[57] Suicide is sometimes interpreted as an affront to society, a "vote of no confidence in the social order." Another type of anti-suicide view assumes that suicide is wrong because it causes additional suicides, though there is an evident circularity in this reasoning. It is true that suicide rates do rise after the suicide of a public figure; that suicide rates are higher among children of persons who have killed themselves and in families where suicide has occurred; and that mimetic suicides frequently occur in which one individual replicates as precisely as possible the manner of someone else's suicide. Even suicides of fashion occur; the prototypes are the epidemic suicides among the maidens of Miletus (put to a stop only by an edict that the bodies of the girls who had hanged themselves be carried naked through the marketplace),[58] and the suicides of 804 males and 140 females who imitated a Japanese student's jump to her death in the Mihara-yama volcano in 1933.[59] But the fact that one suicide causes another does not in itself show that either is wrong; suicide must be shown to be wrong on other, independent grounds, before the fact that it may be the cause of additional suicides will count against it. The Greek and Roman Stoics thought of the noble suicides—Cato, Socrates, and Lucretia, for instance—as *examples* to be imitated by those with sufficient courage and strength to do so. David Hume, centuries later, said:

> *If suicide be supposed a crime it is only cowardice can impel us to it. If it be no crime, both prudence and courage should engage us to rid ourselves at once of existence when it becomes a burden. It is the only way that we can be useful to society—by setting an example which, if imitated, would preserve to everyone his chance for happiness in life and would effectually free him from all danger of misery.[60]*

In considering the various major social arguments against suicide—that it hurts one's family, deprives society of an individual's labor or contribution, and undermines society's system of justice and punishment, we find that none of them independently serves as an adequate basis for a general argument against suicide. This is not, of course, to say that none of them serves as an argument against suicide

[57]Arthur J. Dyck, "An Alternative to the Ethic of Euthanasia," in R. H. Williams, ed., *To Live and to Die: When, Why and How?* (New York: Springer-Verlag, 1973); reprinted in Stanley Joel Reiser, Arthur J. Dyck, and William J. Curran, eds., *Ethics in Medicine* (Cambridge, Mass.: The MIT Press, 1977); citation from the latter version, p. 533, col. 1.

[58]Plutarch, *Mulierum Virtutes*, 249B-D. The suggestion that the bodies of the girls were to be displayed naked is apparently a later embellishment upon this often-told tale.

[59]Iga and Tatai, "Characteristics of Suicides and Attitudes toward Suicide in Japan," (*op. cit.* I/94), p. 258.

[60]Hume, "On Suicide," (*op. cit.* I/49), p. 567, modernizations mine.

in any given case. If we assume, as we undertook to do at the outset of this chapter, that suicide's effects on others are relevant in determining its moral value, then we have encountered a number of cases in which suicide will indeed seem to be impermissible: for instance, where it destroys the psychological well-being of others, where it deprives an interdependent community of an essential service or type of labor, or where it does in fact encourage crime. But we have not undertaken to consider what degree of harm to other individuals or to society as a whole is required to cement the claim that suicide is, in that particular case, impermissible. Must the suicide of a spouse wreak psychiatric devastation upon the mate before it is, under the general assumption of the social arguments concerning suicide, impermissible, or will it be impermissible if the harm it causes is real but relatively slight? In a small, highly interdependent society of the sort we described, must the nonparticipation of one member entail complete destruction for the others, or will a much less radical harm—say, the simple failure to meet certain production or exploratory goals—be sufficient to override any freedom that individual might have to end his life? To answer such questions as these would require a full-scale theory of the relationship between individual autonomy and the claims of society as a whole; various ethical and political theories construe this relationship in quite different ways. The practical conclusions of the social arguments against suicide, then, will rest on acceptance of a particular underlying social theory as a whole. Rather than attempt to produce such a theory here, however, let us turn to the principal social arguments *favoring* suicide instead.

Suicide as a Benefit to the Community

So far, the social arguments have considered suicide wrong because it damages society; this is the core of the original Aristotelian view. But we shall find that the premises of these arguments all appear in arguments *favoring* suicide in certain circumstances as well. Unlike the religious view of suicide, where a certain "invitation" to suicide arises from theological roots quite distinct from those underlying the traditional arguments against suicide, the social arguments favoring suicide tend to be the same as those used against it, simply applied in different circumstances. Since the social arguments are typically teleological or consequentialist arguments, which measure the moral character of suicide in terms of the consequences it produces, they will favor suicide whenever it does not injure society, but benefits it.

Suicide as the Removal of Social Burdens

There are two major classes of circumstances in which suicide constitutes a benefit to society: those circumstances involving persons who constitute a "burden" to society, whose suicides therefore relieve society of this burden, and those circumstances in which suicide provides a direct, often immediate benefit to other persons or groups of persons. We will examine instances of each.

SOCIAL BURDENS IN DOMESTIC SITUATIONS. Perhaps the most familiar situations in which we are likely to view individuals as social burdens are domestic; this is not to say, of course, that we ought to view individuals in this way, only that we often do. For instance, a family situation may include an invalid, incontinent elder parent, who requires uninterrupted care and attention from the younger members of the family; it may include birth-defective, chronically ill, alcoholic, retarded, or mentally disturbed individuals who make considerable demands in terms of time, care, and financial resources on other members of the family. In a great many cases, these individuals have other, salutary effects upon the family—the elder parent may, for instance, provide a cohesive influence or be a source of family wisdom or lore; the Down's child may give unusual affection; the schizophrenic may provide an illuminating alternative view of the world, unconstrained by reality. But some individuals constitute a burden which is not outweighed by benefits they confer upon the family; this is especially likely to be true in extreme cases, for instance when the individual is irreversibly comatose, so severely brain-damaged as to be incapable of any communication, or so pathologically disruptive as to constitute an unrelieved psychological hardship for the family. In the United States, an individual who is chronically or terminally ill or disabled may also constitute a disastrous financial burden to the family, though in countries with comprehensive national-health plans this circumstance is less likely to occur.

In circumstances where an individual constitutes an uncompensated burden on the family, removal of the burden will be a benefit to it. Usually, removal of the burden can be accomplished in a variety of ways: institutionalization of a brain-damaged child, for instance; divorce or eviction of a spouse or dependent whose behavior is so disruptive as to injure the welfare of the family; initiation of social-service or psychological counseling for the family in order to minimize the weight of the burden. But suicide will also remove the burden, and it is here that the social arguments favoring suicide take hold. If an individual does impose severe burdens upon his family, friends, or associates, then suicide, if it will relieve them, might seem to be morally appropriate.

One might object that the psychological harms suicide causes to surviving family members will always outweigh whatever benefits may accrue from removal of a burden. In a previous section, we have discussed the grief/guilt constellation which suicide frequently produces in survivors, and which is frequently extremely damaging to them. Even the suicide of an extremely debilitated or dependent family member may produce this grief/guilt, especially when the survivors blame themselves for the individual's unhappy condition. But some clinical evidence suggests that severe psychological harm does not always result, and that, furthermore, suicide may promote the survivors' long-term well-being. In a British psychiatric study involving interviews of survivors five years after the suicide of the spouse, for instance, one third reported themselves ''worse off'' than before, but an equally large proportion reported themselves ''better off.''[61] Here we see the way in which consequentialist arguments concerning suicide reverse themselves with changing circumstances; whereas it was earlier argued that suicide is wrong because it damages family and friends, a consequentialist argument may also recommend suicide where the welfare of survivors will be improved.

[61]Brian M. Barraclough, ''A Contemporary Look at Suicide,'' Grand Rounds, University of Utah Medical Center, Dec. 7, 1977. Those ''better off'' were generally the younger survivors, and those whose spouses had been alcoholics or psychological burdens. Among all the surviving spouses, there was no evidence of higher mortality or of increased psychiatric morbidity; in short, according to Barraclough, the effects of suicide on surviving spouses is nowhere near as disastrous as is generally believed, and is often beneficial. It should be observed, however, that this study was conducted with spouses only, and may have little bearing on effects on other near relatives or on friends or other associates.

In many cases of suicide, no doubt, other alternatives which would serve to eliminate the burden upon family members, such as institutionalization, medication, or divorce, may be preferable for a variety of reasons. But it may also be the case that these alternatives appear preferable just because of our widespread assumption that suicide is always wrong. In fact, alternatives to suicide may serve only to relocate the burden: the institutionalized senile parent will in the future constitute a burden not to the immediate family but to the state; the divorced dissocial spouse may constitute a burden not to his present family but to a possible future spouse, and the problem arises again. This is especially true where deep-seated psychological problems or irreversible physical conditions threaten to jeopardize any new relationship. If we have admitted an argument which assesses the moral permissibility of suicide in terms of its effects on family, friends, and other larger social groups, we must be prepared to acknowledge that this argument will not only find suicide wrong in some circumstances, but also favor it when alternative arrangements to the present burdensome situation also produce substantial burdens.

Thus, either the original argument that suicide is impermissible because it injures others must be disallowed to begin with, or we must admit that in some cases, the same argument recommends or requires suicide. A set of arguments which condemns suicide on the grounds that it might deprive children of a parent, a spouse of conjugal companionship, and friends, acquaintances, and fellow-workers of "the benefits and pleasures of association with the victim" must recognize that in some unhappy situations, parents are not a blessing, conjugal companionship is uncomfortable and the "benefits and pleasures of association" are a steady torture; it must also recognize that in some particularly unhappy cases there may be no better, less burdensome alternatives. This is not to be morose, but simply to be realistic about the variety of human interactions and experiences. Of course, suicide may not always be forthcoming in situations such as these, and the individual who constitutes the burden may cling very tenaciously to life. But in cases where the individual does contemplate ending his life, we must grant, *if* we accept the underlying assumption of the social arguments concerning suicide, the moral acceptability of such a choice.

BURDENS ON THE SOCIETY AT LARGE.   In some cases, a given individual may constitute a burden not simply to particular, identifiable family units or other social groupings, but to society or to large segments of society. Sometimes this burden takes the form of demands on finances, food, or other resources; it may also involve demands on custodial care. In some cases, the burden an individual constitutes to his immediate social group is acute—one thinks of Captain Oates lying in his antarctic tent, or the Young Comrade in Brecht's *The Measures Taken,* who consents to his own political murder because he sees that he has become a liability to the ongoing work of the communist revolution[62]—but some persons, principally the ill, the disabled, the demented, and the aged, are often said to constitute a more or less chronic burden for the society as a whole.

Whether a given individual is held to constitute a burden to society is relative, of course, not only to the moral climate of a society but to its overall economic and

---

[62]Bertolt Brecht, "The Measures Taken," in *The Jewish Wife and Other Short Plays,* tr. Eric Bentley (New York: Grove Press, 1965), pp. 75–108. The other agitators in the cause of revolutionary action tell the Young Comrade, who has weakened at earlier points and jeopardized the cause, that they must shoot him and throw him into the lime pit, since they cannot take him with them and cannot leave him behind; they ask for his consent, and he says yes.

social condition as well. In contemplorary America, certain kinds of individuals tend to be considered burdens, such as the institutionalized brain-damaged patient and the long-term convict, since they may be maintained at governmental expense. In many traditional societies with marginal economies, such as that on the classical Greek island of Cos, or the Eskimo, various American Indian, and other primitive societies, any individual no longer capable of contributory work was considered a burden: a nonproductive individual is an extra mouth. This view is widely reflected in the euthanasia and senicide practices of these societies, in which those incapable of work were eliminated from the population, sometimes by ceremonial killing, frequently also by institutionally mandated suicide.[63]

Though these views may seem morally primitive, they have also played a role in the central traditions of western culture. Euripides addresses "those who patiently endure long illnesses" as follows:

> *I hate the men who would prolong their lives*
> *By foods and drinks and charms of magic art*
> *Perverting nature's course to keep off death*
> *They ought, when they no longer serve the land*
> *To quit this life, and clear the way for youth.*[64]

He is recommending suicide, or at least refusal of further medical treatment, on social-burden grounds. A similar view, perhaps more forcefully stated, is found in Nietzsche's *Twilight of the Gods:*

> *The sick man is a parasite of society. In certain cases it is indecent to go on living. To continue to vegetate in a state of cowardly dependence upon doctors and special treatments, once the meaning of life, the right to life, has been lost, ought to be regarded with the greatest contempt by society. The doctors, for their part, should be the agents for imparting this contempt—they should no longer prepare prescriptions, but should every day administer a fresh dose of disgust to their patients . . . One should die proudly when it is no longer possible to live proudly. Death should be chosen freely . . .*[65]

Here too, voluntary death is held morally preferable to life as a social burden.

The ill and the aged are most often singled out as the groups which constitute burdens upon society as a whole; the emphasis is still stronger on those who are *both* ill and aged, as many of the elderly members of a population are. This form of social-burden argument has been actively considered in recent years, where social theorists have pointed to the very rapidly increasing proportion of elderly members of society, and to expectations of a very much lengthened but not improved life-

---

[63]See Simone de Beauvoir, *The Coming of Age* (*op. cit.* I/129), and Cavan, *Suicide* (*op. cit.* I/66).

[64]Euripides, *Suppliants* 1109, as quoted by [pseudo-] Plutarch in "A Letter of Condolence to Apollonius," 110C, in *Plutarch's Moralia*, tr. Frank Cole Babbitt (London: William Heinemann; Cambridge, Mass.: Harvard University Press, 1928), II, 153.

[65]Friedrich Nietzsche, *The Twilight of the Idols* 36, in Oscar Levy, ed., *The Complete Works of Friedrich Nietzsche*, 16, tr. Anthony M. Ludovici, (London: George Allen & Unwin, 1927), p. 88.

span. Mary Rose Barrington, a British jurist and administrator of a group of almshouses for the aged, writes:

> *It is future generations, faced perhaps with a lifespan of eighty or ninety years, of which nearly half will have to be dependent on the earning power of the other half, who will have to decide how much of their useful, active life is to be devoted to supporting themselves through a terminal period 'sans everything,' prolonged into a dreaded ordeal by ever-increasing medical skill directed to the preservation of life.*[66]

She believes that in these circumstances, voluntary death should become a frequent, realistic, and socially expected alternative. That suicide might be contemplated and encouraged in order to spare society the burden of caring for its old, ill, and otherwise dependent members may be a serious moral indictment of society, but it is what the social-burdens argument seems to recommend.

OVERPOPULATION. A distinct but closely related issue concerning suicide as the removal of a burden upon society is that of overpopulation. In this case, unlike the special cases of the ill or the aged, the burden which an individual imposes on society does not result from any particular characteristic of the individual involved, but from that individual's mere presence in the society. Earlier writers often argued against suicide on the grounds that it reduces the population and hence weakens society;[67] present concerns with overpopulation threaten to reverse this argument, maintaining that a stasis or a reduction in population would strengthen society.

Both in primitive and contemporary groups, social-policy schemes for controlling overpopulation usually advocate marriage restrictions or birth control to maintain the society within satisfactory size limits. But once the limits are exceeded, removal of present members seems to be indicated, and the suicides of as many members as would reduce the population to optimal size would appear to have beneficial social effects. If the overcrowding is local, alternatives to suicide might include emigration of some members to other regions; if the overcrowding is global, there appears to be no better alternative. Once again, the traditional consequentialist arguments against suicide, based on the notion that population increases benefit society, are reversed; as changing circumstances indicate that population decreases are desirable, the argument becomes one favoring suicide even among those members of the population who have no personal reasons for ending their lives. In the extreme, suicide might be considered a loyal contribution of a loyal citizen.

SOCIOPATHY. A special version of the social-burdens argument favoring suicide is addressed to individuals who are sociopathic or engage in continuing criminal activity. This is a direct counterpart of the "special talents" argument against suicide, in which it was argued that some individuals—musicians, physicists, cancer researchers, etc.—may by virtue of their special gifts and talents have an obligation to continue their contributions to society. Here, we are faced again with a class of individuals with "special gifts," but whose special gifts have negative impact on society: the thief, the arsonist, the rapist, the child molester. If these individuals cannot cease to commit crimes which injure society, according to this argument, they ought to rid society of themselves altogether.

This argument first occurs in little-read passages of Plato's *Laws*, which remain very nearly the only explicit statement of this view in western culture. Plato

---

[66]Barrington, "Apologia for Suicide," (*op. cit.* i/54), p. 101.

[67]Cf. Fedden, *Suicide* (*op. cit.* i/11), p. 42, on the economic basis of the suicide taboo.

argues that those individuals who cannot keep themselves from repeating society's more serious crimes—the particular case is temple-robbing—*ought* to commit suicide. He suggests the following speech be addressed to the compulsive temple-robber:

My good man, the evil force that now moves you and prompts you to go temple-robbing is neither of human origin nor of divine, but it is some impulse bred of old in men from ancient wrongs unexpiated, which courses round wreaking ruin; and it you must guard against with all your strength. How you must thus guard, now learn. When there comes upon you any such intention, betake yourself to the rites of guilt-averting, betake yourself as a suppliant to the shrines of the curse-lifting deities, betake yourself to the company of the men who are reputed virtuous; and thus learn, partly from others, partly by self-instruction, that every man is bound to honour what is noble and just; but the company of evil men shun wholly, and turn not back. And if it be so that by thus acting your disease grows less, well; but if not, then deem death the more noble way, and quit yourself of life.[68]

Of course, as a practical matter the sociopath or recidivist criminal is unlikely to be moved by this exhortation to rid the society of himself; for this reason, the death penalty must be imposed by others. Yet the death penalty is, from Plato's point of view, a substitute measure, one which is to be invoked only when the individual fails in his primary obligation to end his life.[69]

It is not always the case that the recidivist criminal fails to recognize his own sociopathy, and his role as a burden rather than benefit to society. Martin Luther, in *The Table-Talk,* recounts the following severe case:

On one occasion a boy of eighteen years was brought before a judge for theft. The judge was anxious to save him from the gallows, and to release him because of his youth. But the prisoner said, "Make an end of me at once, for that is my destiny. If you release me, I shall assuredly return to the work of stealing."[70]

In a present-day version of the same argument, Steven Judy, a twenty-three-year-old who was convicted of murdering a woman and her three children, told the judge, "I honestly want you to give me the death penalty because one day I may get out"; he had been caught breaking out of his cell the week before.[71] The negative version of the special-talents argument we are considering would hold that in such cases, the requests of these young men for death, at least if the requests are sincere, ought to be honored; they are suicides, we might say, to deprive society of their own special but unfortunate contributions.

SOCIAL DARWINISM. Social darwinism, developed as the application to human social behavior of Darwin's biological theories concerning "survival of the fittest" in a natural competition, is a social theory which sees elimination of the

---

[68]Plato, *Laws* IX, 854B–C, tr. R. G. Bury (Cambridge: Harvard University Press, 1967), II, 201–3.

[69]See Winfried Knoch, *Die Strafbestimmungen in Platons Nomoi,* Klassisch-Philologisch Studien, Heft 23 (Wiesbaden: Otto Harrassowitz, 1960), and my "Philosophers' Death and Intolerable Life: Plato on Suicide." (*op. cit.* i/59).

[70]Martin Luther, *The Table-Talk of Doctor Martin Luther,* 10th Centenary Edition (London: T. Fischer Unwin, 1883), section "Of Princes and Rulers," p. 108 (cf. I/134).

[71]*Salt Lake Tribune,* Feb. 26, 1980. The case was tried in Morgan County, Indiana, Superior Court.

"less fit" members of human society as natural, inevitable, and desirable, in the same way that competition which eliminates the less fit members of other species is said to be natural, inevitable, and desirable as the mechanism of continuing evolutionary advancement. During the late nineteenth century, the spread of these views was associated with a decline in traditional Christian charity, and those perceived as "less fit"—the weak, the needy, the helpless, those who are deformed, disabled, ill, or disturbed, and those whose social relationships are inadequate or criminal— came increasingly to be viewed as threats to the well-being of society.[72] These views of course distorted the biological notion of "fitness" as applying solely to reproductive success. And these views were also very quickly infected with race, class, and age prejudice. Nevertheless, they had increasing impact on social policy, and led to nontreatment of the ill, eugenic breeding schemes, and compulsory thrift-euthanasia. The leading German darwinist biologist Ernst Haeckel argued, around the turn of the century, that putting a high value on life *per se* was a "dangerous sentiment"; he urged the elimination of "hundreds of thousands of incurables—lunatics, lepers, people with cancer, etc." by means of morphine or other drugs.[73] Such policies were in fact practiced on a very wide scale under Hitler's National Socialist regime, involving forcible extermination of millions of people on the grounds that they were of "inferior" genetic stock.[74]

But although social-darwinist views led to large-scale atrocities involving massive violations of human freedom, the social-darwinist view of *suicide,* as distinct from involuntary "euthanasia," may be less easy to defeat on moral grounds. It involves no apparent violation of human freedom, since suicide is conceived of as a voluntary act. Social darwinism simply holds that suicide— chosen and performed by the individual—is to be welcomed as a natural self-cleansing mechanism on the part of the species. Making the empirical assumption that it is the less fit and less well-adapted individuals who choose suicide, the social-darwinist view accepts and encourages suicide as a self-selecting means of purifying the genetic stock of the human race, a beneficial mechanism by which those individuals who are less fit and therefore less content *select themselves* for elimination from the continuing gene pool of the society. Although its immediate emotional impact on particular individuals among the victim's family and associates may be injurious, this view acknowledges, its long-range effects for the society are beneficial.

Such views need not be associated with Nazism or other extermination schemes, and they may be coupled with a considerable charity and sympathy for the individuals involved. The eminent British psychiatrist and geneticist Eliot Slater argues for permitting suicide, even among the insane, on similar grounds:

> Nor should we forget the welfare of society. If a chronically sick man dies, he ceases to be a burden on himself, on his family, on the health services and on the community. If we can do nothing to get a patient better, but do our best to retard the process of

[72]Gerald J. Gruman, "An Historical Introduction to Ideas About Voluntary Euthanasia: With a Bibliographic Survey and Guide for Interdisciplinary Studies," *Omega,* 4, no. 2 (1973) 87–138.

[73]*Ibid.,* p. 109, citing Ernst Haeckel, *The Wonders of Life: A Popular Study of Biological Philosophy,* tr. J. McCabe (New York: Harper, 1904), pp. 118–20.

[74]See Gitta Sereny, *Into That Darkness: From Mercy Killing to Mass Murder* (New York: McGraw-Hill, 1974), for an account of the development of "euthanasia" policies under Hitler to mass extermination.

*dying—extend it perhaps over months and years—we are adding to the totality of ill
health and incapacity . . . There is, of course, absolutely no limit to the burdens we can
go on piling up, by trying to keep badly damaged individuals alive.*[75]

"Mercy" killing, involuntary euthanasia, and other forms of extermination infringe
on the rights of these individuals to remain alive if they wish to do so, according to
the argument we are pursuing, but permissive attitudes towards suicide allow to
happen naturally what is in society's best long-term interests.

This pro-suicide argument can be attacked in various ways. For instance, it
assumes that those who choose suicide are "unfit," though persons like Socrates,
Cato, Joan of Arc, Napoleon, Sir Walter Raleigh (the latter three all unsuccessful
suicide attempters), Ernest Hemingway or Marilyn Monroe may not strike us as
"unfit" individuals, at least in the common sense of that term. Second, it is based
on a misunderstanding. Fitness, to the biologist, is a matter of reproductive success,
and has little to do with the notion of "superb specimen" that the social darwinists
had in mind. Thus, the argument would favor suicide before the onset of reproductive activity, and so prefer suicide among children, adolescents, and very young
adults. The social-darwinist enthusiasm for ridding the world of "lunatics, lepers,
and people with cancer" is not particularly well served by genetic argument, since
these individuals are not the most likely to reproduce. Nor, of course, would the
genetic argument have any bearing on individuals past reproductive age. But the
argument, of course, is not usually understood in a purely genetic way; it is interpreted to advocate the acceptance of suicide among those who are "burdens" of any
sort.

We tend to find the social-darwinist view of suicide repugnant because of its
association with the forced-euthanasia programs of Nazi Germany. But when this
argument is applied to genuinely *voluntary* suicide, it may seem much less so: here,
the individual sincerely desires to end his life, and this coincidentally works to the
benefit of society as a whole. Since the social arguments regarding suicide assess its
permissibility in terms of the effects on society, they will support the social-
darwinist claim in favor of suicide.

Suicide as a Direct Benefit to Society

In addition to those suicides which are said to benefit society by removing
economic, social, custodial, genetic, and other burdens, suicide is sometimes also
said to confer a direct, immediate benefit to individual persons or to larger groups of
persons and societies. Although these types cannot be rigidly distinguished, we
might take as a prototype of the burden-relieving suicide that of the very old or the
very ill; as a prototype of the direct-benefit suicide, we might point to those of
self-sacrifice, martyrdom, and social witness. We have discussed religious forms of
some of these types of direct-benefit suicides in Chapter One; here, we shall focus
on secular examples.

[75]Eliot Slater, "Choosing the Time to Die," *Proceedings of the Fifth International Conference for
Suicide Prevention* (London 1969), ed. Richard Fox (Vienna: The International Association for Suicide
Prevention, April 1970.) Reprinted in Battin and Mayo, eds., *Suicide: The Philosophical Issues, (op. cit.
i/10),* pp. 199–204, quotation pp. 202–03.

SELF-SACRIFICIAL SUICIDE. Self-sacrificial suicides, in which one person directly benefits another by sacrificing his own life in order to spare the life or to promote the welfare of someone else, are familiar in both historical and hypothetical examples. They include such obvious cases as the soldier who falls on a grenade to spare his buddies; the parent who throws himself in front of a train to save a child; the pilot who goes down with his plane in order to steer it away from a populated area; and so forth. Borderline cases of self-sacrificial suicide would include that of the researcher who works with highly dangerous chemical or biological materials; the physician who goes to the jungle to treat an infectious, incurable, and universally fatal disease; the bomb-disposal squad member; and others who undertake high or certainly fatal risks in order to benefit society. In all these cases, the benefit to other persons or society is direct and does not result from the removal of burdens the suiciding person had imposed upon society.

Of course, most of these cases are not called "suicide," but rather "self-sacrifice," "heroism," or "martyrdom." This is largely due to the fact that the term "suicide," like its predecessors in English, "self-murder" and "self-slaughter," carries with it severely negative moral connotations. As we've said earlier, this linguistic distinction rests primarily on the distinction between suicide and laudatory self-death rendered by the traditional Catholic principle of double effect: heroism, self-sacrifice, and martyrdom are situations in which death is foreseen but not primarily intended by the agent; suicide is that situation in which the agent directly and primarily intends his own death. But in a teleological or consequentialist ethic, the benefit to others from an act of suicide occurs regardless of the motivation under which the individual actually kills himself or allows himself to die.

It is crucial to see that some suicide in which death is deliberately and primarily intended, and so termed "suicide" under even the most restrictive definition, may also have strongly beneficial consequences for other persons and for society. For instance, the suicide of one person may make available donor organs which make possible continued life for someone else; the suicide of one member of an orchestra or a team or a faculty will open a position for someone else; the suicide of a rich man will mean wealth for his heirs or perhaps a bequest to charity. In actual cases of suicide, such beneficial consequences are rarely mentioned. Yet, again, any moral theory which weighs an action by its outcomes must acknowledge and take into account the direct beneficial consequences of a suicide, too. In very many cases, of course, they may be outweighed by negative effects, but there are many cases in which they are not.

One particular class of direct-benefit suicides deserves special mention; these are the suicides of "symbolic protest" or "social witness." They are universally labeled "suicide," and yet quite widely also agreed to be of potentially substantial and direct social benefit.

SUICIDES OF SOCIAL PROTEST. We mentioned earlier that suicide is sometimes viewed as an affront to society or a "vote of no confidence in the social order"; this, as we've said, is often taken as evidence of the wrongness of suicide. It is an ancient notion, one which Romilly Fedden, the historian of suicide, sees as an explanation in part for the growth of the suicide taboo. Fedden explains:

> ... suicide shows a contempt for society. It is rude. As Kant says, it is an insult to humanity in oneself. This most individualistic of all actions disturbs society profoundly. Seeing a man who appears not to care for the things which it prizes, society is

compelled to question all it has thought desirable. The things which makes its own life worth living, the suicide boldly jettisons. Society is troubled, and its natural and nervous reaction is to condemn the suicide. Thus it bolsters up again its own values.[76]

But Fedden strikes precisely the point. There are a great many occasions when we think society and its values *should* be disturbed, and when we find a "vote of no confidence" the appropriate response to the prevailing social order.[77] This is true whenever we see society as corrupt or vicious, or as headed for avoidable ruin.

Indeed, some suicides are clearly intended as affronts to society, and are designed both to announce the individual's absolute refusal to live within a society which he conceives of as corrupt or vicious, and to bring to bear social pressure for radical change. Quaker Norman Morrison's self-immolation during the Viet Nam war appears to be precisely this kind of intentional "affront."[78] So does the suicide of Smul Zygielbojm, a leader in the Jewish Socialist Bund who escaped from Poland after his wife and children had been killed by the Nazis; Zygielbojm killed himself in London in 1943, leaving a note addressed to the President and Prime Minister of the Polish government in exile:

By my death I wish to make my final protest against the passivity with which the world is looking on and permitting the extermination of the Jewish people.[79]

The view of suicide as an affront to society is bolstered by the observation that some governments, particularly those which are highly authoritarian, appear indeed to regard suicide among members of their populaces as a loss of face. Fascist Italy and Nazi Germany did not publish suicide figures, and the present USSR and other Communist nations, excepting Hungary, still do not report their suicide statistics to the World Health Organization.[80] Of course, not all suicides in these cultures are

---

[76]Fedden, *Suicide* (*op. cit.* i/11), p. 42.

[77]For an extended discussion of moral reasons for condoning symbolic protest in various social situations, even when such protest will not rectify the situation but will bring harm to the protester, see Thomas E. Hill, Jr., "Symbolic Protest and Calculated Silence," *Philosophy & Public Affairs*, 9, no. 1 (Fall, 1979), 83–102. Hill does not explicitly discuss suicide as an act of symbolic protest, but the central points of his discussion may well be applied to this case.

[78]An account of Norman Morrison's self-immolation can be found in Paul W. Pretzel, "Philosophical and Ethical Considerations of Suicide Prevention," *Bulletin of Suicidology* (July 1968), pp. 30–38; see esp. p. 35.

[79]Sereny, *Into That Darkness* (*op. cit.* II/74), pp. 139 and 219.

[80]The suicide rates for Hungary, the only Communist nation to report suicide figures to the World Health Organization, are considerably higher than median countries like Britain and the U.S., although lower than those of West Berlin. Some observers believe that suicide rates in other Communist countries are extremely high. However, the official Soviet position on suicide, quoted from *The Great Medical Encyclopedia* (Moscow, 1963), may explain the reluctance of these nations to report suicide figures: "Suicide is an important social problem that cannot be solved in capitalist society. . . . In the U.S.S.R. the liquidation of unemployment and rising standard of living of the working masses have resulted already during the period of building socialism in a significant decrease in the number of suicides. With the advent of socialism and the complete liquidation of the socioeconomic causes of suicide, the latter disappeared in the U.S.S.R. as a social phenomenon and ceased to exist as a social problem, similar to the disappearance of unemployment, prostitution, and many other phenomena typical of capitalist society. In socialist society suicide must be considered mainly as a "leftover" of capitalism, a "residual" phenomenon against which a resolute campaign must be waged." Quoted by Jacques Choron, "Concerning Suicide in Soviet Russia," *Bulletin of Suicidology* (Dec. 1968), p. 31.

protest-motivated; nevertheless, the phenomenon of suicide in itself is often interpreted as a symptom of dissatisfaction, and hence is seen as a criticism of the society as a whole.

Although we may have reservations concerning suicides which are intended as affronts to society when we do not approve of the criticism leveled and the societal changes which the suicide aims to bring about, or when we believe it based on a distorted perception of reality, we nevertheless widely regard political "affronts" such as Morrison's and Zygielbojm's laudable when we perceive the circumstances which they protest as in fact morally corrupt. Our view of the morality of the self-immolations of Vietnamese Buddhist monks tends to be associated with our view of the morality of the war. But we also recognize that such acts may have considerable immediate and long-range impact on public opinion (here one might also mention near-suicides such as that of Gandhi by starvation) and on the decisions of political leaders, and that they may actually contribute to the eventual alteration of the social circumstances they were designed to protest.

Lebacqz and Engelhardt, although they generally hold that immediate obligations to other persons, particularly family and friends, will usually override any right to suicide, maintain that social-protest suicide may be justified even when it appears to violate these immediate obligations. They write:

> ... Suicide is occasionally used as an act of symbolic protest against great evil and injustice—e. g., against war or imprisonment—and is meant to support in a radical fashion respect for persons generally.
>
> In such cases, suicide appears to violate one's immediate obligations of covenant-fidelity, since family and friends may be abandoned in order to make symbolic protest. However, the intention of the act is to protest those institutions and structures which undermine the very conditions that make human life and covenant-fidelity possible. When suicide as symbolic protest provides a significant contribution to the struggles against forces which would destroy the freedom of others, taking one's own life can be an affirmation of the dignity of persons. We might say that in this form of suicide, the individual aligns herself with more basic loyalties than those to family and friends—namely the community of moral agents. The need to struggle for justice may in circumstances be more compelling than obligations to one's immediate family and friends.[81]

In the consequentialist terms in which the social arguments against suicide are generally cast, then, it also appears that in some cases of suicide, social benefits may outweigh even quite substantial social harms.

Utilitarian Theory and Suicide

The social arguments concerning suicide, both those favoring suicide and those against it, rest on a consequentialist ethical theory, of which the most fully developed version is that known as Utilitarianism. But when utilitarian ethical theory is applied to suicide, a number of general problems develop.

To begin with the most evident problems, we have been assuming a fairly

---

[81]Lebacqz and Engelhardt, "Suicide and Covenant," (op. cit. II/16), pp. 86–87.

simplistic model of consequences in this discussion; in the real world, a given suicide may have extremely varied effects on others. The suicide of a chronically but not terminally ill person may cause severe grief and guilt to family members, and perhaps professional embarrassment to the physician; it may on the other hand relieve the family of a serious financial burden, and free scarce medical resources to be used by the physician for the treatment of others. Some effects of a suicide cannot be foreseen at all. Consequentialist and utilitarian moral systems usually assume a metric for weighing good and bad consequences against each other; in practice, such calculations are by no means easy to make.

Furthermore, the social arguments assess the moral value of suicide in terms of its effect *on others,* not in terms of the effect on the individual himself. This is because the individual, after committing suicide, no longer exists, and presumably can be neither harmed nor benefited. Of course, negative or positive effects may occur to the individual if he chooses *not* to end his life (e. g., the harm of a continuing painful illness, or the benefit of an unforeseen new opportunity) or if a suicide attempt wounds but is not fatal; it is also the case that an individual who does kill himself may have posthumous interests which can be harmed or benefitted after his death. Strictly speaking, however, completed suicide has *no* consequences for the individual who commits it. Moral judgments regarding the ethical status of a given suicide must be made in terms of its consequences for other people.

In cases where severe injury foreseen for other people suggests that the individual ought not kill himself, considerations of that individual's own welfare if he remains alive (and, say, in great pain) may weigh heavily; here, various forms of utilitarianism supply slightly different procedures for calculating the weights of happiness in the individual and in other persons or society, and thus slightly different views of the degree to which the avoidance of harm to others takes precedence over the satisfactions of the individual himself. These are the cases in which the individual wants to end his life to spare himself shame, loneliness, illness, or pain, but doing so will cause harm to others. Much more philosophically disturbing, however, are those circumstances which favor suicide, even though the individual may not really wish to do it, because the suicide will, in the end, benefit others. The trouble arises here, at least on a no-afterlife theory, because there will be no harm to the individual (since he will be dead),[82] and so no countervailing considerations to keep him from ending his life. He may suffer distress in anticipation of death or in the act of killing himself, even if the act is sufficiently voluntary to count as suicide, but this distress is as transitory as the distress in any other somewhat difficult or dangerous task, and may not at all outweigh the benefits of doing the deed. Indeed, in any case where a balance of benefits over injury will accrue to others from the suicide of an individual, it may seem that the suicide ought to be encouraged, since harm to the deceased will be nil.

Worse still, it may be the case that utilitarian theory *requires* suicide in such cases. In discussing earlier Augustine's view that the only morally acceptable suicides are those performed at the command of God, we pointed out that in Augustine's theory suicide is never merely optional; if God commands suicide, the command must be obeyed. But according to the utilitarian moral theory which underlies most of the social arguments concerning suicide which we've been discussing in this second chapter, it may also be that whenever suicide is permissible, it is

[82]We will discuss this argument further in Chapter 4.

also obligatory.[83] According to a utilitarian theory, the moral rightness or wrongness of an action is a function of the way in which that act affects all persons involved: if the act produces a greater balance of happiness or utility over unhappiness or disutility than any other action would produce, then that is the right act to do. In many of the cases we have discussed in this chapter—the miserably alcoholic husband, whose suicide frees his wife and saddens no one; the dying mother, whose suicide spares her family the agony of watching her suffer; the voluntary organ donor, whose various organs make possible continued life for a number of other people; Captain Oates, walking to his death in the blizzard, thus raising the chances of survival for his comrades—the act of suicide will produce a greater balance of utility for all persons involved, even considering the fairly severe discomfort it may cause the agent, than any alternative act. The positive effects for others of suicide in these cases outweigh the negative ones, and the long-term effect on the agent is nil. It seems, then, that suicide is obligatory in even those cases in which the benefit to others is real, but small. To counteract this difficult conclusion we may be tempted to formulate hypotheses about disruptive generalized anxiety concerning suicide that suicide-favoring attitudes might generate, or about harms to the deceased's interests which are not harms to his person, but it may be that such hypotheses are nothing more than a rather transparent device to ward off a conclusion most of us will find disturbing.

A still more bizarre result of applying utilitarian moral theory to the problem of suicide is the rather curious technical problem sometimes known as the "paradox of utilitarianism"; it is significant because it sheds further light on the sense in which suicide can be said to be obligatory.[84] The problem is this. Utilitarian theory obligates individuals to act so as to increase the average level of happiness or utility in the society as a whole, or (in alternative versions of the theory) to produce a maximum aggregate of happiness. It is usually assumed that this is accomplished by actions which contribute to the happiness of others and/or to the happiness of oneself, and by avoiding actions which cause unhappiness. But raising the overall level of utility can be accomplished in another way: by the *removal* from society of any person who, on the whole, is unhappy enough to bring the overall level of happiness down, or who does not contribute to the aggregate happiness. Richard Henson describes the paradox in this way:

> Now consider . . . a person whose [hedonic, or "happiness"] level is below . . . average. If any such person were to die, the hedonic average of the whole population would rise; this would in itself be a good consequence, the kind which we have just

---

[83]The terminology of 'obligations' and 'duties' is not classically part of utilitarianism; the utilitarian, rather, describes actions as "the right thing to do," or "the best alternative available," and the terms 'obligation' and 'duty' are reserved to describe situations involving special relationships to or claims on other people. Thus, it may be the *right* thing to do to assist any feeble old man across the street, though one may have an *obligation* only to help one's own father. Nevertheless, that action which, for the utilitarian, is the right thing to do, is what we ordinarily would call obligatory, and is similar to the sense in which we said that suicide could sometimes be obligatory under Augustine's religious account. One who refuses to do so in the circumstances would be morally deficient. One might have wanted to praise, say, Samson or Captain Oates for sacrificing themselves; both the religious and utilitarian accounts insist that these figures did exactly what they ought to do.

[84]The problem is formulated by Richard G. Henson in "Utilitarianism and the Wrongness of Killing," *The Philosophical Review*, 80 (July 1971), pp. 320-37, and reexamined by L. W. Sumner in "A Matter of Life and Death," *Nous*, 10 (1976), 145-71.

said a utilitarian should seek to bring about; to bring it about would tend to be right; indeed, to fail to bring it about would—unless one were doing something else instead which had better consequences—be wrong.[85]

The death of a person who is less happy than average is to be welcomed, provided, of course, that death does not produce new unhappiness for surviving individuals. Furthermore, as each unhappy person dies, the average happiness rises: by the so-called "recomputation effect," people formerly above average in happiness may now fall below it, and their deaths are now also to be welcomed. It would not, of course, be appropriate to *kill* unhappy individuals, since killing them against their will would produce extreme fear in others, and widespread fear would lower the overall utility. But to allow or encourage unhappy individuals—those below average—to kill *themselves* when they choose is quite another matter. In the absence of strong social ties or duties, where suicide might adversely affect others, and where the only effect an individual may have in committing suicide is to willingly eliminate his own misery, utilitarian theory suggests that he is not merely entitled, but obligated to do so. The greater his misery, the stronger his obligation to rid the world of himself.

We have discussed so far the problems associated with *act utilitarianism,* that form of utilitarianism which holds that the moral status of a particular act is directly determined by whether it maximizes the general utility or not. But it might be argued that because it is often difficult or impossible in any particular case for someone to predict precisely what consequences an act will have, a prospective suicide cannot know whether the act he contemplates will maximize the general utility or not, and therefore cannot know whether that act would be right or wrong. We can know, however, what consequences acts of a given type *tend* to have, and so whether such acts do, on the whole, maximize the general utility. Thus, we can know whether most such acts are right or wrong, and whether a particular act of that type is likely to be right or wrong. On this basis, it could be argued, we are justified in establishing rules which prohibit or permit any act of a given kind, since such a rule, if correctly formulated, will itself maximize the general utility. So, for instance, we might say that one ought not lie even in a case when no harm would be done, since a rule against lying (rather than a rule permitting lying, or no rule at all) maximizes the general utility by keeping us from acts which are, in general, likely to be wrong. Similarly, we may support a rule generally prohibiting suicide, even if in some few cases suicide might be "rational" or otherwise permissible from an act-utilitarian point of view.

This notion of rules may seem to provide a basis for acceptance of the sorts of legal, religious, medical, and cultural suicide prohibitions which are very much a part of contemporary society. These prohibitions, as we've said earlier in this book, include such barriers as legal sanctions against suicide and/or assisted suicide, legal protection for suicide prevention, restrictions in life- and health-insurance policies, religious penalties such as nonburial and threat of damnation, medical procedures promoting the prevention of suicide, and, more generally, a strong cultural repudiation of suicide, with its attendant stigma for attempters and survivors. Although these very substantial barriers may operate to prevent some suicides which the act utilitarian would allow, the establishment and maintenance of such barriers is jus-

---

[85]Henson, "Utilitarianism and the Wrongness of Killing," (*op. cit.* II/84) p. 325.

tified, on this view, because these barriers operate on the whole to maximize the general utility. Were there no such barriers, the incidence of suicide would be much larger, and hence—since most suicides decrease the general utility—the general utility would go down.

More than a purely theoretical observation suggests the compellingness of this argument. Although many clinicians acknowledge that some cases are rational or well-justified (for example, suicide in terminal illness), they are also quite sensitive to the extreme vulnerability of individuals contemplating suicide. To condone suicide at all—even in terminal illness—would be to open the possibility for others whose reasons are much less sound. Were barriers to suicide weakened, or were open advocacy of rational suicide to be allowed, it might reasonably be supposed that many such vulnerable individuals, who would not otherwise commit suicide, might be led to do so. At a time when teenage suicide rates are skyrocketing, permissive attitudes towards suicide may seem irresponsible or murderous.

But while this argument may seem intuitively compelling, closer inspection reveals it to have a central flaw. For notice its general form: a rule generally prohibiting behavior of a certain sort, although it prohibits some few cases of it which promote or leave unaltered the general utility, is to be accepted because behavior of this sort in general decreases the general utility. But this cloaks a hidden *empirical* assumption concerning the relative frequency of negative and positive outcomes of this kind of behavior: it assumes that in the main, such behavior decreases the general utility and only comparatively rarely promotes it. Thus, for instance, acceptance of a rule against lying depends on the *empirical* assumption that most cases of lying which would occur if the rule were not in force decrease the general utility, although some few cases might have the reverse effect. In the same way, advocacy of general barriers to suicide rests on the empirical assumption that most cases of suicide are, from an act-utilitarian standpoint, wrong: they do not maximize the general utility.

But, with respect to suicide, it is precisely this empirical assumption that can be challenged. Barrington and Kastenbaum have argued that suicide at an advanced but not deteriorated age could become the accepted and preferred way to end one's life. Of course, in such a world there would still be suicides of the hasty, irrational sort: these would continue to decrease the general utility, often very sharply. But such suicides, "wrong," "immoral," or "unacceptable" from an act-utilitarian point of view, would in the world Barrington and Kastenbaum foresee be in the minority; those which are "right," "moral," or "acceptable" from an act-utilitarian point of view would vastly outnumber them, at least if they have become the normal end of human life. If the proportion of "acceptable" suicides is greater than the proportion of "unacceptable" ones, the principles of utilitarianism will justify the establishment of a rule which permits or requires suicide, even if this rule also permits or requires occasional suicides of the irrational or "wrong" sort.

This argument may seem to trade on a science-fiction view of a future world in which death by suicide is the preferred exit, and we may object that there is no evidence that such a state of affairs will occur. But neither is there any satisfactory evidence for the empirical facts which form the basis of the traditional case. We must remember that out present behavior with respect to suicide is already very heavily influenced by the existence of culture-wide suicide barriers of precisely the sort in question. Because of the sustained, culture-wide operation of these barriers, we simply do not know what the empirical facts of suicide behavior uninfluenced by such barriers might be. We do not know what suicide behavior was like in human culture prior to the establishment of these rules, although very early Greek and Hebrew cultures, where there were no apparent prohibitions, may give us some clues. More important, we do not know how such behavior might change in response to new and very different contemporary circumstances. Particularly relevant, of course, is the development of sophisticated medical technology which makes it possible to extend human life to much greater lengths than was possible in the past. The issue of suicide in preference to old age may not have been a pressing issue in a culture in which the average life expectancy was twenty-five or thirty years; but it is becoming a pressing issue now.

The ethical theory I have described above is in fact a form of act utilitarianism modified by rules-of-thumb. The true rule utilitarian advocates action according to a set of rules whose general adoption would have the best consequences, and applies his utility test to rules, not acts. Even if he knows with certainty that breaking a rule in a particular case would produce more utility than observing it, he believes himself obligated to follow the rule. Nevertheless, the problem which we have just seen in connection with rules-of-thumb exists still more forcefully here: would the true rule utilitarian's set of rules include one prohibiting suicide—or one permitting it? Clearly, the empirical issues must be resolved before the rule utilitarian can begin to formulate rules which genuinely maximize the general utility. This, I think, we might call the "paradox" of rule utilitarianism, and I think this paradox may show us that both rule-of-thumb utilitarianism and true rule utilitarianism are theoretically inadequate to serve as a basis for general cultural suicide prohibitions.

Thus, neither act nor rule utilitarianism seems to adequately address the moral issues in suicide. Act utilitarianism appears to yield a conclusion we find very hard to face—that suicide is in some cases obligatory, even if it is not the wish of the person involved. Rule utilitarianism proves to be unsupported in the empirical assumptions which lie at its foundation. Neither objection proves utilitarianism wrong; the act utilitarian's uncomfortable conclusions may in fact be the correct ones, and there may be some way of obtaining the empirical data for the rule utilitarian's case. Rather than belabor these points, however, let us in the following chapter consider a set of arguments which have a nonutilitarian foundation.

CHAPTER 3

Suicide
and the Value of Life

Most of the arguments examined in the preceding chapter are consequentialist arguments: they evaluate the moral status of suicide according to its effects, including its effects on others. One might, however, assert that it is simply *wrong,* as a matter of principle or moral law, to destroy human life—whether the consequences are good or bad. This objection, often termed deontological because of its appeal to abstract moral principles, occurs in a number of arguments which emphasize the value of human life.

The Principle of the Value of Life

The principle of the value of life in western culture is primarily of Hebraic and Christian origin; it is also called the principle of the "sanctity of life." Although the term "sanctity" locates the roots of this argument in conceptions of life as God-created, the term is nevertheless widely used in contemporary discussions in bioethics without religious import, and in most of these discussions "value of life," "respect for life," "sanctity of life," "inviolability of life," and similar expressions are used interchangeably. An adherent of this view might assert that suicide is wrong because life is "of value," "of irreducible value," or "of absolute value"; that suicide fails to "respect life" or to observe the "sacredness of life"; and that it denies the fact that life is "inviolate," "precious," "holy," and "to be revered." Some of these alternatives do have religious connotations, and some differences of meaning may accompany the various formulations of the argument, but the conclusion is the same. Independent of the social effect of an individual's life, and regardless of the value he himself places upon his existence, life is *in itself* of absolute value, and therefore ought not be destroyed. Suicide is therefore always wrong.

The principle of the value of life has not been defended by many philosophers in recent years,[1] although it has provided the rhetoric for various "pro-life" groups. But one might ask, as does the title of a recent paper by Robert Young, "What is so wrong with killing people?"[2] The question is more difficult to answer than it might seem. One might, for instance, claim that killing violates the Sixth Commandment; this claim, however, assumes a religious ethic. One might maintain that it is wrong to kill a person because of the grief and harm it causes to those who are left behind; but arguments of this consequentialist sort, as we've seen, can very easily backfire. Killing might be said to be wrong because it causes social unrest and insecurity, but this would prohibit only killing which could not be successfully disguised. It is also inadequate to claim that killing is wrong because it causes distress to the victim: we still believe killing to be wrong even if the victim is killed in a painless, instantaneous, and unforeseen way, as when hit without warning from behind. Finally, as we will see in the chapter on rationality, we might claim that killing is wrong because it deprives the victim of the *praemium vitae:* the experiences, expectations, and human pleasures of which life is composed. But even if we grant that human experience is in itself good, this still does not always explain objections to killing. Many of us would regard it as wrong to kill someone who was certain to be killed by someone else five minutes later in an equally painful or painless way. The deprivation of *praemium vitae* would be negligible, but the act still morally wrong.

In lieu of a satisfactory way to account for the moral wrongness of killing, it may be treated as a moral axiom. This axiom, however, is a corollary of a still more fundamental axiom, the principle of the value of life. If life is of intrinsic, absolute value, killing will always be wrong. To treat the principle of the value of life as a fundamental moral axiom, not itself requiring any further justification but serving as the foundation for other moral considerations including the prohibition of killing, is not of course to *prove* that it should be so treated; it does, however, identify a major component of our moral thought.

The question here is whether this axiom would in practice prohibit suicide. It appears, initially, that it would. For if life is of value and killing is wrong, then there must be a general duty to live. This is not a duty to live in order to serve God, perfect oneself, spare others grief, accomplish social purposes, or serve any other purpose or function; under this axiom and its corollary, one has a duty to live just because life itself is of value, and killing—of oneself or others—is for that reason wrong.

Under the principle of the value of life, suicide would be wrong regardless of the circumstances. The principle, when consistently defended, is a comprehensive notion of the value of *all* life. We may in fact value different persons' lives in quite different ways, but there is a central value attributed to life, above and beyond whatever social value that individual might have. This fundamental value derives solely from being alive, and inheres equally in every individual. The forlorn vagrant, nursing a whiskey bottle at the edge of the gutter, is still a human being; to

[1]See, however, Kluge's *The Practice of Death* (*op. cit.* I/46), Chapter 2, for a discussion of this principle in connection with suicide.

[2]Robert Young, "What is so Wrong with Killing People?" *Philosophy*, 54, no. 210 (October 1979), 515–28. See also T. Goodrich, "The Morality of Killing," *Philosophy* 44, no. 168 (1969), 127–39, and Thomas Nagel, "Death," *Nous*, 4, no. 1 (1970), 73–80, reprinted in longer form in James Rachels, ed., *Moral Problems*, 2nd ed. (New York: Harper & Row, 1975), pp. 401–409, and in John Donnelly, *Language, Metaphysics, and Death* (New York: Fordham University Press, 1978), pp. 62–68.

allow him to end his life, even though it might succeed in eliminating unproductive behavior, would be wrong. As Erwin Ringel reminds us, "Labels like 'psychopath,' 'drunkard,' and 'addict' have become invectives, and automatically call forth contempt and antipathy. But the people who bear these labels are human beings . . ."[3]

This egalitarian respect for life may also explain our discomfort with the consequentialist arguments favoring suicide, discussed in Chapter Two. When we considered the originally Aristotelian arguments construing suicide as an injury to the community, we saw that this kind of argument can be used to promote suicide when the individual is sick, demented, poor, sociopathic, or old. In the social-darwinist version of this argument, we saw that suicide is regarded as a kind of self-purging mechanism which rids society of diseased or disfunctional members. If these arguments have seemed perverse, it is probably because they violate a common conviction that *every* life is valuable.

The principle of the value of life provides grounds for a general prohibition of suicide, and supports efforts to prevent it. Although some persons who are old, sick, crazy, sociopathic, or otherwise describable as social burdens may decide to end their lives Ringel again reminds us:

> *It is precisely the despised, those people upon whom society heaps contempt, who are particularly endangered. The critical principle of suicide prevention, after all, is that each individual life is important!*[4]

To forget this is to succumb to the temptation to devalue human life. Ringel cites as examples Hegel's supermen who "must necessarily crush many an innocent flower and destroy many a thing along their way," and Napoleon's explanation to Metternich, as he refused to halt a war costing innumerable human lives, that "A man like me doesn't care for the lives of a million people."[5] This devaluation of human life—the denial that *every* human life is important—is, as Ringel quotes Grillparzer, "that first step from humanity to bestiality,"[6] and it culminates, ultimately, in outrages like Nazism. Jonathan Glover quotes passages from letters of the I.G. Farben chemical trust to the concentration camp at Auschwitz,

> *In contemplation of experiments with a new soporific drug, we would appreciate your procuring for us a number of women . . . We received your answer but consider the price of 200 marks a woman excessive. We propose to pay not more than 170 marks a head. If agreeable, we will take possession of the women. We need approximately 150 . . . Received the order of 150 women. Despite their emaciated condition, they were found satisfactory. We shall keep you posted on developments concerning this experiment . . . The tests were made. All subjects died. We shall contact you shortly on the subject of a new load.*[7]

[3]Erwin Ringel, "Suicide Prevention and the Value of Human Life," in Battin and Mayo, eds., *Suicide: The Philosophical Issues*, (*op. cit.* i/10), pp. 205–11, quotation p. 207.

[4]*Ibid.*, p. 207.

[5]*Ibid.*, p. 208.

[6]*Ibid.*, p. 208.

[7]Jonathan Glover, *Causing Death and Saving Lives* (Harmondsworth: Penguin, 1977), p. 58; Glover's reference is to Bruno Bettelheim, *The Informed Heart* (London, 1961), Chapter 6.

It may be argued that permissive attitudes towards suicide, particularly when the weak, discouraged, or needy are allowed or enocuraged to do away with themselves, devalue life to the same degree. Society trifles with the lives of human beings when it permits them to be killed; it trifles with the lives of human beings when it permits them to kill themselves.

Modifications of the Principle

The principle of the value of life, however, is not a principle we appear to accept intact; it is clear from our practices regarding killing that we would accept it, if at all, only in substantially modified form. Let us look, then, at several possible modifications of the principle,[8] and consider whether these modifications would, like the original principle, still prohibit suicide.

The Value of Human Life

First, we might notice that the principle of the value of life is usually interpreted as applying only to human life; plants and animals are not included. It is thus to be distinguished from *vitalism,* a view which assigns value to life *per se,* including that of lower animal and plant forms. There have been thinkers or traditions which have broadened the notion of reverence for life to include non-human life as well; one thinks of Jain Buddhism, for instance, and Albert Schweizer.[9] Within the western Christian tradition, however, the principle of the value of life has usually been applied to human beings alone, by virtue of their having souls and/or the use of reason. (A lively strain in recent normative philosophy has advocated the extension of the respect-for-life principle to include animals[10] on the grounds that respect for human life is a ''speciesist'' (like racist) view and is not supported by an acceptable distinction between humans and other living things.) However, even if the principle of the respect for life is restricted to human beings, we must still account for the fact that we regularly countenance killings in cases like war, capital punishment, and self-defense. In Chapter One, we saw that Augustine explained these apparent exceptions to the commandment ''Thou shalt not kill'' on the grounds that certain cases of killing and even some suicide is divinely ordered, either at the direct behest of God or at the order of officers of a divinely constituted

[8]Several papers particularly useful in this connection are Sanford H. Kadish, ''Respect for Life and Regard for Rights in the Criminal Law,'' in Temkin, Frankena, and Kadish, *Respect for Life in Medicine, Philosophy, and the Law;* Chapter 3, ''The Sanctity of Life,'' in Glover's *Causing Death and Saving Lives* (*op. cit.* III/7); T. Goodrich, ''The Morality of Killing,'' (*op. cit.* III/2) and Philippa Foot, ''Euthanasia,'' *Philosophy and Public Affairs,* 6 (Winter 1977), 85–112.

[9]Albert Schweitzer, *Reverence for Life,* Thomas Kiernan, ed. (New York: Philosophical Library, 1965). For Schweitzer, the principle of reverence for *all* life is the basis of a complete system of values which possesses ''an altogether different depth and an entirely different vitality than one that concerned itself only with human beings'' (p. 57).

[10]See, e.g., *Animal Rights and Human Obligations,* Tom Regan and Peter Singer, eds. (Englewood Cliffs, N.J.: Prentice-Hall, 1976), and a variety of papers by a number of authors on the issue of whether animals can be said to have rights (e.g. not to be killed, not to be raised by ''factory-farm'' methods, not to be used for sport) as humans do.

state. But a theologically based argument cannot be used to excuse violations of a secular principle of the value of life.

The Protection of Other Life

One might hold that *all* killing of humans is wrong, be it in war, capital punishment, suicide, or self-defense: this position is known as pacificism. More frequently, it is argued that certain types of killings are morally permissible if they are performed in order to save other human life. Killing in war would be justified as an attempt to prevent slaughter by an invader of the members of one's family, tribe, or nation; capital punishment would be justified in order to prevent murderers from killing others; killing in self-defense would be justified to prevent the killing of oneself or those whom one is protecting.

If killing is permissible in order to save other human life, then some self-killing is also permissible. Examples are forms of self-killing usually described as martyrdom or self-sacrifice: the pilot who crashes his plane to avoid a crowded schoolyard; the hero who relinquishes a place in an overloaded lifeboat; and the repentant murderer who kills himself to prevent further misdeeds. Most of these cases, of course, are not termed "suicide" by the western religious or secular tradition. But other cases which *are* termed suicide are also allowed under this narrowed interpretation of the value-of-life principle: for example, the self-immolation of protesters who hope their suicides of protest will bring an earlier end to a war.

But saying that life is of absolute value except when taking it spares the lives of others would sanction not only voluntary self-killing, but also judicial murder, scapegoat killing, exemplary capital punishment, involuntary medical experimentation and similar practices, whenever they serve to avoid the destruction of other human life. Except perhaps for some utilitarians, most moralists would consider it wrong, for instance, to hang an innocent person on fabricated charges, even if it were known that this would serve to substantially reduce future murder rates. This practice would be considered wrong whether it serves to immediately spare some particular other life or lives, or whether it simply maximizes the protection of life in general.

We might revise the respect-for-life principle to say that all *innocent* human life is of value, and that human life can permissibly be taken only when it is in an appropriate sense guilty. This would permit killing in capital punishment, but only of those guilty and not merely for purposes of reducing the murder rate; it would permit killing of aggressors in war and self-defense; but it would not permit unjust judicial murder, fatal medical experimentation upon innocents, or scapegoating. This view seems much closer to our ordinary moral beliefs.

However, a respect-for-innocent-life principle presents enormous problems in determining what qualifies as guilt in the appropriate sense. If the principle were to be applied to suicide, it would require differentiation between guilty suicides and innocent ones. Perhaps public standards might evolve which would permit suicide when the prospective victim is guilty in a sense that would normally allow his execution by others (suicide would then serve as an alternative to capital punishment),[11] but this is certainly not the moral system under which contemporary society

---

[11] An example is provided in Plato's *Laws,* at 854C (*op. cit.* II/68).

operates. We prevent suicide even among those already condemned to death, perhaps in part through fear of legal liability or through recognition that jailed convicts might be coerced into suicide, but more probably through insistence that the guilty be punished in some nonvoluntary way. The problem of differentiating innocent from guilty prospective suicides would be complicated in practice by the fact that much suicide is associated with feelings of unworthiness, shame over misdeeds, need for atonement, and other forms of guilt. This is the case not only when some actual misdeed has been perpetrated, but quite frequently when the crime is imaginary only.

Not only does a value-of-innocent-life principle appear to permit suicides not presently acceptable to our society, it would also preclude suicide in those categories which we may pre-critically think are the best candidates for moral legitimization. In particular it would prohibit euthanatic suicide among the terminally ill, unless such an individual might also happen to be guilty in the requisite sense. Yet we can hardly imagine that the privilege of avoiding severe and terminal pain, when a person so desires, should be given to the guilty and not to the innocent.

The Quality of Life

Alternatively, we might restrict the value-of-life principle to pertain only in cases where human life is of minimum acceptable quality. This interpretation has been actively discussed in recent bioethics; those who hold all human life to be inviolable regardless of its characteristics are said to emphasize the *quantity of life* while those who regard human life as of value only when it meets certain minimum standards emphasize *quality of life*.[12]

Those who accept the quality-of-life view would permit the taking of human life, whether innocent or guilty, in cases where the quality of that individual's life falls below certain standards; this is usually called "euthanasia." Thus, the individual whose EEG is flat, for instance, may be said to fall below the minimum quality of life, and hence be a candidate for euthanatic killing. In practice, this view sometimes also involves denying that vital processes which are merely metabolic or systemic and do not involve the higher brain functions qualify as life, so that the term "life" is reserved to cover only those processes which include distinctively human functioning or capacity. Sometimes, a distinction is drawn between "biolog-

---

[12]See, e.g., Richard A. McCormick, "The Quality of Life, the Sanctity of Life," *The Hastings Center Report* 8, no. 1 (Feb. 1978), 30–36, esp. p. 34. McCormick's article, subtitled "A Theological Perspective," includes a brief but useful review of the positions of several other writers on the value-of-life vs. quality-of-life issue.

Easy test cases can be invented to distinguish between the two views. Suppose, for instance, that a neurosurgeon has time enough to operate on only one of two cases reaching the hospital before the worst possible outcome for each occurs. One case, a recent accident victim, can be restored to full health; if not operated upon, he will be severely and painfully permanently disabled. The other patient is already severely and painfully disabled; if not operated upon at once, he will die, but if operated upon, he will remain permanently in his present painful and disabled condition. Those who support the *quantity-of-life* view will tend to recommend that the surgeon operate on the already disabled patient, with the result that both patients will be permanently and painfully disabled, but both alive; those who support the *quality-of-life* view will recommend operating upon the recent accident victim, with the result that he regains full health, but the disabled patient dies. The degree of one's commitment to either view can be assessed by varying the case slightly; for instance, suppose that no pain is involved, though permanent disability is; or suppose that the disability is relatively slight.

ical life'' and "human life," and it is argued that when a person's life falls below certain qualitative standards, biological life is present. It is wrong to take human life, it is then argued, but not to terminate biological life. More straightforward versions of the quality-of-life principle avoid terminological redefinition; they approve of ending human life which is below certain minimum standards.[13]

According to all of these versions, the standards are sometimes fixed quite narrowly at irreversible coma or at brain death; sometimes they are set at intermediate levels which include individuals who show reflex response or minimal EEG activity, but do not give evidence of sentience or of communicative capacity. They are also sometimes set quite high, so that only individuals who are capable of some degree of emotional response, reflection, and reasoning activity are said to have lives of a quality sufficient to be regarded as valuable. The setting of possible standards for use in actual abortion, neonatal and adult treatment, and euthanasia decisions has, of course, generated an enormous amount of philosophic, medical, and legal discussion in recent years. In general, the higher standards are exercised in abortion and neonatal treatment cases, the lower ones in cases of euthanasia or withholding treatment to nonconsenting adults. A fetus or neonate is often regarded as a candidate for abortion or nontreatment if its deficiencies preclude a fair measure of emotional response, reflection, and reasoning, as in mental retardation, whereas the life of an adult will be declared brain-dead and his life actively terminated only if he or she shows little or no brain or reflex activity at all.[14]

Suicide, however, would seem to presuppose life which is well above even the highest minimum standards. This is because suicide is by nature voluntary, and anyone capable of making a voluntary decision, whether to commit suicide or to perform any other course of action, is *ipso facto* capable of a certain level of human experience: he can think, intend, project, and perhaps also feel pain. But if so, suicide, according to a quality-of-life criterion, is wrong, since it constitutes the taking of a life of above-minimum quality. Thus, whether the highest or lowest version of the value-of-life principle is used, suicide cannot be permitted.

There are, however, cases in which this conclusion does not follow. First, an individual, while still capable of full human experience, may direct *in advance* that, if incapacitated at some future time, his life is then to be terminated;[15] in such cases, because of the temporal disparity between the decision to have one's life terminated and the actual accomplishment of it, the so-called "suicide" or euthanasia decision is voluntary though it does not result in the termination of an above-standard life.

Second, an individual may voluntarily choose now to end a life which will fairly shortly become vegetative or severely deficient in experience. This may be the case in many kinds of terminal or deteriorative illness. Of course, the line between

---

[13]See David J. Mayo and Daniel I. Wikler, "Euthanasia and the Transition from Life to Death," in Wade Robison and Michael Pritchard, eds., *Medical Responsibility: Paternalism, Informed Consent, and Euthanasia* (Clifton, N.J.: Humana Press, 1979), pp. 195–211, for a discussion of the risks of terminological redefinition of such notions as "death."

[14]Application of these standards varies widely, and it is apparent that passive euthanasia is becoming increasingly common in non-brain-dead patients. Nevertheless, the generalization holds: the higher standards tend to be exercised in abortion and passive infanticide (i.e., withholding of both extraordinary and ordinary treatment from newborns, including surgery and feeding); the lower standards are typically applied to nonconsenting adults. Cf., however, footnote 33 to Chapter Five, on the Quinlan case.

[15]The widely-distributed Living Will does involve advance instructions concerning medical care in case of incapacitation, but directs only that heroic treatment not be introduced or continued; the Living Will does not give instructions for active euthanasia, or what we might call pre-directed assisted suicide.

above-standard experience and severely deficient or merely vegetative existence is not sharp, and most cases involve a more or less extended period of decline. Consequently, the principle which requires respect for life only of a certain quality will sometimes be invoked to terminate lives which are not yet below this level but are expected to become so within a fairly short time. The individual who chooses voluntarily to end his life now, and who performs that action himself, will in fact terminate a human life still involving above-standard human experience, though there will be very little of it left. Nevertheless, some thinkers would consider such a suicide to observe rather than violate the respect-for-life principle. The difficulty is a practical one; as Charles Wertenbacker emphasized when planning his own suicide to avoid the final stages of terminal cancer, the difficulty is to pick a point for performance of this action which maximizes the amount of good life left, and yet is not delayed so long that one becomes incapable of the action.[16]

Medical, legal, and philosophical attempts to define a minimum quality of life have almost all equated the absence of experience with minimum quality, and the presence of experience with above-standard quality. For instance, an individual who displays a flat EEG may be a candidate for discontinuation of treatment, whereas one whose brainwaves show some activity is not. But experience is of several sorts: it includes painful as well as pleasurable sensations. One might consider redefining the minimum-quality concept in terms of the *kind* of experience undergone, rather than simply the presence or absence of it. For instance, one might insist that a low-quality life is not merely one in which there is no experience, but also one which involves continuous, unremitting pain, drugged but conscious torpor, continuous and unrelenting confusion, or even vivid and terrifying delusions.[17] These are experiential states, of course, and may be difficult for others to diagnose reliably; this fact in itself provides a very strong argument against killing persons who appear to be in such states. But difficulty of diagnosis of experiential states is *not* an argument against suicide, since the individual is in a privileged position to know how painful particular experiences or circumstances are to him. He may miscalculate the painfulness of future states, but always has immediate knowledge of his present experience. Of course, just as some comas are temporary and some (to the best of our present knowledge) are not, some psychological states are temporary and some are not. If psychosis, trauma, or disease produces an experiential life which (to the best of our present knowledge) is irreversibly below a given level of quality, the arguments which are advanced for the permissibility of ending life where substandard quality is defined in terms of total absence of experience might apply here, too. Suicide in these conditions would be permissible, and yet not violate the principle of the value of human life.

On the other hand, one might maintain that life itself is a benefit or good, regardless of the experiences or absence of experiences it involves. If so, then we ought not simply weigh good experiences against bad ones in determining the quality of our own or others' lives; the goodness of life *per se* outweighs even an experiential life which is on the whole bad or nonexistent. In this sense, *all* life is

[16]Lael Tucker Wertenbacker, *Death of a Man* (Boston: Beacon Press, 1974), on assisting suicide in the cancer death of her husband, Charles.

[17]Bernard Haring, however, defines his distinction between mere biological life and human life in terms of the capacity of "reasonable use of freedom," and says the reasonable use of freedom can be defeated not only by total lack of consciousness, but by "grave defects and suffering of all kinds." *Medical Ethics* (Notre Dame: Fides, 1973), p. 142.

above-quality life; there is no human life, however deficient in experience or in good experience, which falls below some level of quality at which it first begins to be of value. This, of course, is simply to reject the quality-of-life variation of the argument that life is of value, and to revert to the original view.

Kant and Respect for Human Moral Life

An alternative value-of-life view, associated with the thought of Immanuel Kant, assigns value not directly to human biological processes or the mental capacities associated with them, but to human *moral* life. For Kant, that which is of value is distinctively human: the capacity to generate and observe moral principle or law. Kant's argument, briefly, is this: because individual human beings are, by virtue of their capacity to reason, capable of creating moral law, they are worthy of our respect; we must therefore not destroy their capacity to function as moral agents. To take someone's life would be to destroy this capacity, and therefore wrong. Since in suicide one takes the life of a person who would otherwise have this capacity, suicide is also wrong.[18]

Kant acknowledges only one exception to the rule that suicide is always wrong, and since it is from his *Lectures on Ethics*—notes taken by a student, published after Kant's death—it may not genuinely reflect Kant's views. Nevertheless, in the *Lectures* Kant describes Cato's suicide as an action which Cato took because he saw, as he was about to fall into Caesar's hands, that he, Cato, would no longer be able to live "conformably to virtue and prudence," but as a slave who had sacrificed the interests of his people to secure his own survival. Kant admits that, in this case, "appearances are in its favor."[19] But he insists that Cato's is the only such case the world has ever offered: Cato's is the only morally correct suicide, and suicide is otherwise morally wrong.

In the *Grundlegung* Kant proposes various ways to determine that suicide is wrong: these are the principal formulations of what he calls the *categorical imperative,* that absolute criterion which serves as a test for the morality of any action. First, he says, a person can discover whether an action he proposes—suicide, for instance—upholds the moral law by asking whether he can consistently desire that the maxim or formula which describes it to be a universal law. But, he says,

A man reduced to despair by a series of misfortunes feels wearied of life, but is still so far in possession of his reason that he can ask himself whether it would not be contrary to his duty to himself to take his own life . . . His maxim is: From self-love I adopt it as a principle to shorten my life when its longer duration is likely to bring more evil than satisfaction. It is asked simply whether this principle founded on self-love can become a universal law of nature. Now we see at once that a system of nature of which it

---

[18]Kant mentions or discusses the morality of suicide in six places within his ethical works. The earliest discussion occurs in the *Lectures on Ethics* (*op. cit.* I/37), pp. 148–54; suicide is twice used as an illustration of the categorical imperative in the *Fundamental Principles of the Metaphysic of Morals,* or *Grundlegung* (tr. Thomas K. Abbott, New York: The Liberal Arts Press, Inc., 1949, pp. 39–40 and 47–48), and, similarly, in the *Critique of Practical Reason* (tr. Beck, New York: The Liberal Arts Press, 1956, pp. 45 and 72), and is given extended discussion in the *Metaphysics of Morals* (volume entitled *Metaphysical Principles of Virtue,* tr. Ellington, New York: Bobbs-Merrill, 1964), pp. 82–85.

[19]Kant, *Lectures on Ethics* (*op. cit.* I/37), p. 149.

should be a law to destroy life by means of the very feeling whose special nature it is to impel to the improvement of life would contradict itself, and therefore could not exist as a system of nature; hence that maxim cannot possibly exist as a universal law of nature . . .[20]

Although the "contradiction" here is sometimes said simply to reside in the fact that we cannot universalize a maxim favoring suicide, since this would invite the annihilation of the human race, some thinkers have entertained such a view.[21] I think the contradiction Kant finds is this: we cannot will that self-serving suicide (to protect oneself from misfortune) become a universal law, since it would destroy the very selves which are to be served. Since suicide destroys humanity, it cannot serve it.

Under a second but, according to Kant, equivalent formulation of the supreme principle of morality, an action can be determined to be right if it treats its human objects as ends in themselves, never merely as means to some other end. By this test too, Kant believes, suicide is clearly prohibited.

He who contemplates suicide should ask himself whether his action can be consistent with the idea of humanity as an end in itself. If he destroys himself in order to escape from painful circumstances, he uses a person merely as a means to maintain a tolerable condition up to the end of life. But a man is not a thing, that is to say, something which can be used merely as a means, but must in all his actions be always considered as an end in himself.[22]

Finally, put in a third, again still slightly different way, suicide is seen to be a morally wrong act because suicide would destroy the being which first makes morality possible. Morality, for Kant, is rationally constituted by each autonomous human being, so that to destroy a human being is to destroy the very possibility of morality.

To destroy the subject of morality in his own person is tantamount to obliterating from the world, as far as he can, the very existence of morality itself.[23]

To destroy the possibility of morality cannot be consistent with performing a morally correct act; it would be self-contradictory to act so as to perform a morally correct act and yet, in that same act, destroy the very possibility of so doing. Suicide, therefore, is morally wrong.

These are the three central ways of showing suicide to be wrong in Kant's critical ethical theory; they announce an uncompromising, unconditional, general

---

[20]Kant, *Grundlegung* (*op. cit.* III/18), pp. 39–40.

[21]See Chapter Two on the problem of universality. Bertrand Russell, in his *History of Western Philosophy* (New York: Simon and Schuster, 1945), notes that Kant's principles do not suffice here to show suicide wrong: ". . . it would be quite possible," Russell says (p. 711) "for a melancholic to wish that everybody should commit suicide." Furthermore, Ronald Glass, in "The Contradictions in Kant's Examples," *Philosophical Studies* Vol. 22, nos. 5–6, October–December 1971, points out (p. 67) that Kant's argument "leaves all other kinds of suicide (those not due to self-love) untouched, including those from duty, those from whim, and those of martyrs."

[22]Kant, *Grundlegung* (*op. cit.* III/18) p. 47.

[23]Kant, *Metaphysics of Morals* (*op. cit.* III/18), pp. 83–84.

opposition to suicide. Nor is suicide a minor point in Kant's ethical theory. As Novak points out, morality is for Kant rooted in the constitution of the individual, and suicide is an ever present possibility for the individual. It is therefore a problem of immediate significance in Kant's moral theory.[24] Yet despite the use of suicide as an example of an act which is unconditionally morally wrong, and despite Kant's very strong opposition to suicide, it is not, I think, clear that Kantian principles preclude suicide in every case.

In stating his position against suicide, Kant discusses two life-or-death cases to illustrate his position:

1. A woman is threatened with rape. If she consents, she will continue to live, but will do so in degraded condition. If she does not consent, she will be killed.
2. A man, justly or unjustly convicted, is sentenced to servitude in the galleys of a ship; he will be degraded by contact with criminals of the lowest degree. However, he is offered death as an alternative.[25]

One ought to go on living, Kant asserts, as long as one can do so honorably; but the duty to preserve one's life is subordinate to a higher duty: the duty to conform to the moral law. Kant says:

> ... there is much in the world far more important than life. To observe morality is far more important. It is better to sacrifice one's life than one's morality. To live is not a necessity; but to live honourably while life lasts is a necessity.[26]

Consequently, in both cases described above, one ought to allow oneself to be killed rather than consent to moral degradation.

For Kant, to allow oneself to be killed is not the same as to commit suicide; Kant sharply distinguishes suicide from circumstances in which one sustains death at the hands of others because one refuses to comply with their immoral demands.[27] Nevertheless, although Kant's theory appears to require allowing oneself to be killed in certain circumstances, but never suicide, it may be that the principles of this theory permit suicide even as voluntary, deliberate self-killing, of which Kant so strongly disapproves. Consider the cases Kant describes: the woman about to be raped, and the man sentenced as a galley-slave. In each of these cases, death is the automatic alternative to consent: the assailant will kill the woman, or the state will execute the man. In each case, Kant believes death to be the proper choice, since consent involves moral degradation and being killed does not.

However, both cases are constructed so that being killed is the only apparent alternative. Suppose, however, that the woman's assailant did not threaten to kill her: the possible alternatives in this situation are now only consent, or forcible subjection to rape. Provided the assailant is physically stronger than she, he can

[24]David Novak, *Suicide and Morality* (*op. cit.* II/28), p. 84.

[25]Kant, *Lectures on Ethics* (*op. cit.* I/37), pp. 155 (the galley-slave case) and p. 156 (the rape case); for the rape case, see also pp. 149–50, on Lucretia.

[26]*Ibid.*, p. 152.

[27]*Ibid.*, p. 150: "it is no suicide to risk one's life against one's enemies and even to sacrifice it, in order to observe one's duties towards oneself."

impose sexual violation (and, thus, Kant holds, moral degradation) upon her without killing her. The choice to let herself be killed instead is not an option.

The man's case, however, appears to be somewhat different. If he resists servitude in the galleys, he will be beaten; if he continues to resist, he will continue to be beaten, and so on, but he cannot ever be *forced* to serve: he can always resist and suffer the consequences, though he will eventually be beaten until he is dead. It is this latter sort of picture, apparently, which is behind Kant's claim that "We can at all times go on living and doing our duty towards ourselves without having to do violence to ourselves."[28]

But Kant ignores those situations in which degradation threatens but death will not automatically result from resistance to that degradation. If the woman consents to the rape, she will be degraded by this sexual contact; if she does not consent, she will be raped anyway and still be subjected to degrading sexual contact. The man cannot be forced to pull the oars of the ship, but he can nevertheless be forcibly transported to the galleys, and thereby subject to the degradation of (as Kant puts it) "contact with criminals of the lowest degree." In neither case does death, imposed by others, offer itself as an inevitable alternative to moral degradation, and if death is the only morally acceptable alternative, the only way to achieve this alternative would be to take death upon oneself.

Two other authors, Plato and Thomas De Quincey, describe circumstances in which degradation threatens but death will not automatically result from resistance to it, and *do* recommend suicide as an alternative. We've seen earlier that Plato requires suicide of the recidivist temple-robber who cannot control his criminal urges: if this continuing self-degradation threatens, one's duty to oneself and to one's society is to end the degradation by ending one's life.[29] De Quincey considers corporal punishment a form of sexual degradation for men, analogous to rape of women; like rape, corporal punishment cannot always be evaded by allowing oneself to be killed, and De Quincey defends the man who chooses to die rather than submit to "that ignominy."[30] Taking the clearly Kantian view that corporal punishment is not simply an offence to "the poor transitory criminal,"[31] but is an injury to the very nature of the human being, who is thus "exhibited in a state of miserable abasement,"[32] De Quincey argues that when corporal punishment threatens "it will be the duty of a man to die [by suicide, if need be] rather than to suffer his own nature to be dishonored in that way."[33]

Kant, of course, makes no such recommendation of suicide, even when it is the only way of avoiding moral degradation; yet such a recommendation may be permitted by his theory. He says that when one cannot live honorably, one has an obligation not to continue to live:

> . . . *what matters is that, so long as he lives, man should live honorably and should not disgrace the dignity of humanity; if he can no longer live honorably, he cannot live at*

[28] *Ibid.*, p. 152.

[29] See Chapter II, pp. 100–101, on sociopathy.

[30] Thomas De Quincey, "On Suicide," from *Essays in Philosophy* (Boston and New York: Houghton Mifflin, 1856), p. 211.

[31] *Ibid.*, p. 211.

[32] *Ibid.*, p. 213.

[33] *Ibid.*, p. 213.

all; his moral life is at an end . . . If, then, I cannot preserve my life except by disgraceful conduct, virtue relieves me of this duty because a higher duty here comes into play and commands me to sacrifice my life.[34]

But in the cases described above, degradation is inevitable, yet death will not automatically result from resistance to it. The issue is this: If your life will not be "sacrificed" for you, and yet if you remain alive you cannot avoid breaking the moral law, must you then sacrifice your life yourself?

Of course, it may be that what Kant would find degrading is consent to rape or galley-slavery when there is the option of being killed instead, though he would not find degrading such consent when the only alternative is suicide, because although death (at another's hands) is preferable to such degradation, suicide is not.[35] But this argument succeeds only if it can be independently established that suicide is seriously wrong, a point which—though believed by Kant—is not established by his other claims.

In his mature philosophy Kant is confronted by the fact that cases of this sort can happen rather more frequently. In the *Metaphysical Principles of Virtue*, written well after the major works of his ethical theory, Kant presents a number of "casuistical questions," practical moral problems to which his theories are to be applied. Some of these appear to raise the issue of whether suicide will in some cases be the only way to satisfy the requirements of the moral law. Two of the five questions are:

> *Is it self-murder to plunge oneself into certain death (like Curtius) in order to save one's country? Or is martyrdom—the deliberate sacrifice of oneself for the good of mankind—also to be regarded, like the former case, as a heroic deed?*
>
> *Can one attribute a criminal intention to a great, recently deceased monarch [Frederick the Great] because he carried a fast-acting poison with him, presumably so that if he was captured in war (which he always conducted personally), he might not be forced to submit to conditions of ransom which might be harmful to his country? (For he can be credited with such a purpose without one's being required to presume that he carried the poison out of mere arrogance.)*[36]

These cases do not involve conflicts simply between the individual's duty to preserve himself as an agent of the moral law and his own self-centered desires to avoid pain or despair, but conflicts between two kinds of moral interests: those regarding preservation of the individual, and those regarding the preservation of society.[37] Both the individual and society are agents of the moral law; both are ends in themselves, and not to be treated as means. But if Kant has held Cato's choice to prefer the interests of society to his own to be the morally correct one, then in consistency he should find Frederick the Great's taking of the poison and Curtius' leap into the abyss morally correct, since they involve putting the interests of others before one's own. Kant does not resolve these cases. And it must be remembered that Kant's is not an ethic of self-sacrifice; one must always include oneself among

[34]Kant, *Lectures on Ethics* (*op. cit.* I/37) pp. 156–57.

[35]I thank the editors of the *Philosophical Review* and, independently, Mendel Cohen, for this objection.

[36]Kant, *Metaphysics of Morals* (*op. cit.* III/18), p. 84.

[37]See Novak's discussion (*op. cit.* II/28), p. 104ff.

the kingdom of ends. But when both ends cannot be served, the Cato case suggests that it is the preservation of society that is to be favored over preservation of the individual. This, then, is another kind of case in which Kant's theory will appear to permit suicide, though only in the Cato case does Kant acknowledge this conclusion.

More interesting are those situations—though the only examples Kant provides are the galley-slave and rape cases—which do not involve conflicts between individual interests and social interest, but a self-respecting situation in which, if one remains alive, one will become unable to uphold the moral law with respect to the humanity in oneself. Kant does not seem to see that cases of this sort can happen very frequently. They may occur not only when one is subject to physical degradation, forced into circumstances in which contact with degrading influences is inevitable, but they may occur too when one is subject to irresistible criminal impulses[38] or when one is afflicted with mental or physical disorders or diseases which make it impossible to uphold the moral law. Kant, of course, holds that one is never wholly at the mercy of his physical being, and yet among the casuistical cases in the *Metaphysical Principles of Virtue* he presents a case in which it is not possible to overcome degradation:

> *Bitten by a mad dog, a man already felt hydrophobia coming upon him. He declared that since he had never known anybody cured of it, he would destroy himself in order that, as he said in his testament, he might not in his madness (which he already felt gripping him) bring misfortune to other men too. The question is whether or not he did wrong.*[39]

Since the madness produced by rabies would preclude his continuing to uphold the moral law forbidding harm to others, we might see his action as intended to uphold his obligation to this law, even at the cost of his life. Of course, once the rabies develops he will lose his power of choice and so no longer be morally responsible, but he can choose *now,* while he is responsible, to avoid the harm to others which he knows will inevitably occur.

But this is a very specialized case, and I think the range of cases to which Kant's theory might apply is much wider than we at first suspect. We've mentioned criminal recidivism; Kant would include rape and degrading environments, and De Quincey would add corporal punishment. But the problem may arise in still more frequent, ordinary cases. For instance, there is much talk among medical practitioners and patients'-rights advocates about the "degradation" of severe and sustained physical illness, and among gerontologists about the degradation of extreme old age. Both are a kind of physical humiliation, of course, and what Kant has in mind is *moral* degradation. But poor health, pain, discomfort, financial limitation, lack of employment or satisfying occupations, failing senses, and dependency can all produce a kind of selfishness which Kant might well describe as moral degradation: a kind of decrepitude in which one is no longer able to treat others as ends in themselves, but uses them only to service one's needs. One ought, of course,

---

[38]Cf. Jeffrie Murphy's "Moral Death: A Kantian Essay on Psychopathy," *Ethics* 82, No. 4 (July 1972), 284-98. Murphy's view is that psychopaths, because they do not accept moral responsibilities, are "morally dead," like animals, and should neither be held morally responsible nor accorded moral respect.

[39]Kant, *Metaphysics of Morals (op. cit.* III/18), pp. 84-85.

according to Kant, resist such a condition, but resistance to serious illness or advancing age is unlikely to be successful. Kant might object that man as a moral being (*homo noumenon*) is always independent of the claims of man as a physical being (*homo phainomenon*), but if *moral* degradation can be produced, as Kant seems to believe it can, by rape, hydrophobia, or association with criminal elements, it can surely also result from illness, age, and other irresistible physical conditions. It may seem perverse to suggest that old age or serious illness bring with them moral as well as physical degeneration, but—given Kant's demanding view of moral rectitude—there is unfortunate evidence to suggest that they sometimes do. If so, Kant's theory might be read to permit or even require suicide for those who are ill or approaching old age, if there is reason to think that physical or mental infirmity will diminish their adherence to the moral law.

In his influential volume *Morals and Medicine,* Joseph Fletcher recounts the desperate end of Jonathan Swift. It was a death, Fletcher says, "degrading to himself and to those close to him." He suffered a brain tumor for eight years, and the pain in his eye became so acute that it took five men to hold him down to keep him from tearing out his eye with his own hands. He sat and drooled for the last three years of his life; knives had to be kept out of reach, and his final convulsions lasted thirty-six hours. Fletcher says:

> ... let us not forget that in such tragic affairs there is a moral destruction, a spiritual disorder, as well as a physical degeneration ... our present customary morality ... sometimes condemns us to live or, to put it another way, destroys our moral being for the sake of just being.[40]

If Fletcher is correct that continued life in such cases "destroys our moral being," we may wish to consider whether a theory like Kant's—asserting the absolute and intrinsic value of human moral life—would not permit or even require suicide in tragic circumstances like these. It is difficult in so short a space to do justice to Kant's complex account, but I think we can see the kind of problem to which an ethic of respect for moral life would give rise.

Only the broadest interpretation of the principle that life is of value prohibits suicide in all circumstances. But this interpretation would also prohibit killing of animals, killing of humans in war, capital punishment and self-defense, sacrifice of one's life in heroic or martyrdom situations, voluntary euthanasia, and a variety of other kinds of killing, some of which are regarded by much of traditional and contemporary moral theory as permissible. If, on the other hand, the principle is limited to accord with our ordinary practices, it then also often permits suicide.

Of course, there may be general objections to the value-of-life principle itself. It may be difficult to state the principle coherently, and difficult to provide justification for it. Frequently, as we've said, the principle is simply treated as a moral axiom, one of the fundamental principles a system of morality may include. Western legal systems have incorporated only substantially modified versions of the principle,[41] and it is sometimes argued that we do not in fact accept this principle at

---

[40]Joseph Fletcher, *Morals and Medicine (op. cit.* I/18), pp. 174–76.

[41]Kadish, "Respect for Life and Regard for Rights in the Criminal Law," (*op. cit.* III/8), esp. pp. 70–72.

all.[42] However, to provide a fundamental critique of the principle is not our purpose here; what is crucial is that according to interpretations of the principle which are more or less consistent with our other practices concerning killing, or with ethical theories we respect, suicide will be allowed in a number of distinct situations. Thus, what may have seemed to be the firmest and most general objection to suicide in principle turns out not to prohibit it so strictly after all, and will permit it in many of the circumstances in which it is likely to be most earnestly considered.

There is one last way in which we might apply the principle of the value of life to the issue of suicide. Imagine, for a moment, a man on a permanently deserted and inescapable island: he is the sole survivor of a nuclear holocaust, the last man in the world. There are no social obligations or ties to bind him, and his survival or nonsurvival will have no impact on the future course of the world. There is no God, and the man has no religious beliefs. He has no moral obligations, except perhaps to himself, since there are no longer any other persons to whom such obligations could be owed. The island provides him with the necessities of life; he is not in pain, nor ill, nor psychologically disturbed. In fact, being a somewhat solitary man, he is not even particularly distressed by his isolation, though he sees no reason to continue his life. Nevertheless, he is alive. Does he have an obligation to stay alive, that is, a duty to live? Those who accept the notion of an intrinsic value of life must answer yes; those who do not accept this principle will answer no. The case is contrived, but it is the kind of case which allows us to see most clearly the issues at stake.

[42]Glover, *Causing Death and Saving Lives* (*op. cit.* III/7), see p. 42. Glover says that although the doctrine of the sanctity of life is not acceptable, "there is embedded in it a moral view we should retain." This is the view that killing is normally "directly" wrong, that is, that killing is normally wrong even though it does not produce harmful side-effects. However, Glover does not regard killing as *intrinsically* wrong.

PART TWO

Contemporary Issues in Suicide

CHAPTER 4

The Concept
of Rational Suicide

Although traditional moral arguments still inform many of the pre-critical assumptions we make about suicide, they have fallen into disuse. We now tend to treat suicide as the product of mental illness, or as a desperate and dangerous "cry for help" used by someone who does not really want to die. Both of these views suggest that the traditional moral arguments no longer have relevance either for persons contemplating suicide or for bystanders who would intervene. But these views sidestep a crucial issue: can suicide ever be a *rational* act? If so, we may need to reconsider our moral assessment of suicide. That an act is rational does not mean, of course, that it is also morally good, but to find potentially rational an act we had thought could only be crazy may invite reinspection of our views. This means both that we may wish to reassess the traditional arguments concerning suicide, and that we may want to approach the moral issues from a contemporary viewpoint.

The Characterization of "Rational Suicide"

To determine whether suicide can ever be rational, we must first define a rational act; then we must decide whether suicide could ever fit such a definition. Perhaps none of our acts are ever *wholly* rational, in that they are never wholly free from emotion, training, circumstantial coercion, or other arational components. Yet we readily distinguish between things which we choose rationally to do, or which it is rational for us to do, and alternative acts which could be done in the same circumstance but are not rational acts. The question, then, is this: can suicide be as rational as our other "rational" acts?

"Rational suicide" may seem easy to characterize in negative terms. Presumably, it is suicide in which the individual is not insane, in which the decision is reached in unimpaired, undeceived fashion, and in which the choice made is not a bad thing for that individual to do. Alternatively, one might attempt to characterize "rational suicide" in positive terms. Choron, for instance, asserts:

"Rational" here implies not only that there is no psychiatric disorder but also that the reasoning of the suicidal person is in no way impaired and that his motives would seem justifiable, or at least "understandable," by the majority of his contemporaries in the same culture or social group.[1]

Choron's claim that the rational suicide's motives must seem "justifiable" or "understandable" to "the majority of his contemporaries in the same culture or social group," however, overlooks the fact that in contemporary culture, suicide has been a phenomenon very heavily enveloped in taboo; the majority of almost any individual's contemporaries within this culture will find suicide unjustified, whatever the circumstances, except perhaps in terminal illness. Consequently, we can hardly appeal to the criterion Choron suggests; it will only reflect the existing taboo. As an alternative, we shall attempt to construct a set of criteria for rationality which will be as independent as possible of the prevailing suicide taboo.

These criteria fall into two broad groups. The first three, ability to reason, realistic world view, and adequacy of information, are what might be called the "nonimpairment" criteria. The final two, avoidance of harm and accordance with fundamental interests, are what might be called the "satisfaction of interests" criteria in that they assure us that a rational decision is one which serves the agent's own interests, both in avoiding harm and achieving his goals. We typically speak of a decision as "rational" or "rationally made" if it is made in an unimpaired way; we also speak of a decision as "rational" or as "the rational thing for someone to do" if it satisfies his interests in avoiding harm and achieving his goals. The question of rational suicide, then, may be restated as a compound issue: can suicide be chosen in a rational way, and can it be the rational thing for a particular person to do?

The five criteria we will use to assess the rationality of suicide are the same criteria we would use to assess any other act or choice. Of course, such a list of criteria will itself invite philosophic dispute. There is little consensus among philosophers on the precise characterization of rationality in general, and so no agreement on what might count as standards for a rational suicide or for a rational choice of any sort. Nor is there agreement on which of these conditions, if any, are necessary for rationality, and whether any combination of them is jointly sufficient. Rather than divert ourselves with these preliminary difficulties, however, we shall simply posit the five rationality criteria to be discussed, and suggest that a suicide which is rational will meet all or most of them. Rational suicide may be quite rare in contemporary culture; the pressing question is whether there can be, by even an approximate set of criteria, any such thing as rational suicide at all.

Criteria for Rational Suicide

Ability to Reason

Traditionally, a rational person has been defined as one who has the use of reason, or the ability to reason; a rational decision is one in the reaching of which reason is employed. But to say that a person is able to reason implies at least two

[1]Choron, *Suicide* (*op. cit.* i/2), pp. 96–97.

distinct things: 1) that in moving from the premises from which he begins to the conclusion he reaches he maintains good logical form—that is, he doesn't make mistakes in logic—and 2) that he can see the consequences of the positions he adopts or of the actions he plans to take.

Suicidologists Shneidman and Farberow have examined a large number of suicide notes collected from the Los Angeles County Coroner's Office, and on this basis attempt to recreate what they call "suicidal thinking."[2] Suicidal thinking, they claim, involves both syntactic and semantic fallacies, the most characteristic of which is a confusion between "oneself as experienced by oneself," and "oneself as experienced by others." For instance, in the quite typical bit of reasoning, "People who kill themselves get attention; I will kill myself; therefore I will get attention," the prospective suicide uses the pronoun 'I' to refer to himself *as experienced by himself* in the second premise, but in the conclusion he uses it to refer to himself *as he will be experienced by others* after he is dead. What this equivocation disguises is the fact that the 'I' who is now doing the experiencing and is now eager for attention is not the same 'I' as the one who will get attention: after death, the 'I' who now craves attention will not be present to experience it.

This error in reasoning is very closely related to the second condition for 'being able to reason': a person who has the use of reason is one who can see, at least to some degree, not only the logical but also the causal consequences of his beliefs, statements, and actions. The "rational suicide" is one who is able to foresee the probable consequences of his act of suicide, both for others and for himself. It may, of course, be very difficult to foresee with full accuracy the impact of one's suicide on others, but there is one consequence of suicide which can be foreseen with certainty: the individual who commits suicide will be dead.

But this is precisely what a great many suicides do not accurately foresee; they tend to assume that even after death, they will continue to have experiences, to interact with other persons, and to play some continuing causal role in the world. This is characteristic of psychotic suicides. Some researchers also suggest that almost all child suicides are "irrational" in this way; influenced perhaps by television and cartoon figures who die but revive unharmed, children are not able to think of themselves as dead, but instead think of the death that follows suicide as a kind of sleep from which they will reawaken.

Many adults, too, do not accurately foresee the consequences of suicide, namely, that they will be dead. Freud claims that this is true of all people, insofar as the human unconscious "believes itself immortal."[3] Others point to the fact that when we imagine ourselves dead, we characteristically imagine an external view. This view typically shows our own dead body surrounded by grieving relatives or located in a grave, but this view itself presupposes a subject of experiences, and so shows that we do not accurately imagine death.[4]

---

[2]Edwin S. Shneidman and Norman L. Farberow, "The Logic of Suicide," in Shneidman and Farberow, eds., *Clues to Suicide* (*op. cit.* i/36), pp. 31–40.

[3]Sigmund Freud, *Thoughts for the Times on War and Death,* Chapter Two: "Our Attitude Towards Death," *The Standard Edition of . . . Freud,* (*op. cit.* I/68) 14, pp. 273–302, p. 289: "It is indeed impossible to imagine our own death; and whenever we attempt to do so we can perceive that we are in fact still present as spectators. Hence the psycho-analytic school could venture on the assertion that at bottom no one believes in his own death, or, to put the same thing in another way, that in the unconscious every one of us is convinced of his own immortality."

[4]See, e.g., Shneidman and Farberow, "The Logic of Suicide," (*op. cit.* IV/2) p. 33, and, for the same notion in a philosophic context, Thomas Nagel, "Death" (*op. cit.* III/2). As a *Gedankenexperiment* to

Joyce Carol Oates points out another kind of error in reasoning committed by those who are unduly influenced by romantic literary accounts of death: they conceive of death in what she calls "metaphorical" terms: as alluring, inviting, liberating, and deep. A metaphor like Jung's "the profound peace of all-knowing non-existence," Oates thinks, breeds tragic error:

> To so desperately confuse the terms of our finite contract as to invent a liberating Death when it is really brute, inarticulate Deadness that awaits—the "artist" of suicide is a groping, blundering, failed artist, and his art-work a mockery of genuine achievement.[5]

Most common among the errors in reasoning committed by those who kill themselves or attempt to do so, however, may be the kind of assumption underlying much of so-called "dyadic" suicide.[6] In these suicides, the intention of the individual is to injure, manipulate, insult, or impress the important other person in his life. "I'll get even with you," is an expression typical of the dyadic suicide; so is "I'll make you love me after all," or "I'll make you finally see how much you really need me." But, some suicidologists claim, this kind of assumption is fundamentally irrational in suicide contexts, since if the gesture is effective there will be no "I" to appreciate that fact.

Most suicide attempts, and some completed suicides, are of this dyadic form,[7] and thus subject to the kind of fallacy in reasoning which such motivation invites. But this does not establish that all such suicide is irrational. A person may in fact succeed in "getting even" with another even though he is no longer available to appreciate that fact: for instance, an intolerant parent may "get even" with a wayward child by striking him from his will, even though the will does not go into effect until after the parent has died. Similarly, we can imagine cases in which a person intends to "get even" with someone else by suicide, even though he knows that he will be unable to savor his success and that his own sacrifice will be great; although such cases may be infrequent, they can in principle occur.

There are, in addition, two important classes of suicides which are not necessarily irrational. First, for those individuals whose religious or metaphysical beliefs include the possibility of a sentient afterlife, it is not irrational to assume that one will have continuing experiences or relationships after suicide. And, second, some individuals place little or no value on themselves as subjects of experiences or participants in relationships, but place great importance on the ways in which they are viewed by others. Typically, reputation and honor are paramount to these individuals; continuing experience is not. These individuals too rarely confuse the

---

support this claim, one might also notice that it is typically much more difficult to imagine oneself dead and cremated than dead and buried.

[5]Joyce Carol Oates, "The Art of Suicide," *The Re-evaluation of Existing Values and the Search for Absolute Values,* Proceedings of the Seventh International Conference on the Unity of the Sciences (Boston, 1978); also in Battin and Mayo, eds., *Suicide: The Philosophical Issues,* (*op. cit.* i/10). pp. 161-68.

[6]The term is Edwin Shneidman's; see his "Classifications of Suicidal Phenomena," *Bulletin of Suicidology* (July 1968), pp. 1-9.

[7]According to Maris, in *Pathways to Suicide* (*op. cit.* i/2), p. 291, most completed suicides are escapist; the remainder, and almost all nonfatal attempts, are aggressive.

notion that they will be viewed in a certain way after death with the erroneous notion that they will be able to observe or experience this view; such suicides are not irrational in this respect. The religious suicides of Chapter One might be taken as examples of this first class of exceptions; Lucretia or the Japanese suicides of honor as examples of the second.

To establish in a positive way, however, that some suicides meet the criterion of "ability to reason" may prove more difficult, for a detractor can always claim such individuals must have made some other fundamental error in reasoning. But this, I think, is often a symptom of the *post hoc* argumentation so common in discussions about suicide. It might be equally difficult to prove that we reason in nondefective ways in making other important life-choices: do we avoid all equivocation? Do we have adequate conceptions of the future? It is very easy to grant that some, perhaps even most, suicides do reason in fallacious ways—the juvenile and psychotic suicides who do not understand that they will be dead; the romantic adults who glamorize death, the get-even revenge-seekers who assume that they themselves will continue to exert influence on their survivors. But although we may readily grant this point, this is not to establish that all suicides commit these errors. In the absence of any compelling evidence to the contrary, we must simply leave open the possibility that some persons do choose suicide in preference to continuing life on the basis of reasoning which is by all usual standards adequate.

Realistic World View

We may assume that a rational decision is one based upon a realistic view of the world; this criterion is closely related to that of ability to reason. Many types of suicide are clearly highly irrational in this respect. For instance, suicides among schizophrenics are quite often based on bizarre beliefs about the nature of the world, and the methods employed in such cases can be equally bizarre. A schizophrenic may throw himself from a window believing that he will be transformed into a bird; this sort of suicide is irrational because it results from a world view which is very clearly false.

In less severe sorts of disorders, an individual may have a relatively realistic picture of the world as a whole but fail to have a realistic conception of his own life situation, including his identity, his position in the world, and his particular talents and disabilities. Some milder afflictions are quite common: extremely low self-esteem and the overly inflated ego. As these conditions become increasingly pronounced we are increasingly likely to say decisions made on such bases are irrational.

For Jerome Motto, whether an individual has a realistic assessment of his life situation is crucial in determining the psychiatrist's approach towards the prospective suicide. Acknowledging that the psychiatrist, like anyone else, can offer only his own perception of reality, he nevertheless claims that

> Some persons have a view of reality so different from mine that I do not hesitate to interfere with their right to suicide. Others' perceptions are so like mine that I cannot intercede. The big problem is that large group in between.[8]

[8]Jerome Motto, "The Right to Suicide: A Psychiatrist's View," *Life-Threatening Behavior*, Vol. 2, no. 3 (Fall 1972), reprinted in Battin and Mayo, eds., *Suicide: The Philosophical Issues* (*op. cit.* i/10), pp. 212-19.

The notion that rational suicide requires a realistic world view, however, raises difficulties concerning suicides based on strong religious convictions. In Chapter One we discussed metaphysical and religious doctrines which assert the existence of an afterlife, often including continuing sensation, intellection, and heightened spiritual experience. Yet we are reluctant to call holders of these religious beliefs "irrational," even though no evidence supports their beliefs. Consequently, we find it difficult to term irrational a suicide performed in order to enter into this state. Similarly, it is difficult to label irrational a great variety of institutional suicides, even though the world view involved is different from our own. For instance, among certain African groups, it was common for kings to kill themselves or have themselves killed, either after a fixed term or at the first signs of debility, in order to promote their transformations into the next stages of divinity. The Scandinavian peoples practiced suicide in the belief that those who died by violence, rather than allowing themselves to succumb to sickness, age, or captivity, were assured of a place in Valhalla. Many primitive religions have held that an individual reaches the afterlife in the same condition in which he or she leaves this one; suicide is frequently practiced in these societies to avoid degenerative disease, senility, and so forth. Some religiously motivated suicides are irrational in the extreme, but, as H. J. Rose puts it,

> . . . religious suicides are not always maniacs . . . Nor can one justly class as maniacs those persons who hold that by killing themselves they can attain future happiness . . . or will return to life in this world stronger or wiser than before.[9]

While suicide in these cases is similar to that of the psychotic, in that both are based on apparently unrealistic world views, it is clear that the rationality or irrationality of an individual's views of the world is relative to the environment in which he lives. We term the schizophrenic who thinks he can fly "irrational" because he has come to have this belief in a culture which offers no evidence for it; in the context of religious cultures, however, we do not usually label "irrational" those who adopt the views of the group, even if we believe them wrong. No doubt we take odd metaphysical beliefs as evidence of irrationality not because they are any more false than usual metaphysical beliefs, but because we suspect that the person who has odd beliefs, unlike his peers, has them because of some mental disability: he has reacted in an "abnormal" way to the cultural dogmas of his society. This issue may, of course, raise larger questions of rationality and irrationality within cultural and religious systems,[10] but it is important for our present examination because so much suicide is associated with it. In order that a suicide count as rational, it is only necessary that it be based on a world view which is consonant with the surrounding culture; we do not consider whether the world view

[9]Rose, "Suicide (Introductory)," (op. cit. I/9), p. 22.

[10]For instance, Dan Wikler, in a private communication, observes: "Suppose that someone grew up in a society believing some religion but was isolated within that society and was never transmitted the dominant religious belief. Suppose then that this person, quite on his own, began to believe these things. It would seem to me that we would have evidence that this person was irrational, even though his beliefs were precisely consonant with those of the dominant group, in this case. Similarly, someone who went on the warpath because of a belief in Valhalla would be suspect here even though his beliefs are quite consonant with the beliefs in another culture." Wikler's conclusions are consistent with the view presented here.

of the culture as a whole is realistic or not. There may of course be considerable variation in world views within a culture; contemporary western culture, for instance, includes both those whose view of the universe is materialistic and those whose view includes spiritual entities; individuals of neither sort would be counted *irrational* in a suicide predicated upon such beliefs, though adherents of the opposite view would surely regard them as foolish.

Adequacy of Information

A rational action is one performed not only in accordance with acceptable logical principles and based on a realistic world view, but one also based on adequate information. This third criterion is the basis of many claims that suicide can never be rational.

One quite poignant type of inadequately informed suicide is the person who reasons that if he has a painful terminal illness he will be better off to put an end to his life, and on the basis of a puzzled glance by his physician, or imagined but undiagnosed pains wrongly assumes he is dying. One of the Los Angeles suicide notes collected by Shneidman and Farberow reflects this sort of irrationality:

> *Dearest Mary. This is to say goodbye. I have not told you because I did not want you to worry, but I have been feeling bad for 2 years, with my heart. I knew that if I went to a doctor I would lose my job. I think this is best for all concerned. I am in the car in the garage. Call the police but please don't come out there. I love you very much darling. Goodbye. Bill*[11]

A large number of similar cases, frequently involving fear of cancer, occur each year; in comparatively few of them is there any evidence of malignancy. An analogous type of case, also quite frequent, involves fear of pregnancy.

The suicide who mistakenly fears a terminal disease or unwanted pregnancy is a special case of a more general type: the suicide whose act, though not necessarily the product of illogical thinking or a distorted world view, is based on inadequate or faulty information. This may be information about present circumstances: the author of the suicide note just cited, for instance, displays inadequate information about his own present physical condition, in that he has not had his alleged heart trouble diagnosed by a doctor. But he also displays inadequate information about the future: he believes that he will be fired if he consults a doctor, and he no doubt also believes, though he does not say so explicitly in his note, that his heart condition will involve progressive deterioration, dependency, and pain.

Inadequate information about present circumstances may involve simple ignorance of some important fact—that help is on the way, that a reprieve has been granted, or that a drug to reverse one's condition has just been synthesized—or it may involve distortion of all information about one's circumstances and environment, ranging from the slightly unrealistic to the gross dislocations of the schizophrenic.[12] Of course, we do not consider choices irrational if they are made in the

---

[11]Shneidman and Farberow, *Clues to Suicide* (*op. cit.* i/36) Note 3A, p. 200. The names of the authors of these genuine suicide notes have been changed by Shneidman and Farberow for publication.

[12]See Jerome A. Motto, "The Right to Suicide: A Psychiatrist's View," (*op. cit.* IV/8). Motto discusses, among other things, the psychiatrist's conception of "realistic life-assessment" and its use in suicide situations.

absence of important relevant information which one has no way of knowing or cannot be expected to have; a suicide committed to avoid torture is not therefore irrational if help turns out to have been on the way but the victim had no way of knowing that this was the case. We tend to judge a choice inadequately informed only if it has been made without a substantial attempt to obtain information from reliable sources, or if it involves distortion of whatever information is actually available; the same criterion applies in suicide.

Some choices are irrational because the agent does not have access to adequate information from outside sources; but in another very large group of cases, the inadequacy of information is due to factors within the agent himself. This is particularly conspicuous in depression. In his widely reprinted paper "The Morality and Rationality of Suicide," Richard Brandt describes the way in which depression can constrict normal information-gathering processes when one approaches a decision, and result in reasoning which is impaired.

> In the first place, depression, like any severe emotional experience, tends to primitivize one's intellectual processes. It restricts the range of one's survey of the possibilities. One thing that a rational person will do is compare the [future] world-course containing his suicide with his best alternative. But nis best alternative is precisely a possibility he may overlook if, in a depressed mood, he thinks only of how badly off he is and does not contemplate plans of action which he has not at all considered.[13]

Thus, a depressed person's view of the range of possibilities for alternative actions may be severely restricted. His judgment about probabilities may be seriously affected: he may pessimistically select data upon which he forms a gloomy self-image, subconsciously suppressing data which might lead to a more optimistic prediction. Good things in the future tend to seem less significant than bad things occurring now; this is the familiar goal-gradient phenomenon, under which we agree to read a paper or visit an unpleasant relative a year in advance, though we would not dream of committing ourselves to do so in just a month. Finally, depression tends to warp our recollections about our preferences for and enjoyment of certain types of things: when depressed we may be quite unmoved by things or prospects which would normally excite us, and the focal object of the depression, say a jilting lover, failing health, or a dwindling fortune, tends to assume all-consuming importance. In short, depression, because of its characteristic effects on the way in which we store, process, and utilize information, and because of the way in which it affects our preferences, can seriously interfere with the "rationality" of a decision. This observation is often used to promote a general argument against suicide: as we have seen, many researchers claim that depression is present in the majority of suicide cases. Thus, it is inferred, most if not all suicide is irrational.

However, although a great many suicides in depression involve inadequate information, not all depressive suicides are irrational in this way. Not all predictions of the future are inadequately informed, even when associated with depression. There are some situations in which the narrow view produced by depression cannot

[13]Richard B. Brandt, "The Morality and Rationality of Suicide," in Seymour Perlin, ed., *A Handbook for the Study of Suicide* (Oxford: Oxford University Press, 1975), p. 380; a portion of this essay is reprinted as "The Rationality of Suicide" in Battin and Mayo, eds., *Suicide: The Philosophical Issues* (*op. cit.* i/10), pp. 117-32.

be greatly broadened. For instance, depression is a frequent concomitant of Parkinson's Disease, and the Parkinson's victim is likely to see his future as extremely bleak. But the future may in fact be quite bleak. Severe parkinsonism may mean decreasing mobility, conspicuous tremors, fixation of the eyes, unintelligible speech, and ultimately nearly total incapacitation. On the other hand, much parkinsonism responds dramatically to levadopa therapy. There may even be compensations: L-dopa often acts as an aphrodisiac in male patients, and many Parkinson's victims have extraordinarily satisfying sex lives. But for the patient for whom levadopa therapy is medically ineffective, for whom other side effects are too great, or for whom increased sexuality is a burden, the future is dismal, and although he may be distorting information, he may nevertheless have an adequate view of what the future is likely to bring.

Inadequacy of information about the future may also affect suicide decisions even where depression is not involved. Much suicide is undertaken to avoid future evils: physical or mental suffering, torture, falls from honor, the discovery of misdeeds, bankruptcy, old age, or even boredom. But in the real world it is difficult to be certain exactly what will occur, and one can never be entirely sure that a particular event will happen.[14] Effective suicide means certain death, whereas torture, bankruptcy, or boredom are, at worst, only likely.

This component of our rationality criteria is often used as an explicit argument against suicide. Josephus, under pressure from the remnants of the Jewish forces at Jotapata to initiate a mass suicide in which he would be obliged to participate, attempts (unsuccessfully) to convince them to surrender to the Romans rather than kill themselves:

> What is it we fear that prevents us from surrendering to the Romans? Is it not death? And shall we then inflict upon ourselves certain death, to avoid an uncertain death, which we fear, at the hands of our foes? . . . in my opinion there could be no more arrant coward than the pilot who, for fear of a tempest, deliberately sinks his ship before the storm.[15]

Josephus' underlying argument, that the future is never fully certain, is fed not merely by exorbitant hope, but by many actual occurrences: history is full of tales of narrowly missed cataclysms, impossible rescues, stays of execution, and miraculous cures of hopeless disease. Dostoevsky was spared from a firing squad after the rifles were already loaded, cocked, and aimed. Indeed, there is a general epistemological sense in which no future event is entirely certain. We do, of course, know that certain sequences of events have always occurred in the past and that fundamental physical laws predict that they will do so in the future, but we can never be certain that our formulations of these laws are fully accurate, or that our descriptions of events are entirely complete.

---

[14]See Antony Flew, "The Principle of Euthanasia," in A. B. Downing, ed., *Euthanasia and the Right to Death* (London: Peter Owen, 1969), p. 37.

[15]Josephus, *The Jewish War* III 367–368 (*op. cit.* I/10). Josephus, seeing that he was unable to persuade his companions to abandon their suicide plan and surrender, proposed that they all draw lots and kill one another in turn, so that "we shall be spared from taking our lives with our own hands" (III 389). Josephus drew the next-to-last lot; when each of those preceding had been killed in turn, Josephus persuaded the man behind him that they should both remain alive. This episode is often taken to cast doubt on the sincerity of Josephus' views concerning suicide.

This argument is most pressing in medicine. Few physicians would agree that any particular case is *absolutely* certainly hopeless: though physicians are well acquainted with fatal diseases, they are also familiar with cases in which patients unpredictably and quite inexplicably recover. This is true of advanced malignancies, organ failures, and near-flat EEG's, as well as other sorts of illnesses; spontaneous recoveries can and do occur. If it is possible that the feared event—whether slaughter by the Romans, execution by a firing squad, or death by cancer—may not after all occur, then, according to this argument, suicide is irrational: it brings about certain death in a case where it is not entirely certain.

But this does not succeed as an argument against the rationality of suicide in general. Although there may be some chance of a striking change in the future—the rescue, the reprieve, the cure—it is not therefore rational to act in accordance with these hopes, or irrational to choose to avoid what the future is highly likely to bring. It is rational to bank on a likely event, not a highly unlikely one. The terminal patient may survive an extended period of severe pain and recover entirely, but it is irrational for him or others to behave as though this were going to occur; the very strong chance is that it will not.

It is important to see clearly the consequences of the anti-suicide argument here. When the claim that future circumstances are never fully certain is used as an argument against suicide, it condemns the potential suicide to almost certain suffering, by encouraging an irrational hope.[16] In terminal-illness situations, this is almost always the case. To insist that the victims of extremely serious burns or irreversible cancers ought to stay alive because there is a slight chance that they will survive may mean that a few persons who would otherwise have ended their lives do survive; but it will also mean that many, many others will die in greater suffering than they might otherwise have chosen to undergo. Users of the "there's always hope" argument against suicide, although beginning from a premise which is technically true, must accept responsibility for the suffering they cause in offering unrealistic hopes as well as for the pleasure of those whose remote hopes come true.

One might object that although it is not rational to *believe* that the unlikely event will actually occur, it can nevertheless be rational to act in accord with that belief: one can rationally bet a penny to win a million dollars, even though the likelihood of winning is extremely small. In betting pennies for millions, this is certainly true. And it is true that the rationality of a wager depends on the attractiveness of the stakes; indeed, if a million dollars is an attractive win, surviving with one's life is even more so. But the rationality of a wager is also a function of the magnitude of the likely loss, and this is where the cases diverge. If you bet a penny to win a million, what you almost certainly will lose is the single penny. But when someone is encouraged to forgo suicide on the outside chance that he may survive an ordinarily painful and fatal condition, the likely loss is considerably more than a penny: it is an end of one's life in perhaps excruciating physical and emotional pain.

Thus, the "there's always hope" argument against suicide is a particularly dangerous one in practice, especially when it is used to override someone's choice of an earlier, less painful death. For every individual who, forgoing suicide when his situation seemed hopeless, survives to a complete and full life, countless more die in misery. Suicide to avoid likely future evils, then, is not irrational as a

---

[16]See Flew's discussion of the fallibility of medicine and the consequences of this circumstance, "The Principle of Euthanasia," (*op. cit.* IV/14), pp. 37–40.

calculation of future interests; where the likely loss is great enough, to bet against such evils would be folly, to act to avoid them wise.

This, of course, applies only to future evils whose likelihood we can predict with a strong degree of assurance. Many of the future evils for which suicide may be contemplated cannot be predicted with any real degree of confidence, and many fears are based on only the flimsiest evidence. Firm diagnoses are sometimes wrong, and many seemingly secure predictions of future catastrophes are false. Of course, it would be irrational to end one's life to avoid a future evil foreseen on only scanty evidence, or where there is some substantial chance the future evil will not occur. However, there may be exceptions, such as when the future evil predicted is so calamitous that no chance of other experience outweighs the risk of suffering it. For instance, if we were to assume that the paranoia associated with certain illnesses would preclude suicide after the onset of symptoms adequate to diagnose the disease, one might suggest—if the end stages of the disease often involve severe dementia as well as physical deterioration—that suicide on the basis of even slight, insidious early symptoms, in the presence of genetic or other risk, might be a rational choice. Virginia Woolf's suicide appeared to be of this form.

A separate but very closely related issue regards the difficulty for the prospective rational suicide of accurately predicting how he will *react* to predictable future events.[17] A financial magnate may be able to accurately predict forthcoming ruin and poverty, but may be quite unable to tell whether he will resent or—released from his responsibilities and a heavily material life—perhaps enjoy it. A person severely injured in an accident may accurately foresee a life involving severe physical limitations, but not realize that they will constitute little hindrance to his real, cerebral interests. Reactions to past though perhaps dissimilar evils may provide some basis for predicting one's own reactions to future evils, but one's prediction may be warped by depression and other strong emotional states; some future evils turn out to be "not so bad" after all. But this fact does not make avoidance of future evils theoretically mistaken. The problem of predicting one's reactions to future events is a general problem not confined to suicide; it is equally a problem in setting positive goals. Yet we do not consider it irrational to set positive goals, even if we cannot be sure how we will respond to attainment of them. What the prospective rational suicide must calculate is just how damaging it will be to him if things turn out as he fears, and whether this risk is offset by the possibility of other, better outcomes.

Finally, there is a general sense in which, as we have seen earlier, no suicide decision can be adequately informed—since, as Philip Devine has pointed out, we can never have knowledge of what death actually is: suicide is a leap into the wholly unknown.[18] Strictly speaking, this argument is correct. But each individual will have his firm convictions of what is to come after death; just as we do not consider beliefs irrational which are consonant with the beliefs of the individual's cultural group, so we do not count as irrational a choice made with respect to alternatives about which the individual, in concert with his religious group, believes himself fully informed. The traditional Christian believer cannot be said to lack adequate information in his choice of suicide over life: he knows perfectly well he will burn in

---

[17]See Brandt's discussion in "The Morality and Rationality of Suicide," (*op. cit.* IV/13) especially in the section titled "Whether and When Suicide is Best or Rational for the Agent."

[18]Devine, *The Ethics of Homicide* (*op. cit.* I/84), pp. 24–28.

the fires of hell (though we might count him irrational for making such a choice). The general sense in which we are inadequately informed about the nature of death is part of the sense in which we are inadequately informed about the metaphysical character of the universe and about which religious claims, if any, are true. This does not show the suicide's act any more inadequately informed, or less rational, than any of our other important moral choices.

Avoidance of Harm

We also widely assume that an action, to be rational, must accord with the agent's own interests in the protection of his person and body from harm. For instance, self-mutilators strike us as irrational, since they cause themselves harm; suicides may strike us in the same way, since we assume that it is in one's own prudential interests to remain alive.

It may be argued, however, that death is not a harm to the individual who is dead. The process of painfully dying or knowing one is going to die, of course, can constitute an extraordinary harm, but once dead, the individual no longer exists, and therefore is no longer harmed. For this reason, the suicide, provided he selects a reasonably painless and expeditious method of carrying out his plan, cannot be said to act contrary to his own prudential interests, since he does himself no harm. In fact, R. M. Martin argues that even the suicide which is hastily planned, irrationally chosen, or undertaken for wholly inadequate reasons is not a harm to that individual, since that individual is dead.

> The man who believes that death will bring him to paradise will not be disappointed; not because he will go to paradise, but because there won't be any him left after his death to be disappointed. Neither will the man who kills himself because he falsely believes he has a terminal disease regret his decision. The man who didn't know about therapy won't be worse off than he could have been had we intervened, after his suicide, since he won't exist at all. And the man who had the fleeting desire to kill himself and did won't suffer as a result of his desire's being only a fleeting one, as the man who went to live in the woods would.[19]

We might object as we suggested in discussing the value of life, that if a view like this were correct, it would be no harm to someone else to kill him either, at least if we can do it quickly, painlessly, and without warning. But we do think that to kill someone, even quickly, painlessly, and without warning, is to harm *him;* death is a harm, and a harm to the person whose death it is. Are we correct in thinking so? One way in which we might make sense of this assumption is to understand ''harm'' not simply in terms of bodily injury or discomfort, but also in terms of deprivation of pleasures, satisfactions, and other goods,[20] or what we called the *praemium vitae.* It is wrong to kill someone—even though swiftly, painlessly, and without his knowing it—because he is thereby deprived of these goods. Indeed, since killing him deprives him of *all* such goods, killing him

[19]Robert M. Martin, ''Suicide and False Desires,'' in Battin and Mayo, eds., *Suicide: The Philosophical Issues,* (*op. cit.* i/10), pp. 144–50 quotation from earlier version.

[20]This is the strategy Nagel uses in his paper ''Death.'' (*op. cit.* III/2).

is the greatest harm. Similarly, it can also be argued, since suicide too will deprive one of pleasures, satisfactions, and the other goods of life, it must also be a harm. Thus, since it is irrational to do an act which constitutes a harm to oneself (unless of course some greater good is thereby to be obtained), it is irrational to commit suicide.

Thus suicide, viewed this way, is always irrational, even if logically chosen on the basis of adequate and correct beliefs, because it brings about the greatest possible harm. But this view, although widespread, may not be correct. Note that we have defined "harm" in terms of the deprivation of *goods:* pleasures, satisfactions, and whatever else life may make possible. We do not ordinarily think it a harm to be deprived of evils: pain, suffering, terror, or want; and we do not count it irrational when one acts to avoid harm. If so, then surcease suicides, undertaken to avoid either physical or emotional harm, are not irrational after all: they serve to avoid harms, not to deprive one of goods.

It is certainly clear that we count most harm-avoiding activities as rational. But this does not tell us whether harm-avoiding *suicides,* as distinguished from other harm-avoiding activities, can be considered rational. The answer depends in part on whether we consider death or suffering to be the greater evil. If death is the greater evil it is irrational to seek it, even if suffering can thereby be avoided; if, on the other hand, suffering is viewed as the worst thing that can befall a human being, then death undertaken to avoid it is not irrational.

We might try to resolve this issue by counting life in itself as a good, regardless of the kinds of experiences or suffering it involves; this is a version of the view that life has intrinsic value. Thus, we consider it a benefit to save someone's life, even though his life may involve pain. But we do not always consider preserving life a good, as Philippa Foot's examples may show:

> *Suppose, for instance, that a man were being tortured to death and was given a drug that lengthened his sufferings; this would not be a benefit but the reverse. Or suppose that in a ghetto in Nazi Germany a doctor saved the life of someone threatened by disease, but that the man once cured was transported to an extermination camp; the doctor might wish for the sake of the patient that he had died of the disease.*[21]

Life, she grants, is *normally* a benefit to the person whose life it is, but this is not always so; there may be cases in which it is better for a person to die earlier than later. Presumably, then, life is a harm if it consists wholly of harmful or painful experiences; if it is rational to avoid harm, then it is sometimes rational to avoid life.

Of course, it is not rational to avoid harm when there is some purpose to be served by undergoing it: we rationally submit to dental pain in order to prevent decay. This is precisely the view many Catholic writers take in arguing against the rationality (and moral permissibility) of surcease suicides. As we've seen in Chapter One, the contemporary Catholic doctrine, first explicated with reference to suicide by Mme. de Staël and later by Paul-Louis Landsberg, teaches that enduring even severe pain and suffering is of important spiritual value. The Christian should regard suicide as depriving himself of a possible good—suffering—and thus causing himself harm. Thus, the Christian may *rationally* choose to endure the pain, while his non-Christian counterpart may rationally choose to evade it.

This distinction rests, of course, on the thesis that pain and suffering may

[21]Philippa Foot, "Euthanasia," (*op. cit.* III/8), p. 88.

serve some further purpose. As we've noted earlier, even within the Christian religious tradition some thinkers distinguish between "constructive" and "destructive" pain, or pain which serves some further purpose and permits some further spiritual growth, as against pain which does not. A similar secular distinction between productive and destructive pain can also be drawn on the basis of other purposes which may be served. It may be easy to distinguish pain which serves some further purpose from pain which does not in cases like childbirth, dentistry, or first-aid treatment for accident victims. It might be harder to make this distinction in cases of severe burn treatments or repeated amputation, and perhaps impossible in terminal cancer or in burn cases where survival is unprecedented. No doubt one would be tempted to formulate a kind of rule-of-thumb approximation: the longer-term and less transitory the pain threatens to be, and the dimmer the outlook for pain-free recovery, the more rational an attempt to avoid the pain by suicide.

Fortunately, enormous progress has been made in the medical control of pain; new drugs and methods of anesthesia and analgesia are under continuous development. Perhaps most promising in this respect is the Hospice movement's technique of pain prevention in terminal illness, which is based on administration of pain-relief mixtures on a scheduled basis prior to need, designed to anticipate and prevent pain rather than subdue already occurring pain.[22] Presumably, it would not be rational to choose suicide in order to avoid pain when in fact there will be little or none; we are already beginning to see the day when terminal cancer will be, as are kidneystones and gout, another outmoded example of irremediable pain.

Presumably, it would also be irrational to choose suicide to avoid pain when, although the pain itself serves no further purpose, another positive experience may occur which it is rational to seek. Lael Wertenbacker describes the cancer death of her husband as involving episodes of extreme pain, but describes the pain-free periods between those episodes as times of remarkable intimacy and preciousness.[23] Hospice workers often report that the most valued human relationships arise in the period between diagnosis and death. Literature, too, offers many accounts of experience of great spiritual depth and importance even in the immediate accompaniment of severe pain: for instance, the experience of (religious) enlightenment which occurs two hours before the death by cancer of the title figure in Tolstoi's *The Death of Ivan Ilych*.[24] Nevertheless, some kinds of pain are simply resistant to treatment,

[22]Hospice, founded and directed by Cicely Saunders, is a movement devoted to the development of institutions for providing palliative but medically nonaggressive care for terminal-illness patients. In addition to its extraordinary contribution in developing methods of prophylactic pain control, according to which analgesics are administered on a scheduled basis in advance of experienced pain, Hospice has also emphasized attention to the emotional needs of the patient's family. An account of the theory and methodology of Hospice can be found in a number of the publications of Cicely Saunders, including "The Treatment of Intractable Pain in Terminal Cancer," *Proceedings of the Royal Society of Medicine* 56 (1963), p. 195, and "Terminal Care in Medical Oncology," in K. D. Bagshawe, ed., *Medical Oncology* (Oxford: Blackwell, 1975). pp. 563–76. A careful assessment of potentials for abuse of the Hospice system may be found in John F. Potter, M. D., "A Challenge for the Hospice Movement," *The New England Journal of Medicine* 302, no. 1 (Jan. 3, 1980), 53–55.

[23]Wertenbacker, *Death of a Man* (*op. cit.* III/16); see also two other intimate accounts of deaths by cancer, Jessamyn West's *The Woman Said Yes* (New York: Harcourt Brace Jovanovich, 1976), and Derek Humphrey with Ann Wickett, *Jean's Way* (London, Melbourne, New York: Quartet Books, 1978).

[24]Leo Tolstoi, "The Death of Ivan Ilych," in *The Death of Ivan Ilych and Other Stories* (New York: New American Library, 1960).

or occur in locations (for example, battlefields or remote territories) where treatment is unavailable, or in establishments (some hospitals, nursing homes, and unhappy families) where treatment is only erratically or ineptly offered, and preclude experience of any other sort. In some of these situations suicide may be the rational choice.

Furthermore, not all suffering is a matter of pain. The Hospice program is extremely effective in controlling physical pain, but reports much less success with other problems like difficulty in swallowing. Then, too, much physical pain is accompanied by severe emotional pain, and it is not always easy to differentiate the two. But it is important to discriminate between them because our responses to suicide based on avoidance of physical and of emotional pain are often quite different. We regard both as in principle transitory. Yet we recognize, and are beginning to acknowledge as grounds for suicide, a category of terminal physical pain which we do not recognize in cases of emotional suffering. However, many psychotics live in considerable mental agony, and can expect no cure; though contemporary society is beginning to acknowledge suicide as a remedy in cases of irremediable, terminal physical pain, it does not respect a suicide decision reached by a person suffering permanent and irreversible psychosis.

Of course, most emotional pain, like most physical pain, *is* transitory, and will recede to permit other intrinsically valuable experience in the future. Mme. de Staël remarks:

> *Observe, after a period of ten years, a person who has sustained some great privation, of whatever nature it may be, and you will find that he suffers and enjoys from other causes than those from which ten years ago his misery was derived.*[25]

The transitoriness of most depression can hardly be emphasized strongly enough, since depression is so widely associated with suicide. Yet one can also imagine cases of permanent emotional pain, either circumstantially caused, as in lasting public disgrace or social ostracism, or produced by an individual's own psychological constitution, as in untreatable depression or psychosis. Robert Burton, in 1621, says of "melancholics" or the mentally ill that:

> *In the day time they are affrighted still by some terrible object, and torn in pieces with suspicion, fear, sorrow, discontents, cares, shame, anguish, &c. as so many wild horses, that they cannot be quiet an hour, a minute of time, but even against their wills they are intent, and still thinking of it, they cannot forget it, it grinds their souls day and night, they are perpetually tormented, a burden to themselves, as Job was, they can neither eat, drink, nor sleep.*[26]

Modern psychotherapeutic drugs have done a great deal to change this, but they have by no means eradicated the sufferings of mental despair and illness from the face of the earth. In many cases of mental suffering, suicide may be an irrational choice, since most such suffering is transitory and treatable, and suicide precludes the real possibility of having other, subsequent experience which it is rational to seek. Nevertheless, where the possibility of such other experience is small,

---

[25]Mme. de Staël, "Reflections on Suicide," (*op. cit.* I/85), p. 102.

[26]Burton, *The Anatomy of Melancholy* (*op. cit.* I/61), p. 368.

suicide—in mental illness as well as physical illness—appears to be the prudent, rational choice.

This indicates a remaining problem: if we do acknowledge the rationality of surcease suicide in cases where pain and suffering, either mental or physical, serve no further purpose, it is still not clear what degree the pain and suffering must reach before it becomes rational to avoid them by death. Contemporary western culture appears to assume that only intense, unrelenting, and terminal physical pain makes death a rational choice, if ever. The Stoics, on the other hand, admitted both physical and emotional suffering as legitimizing reasons for suicide, and held that any modest preponderance of pain of either sort was sufficient to make death the rational choice. They did, of course, school themselves to resist pain, but did not hold that only severe or terminal pain could provide a reason for suicide. Seneca remarks:

> And there are many occasions on which a man should leave life not only bravely but for reasons which are not as pressing as they might be—the reasons which restrain us being not so pressing either.[27]

Need pain be terminal, or need it reach excruciating levels before it is rational to avoid it by suicide? Again, one might attempt to formulate a rule-of-thumb answer; it would depend on the amount of *other* experience permitted by the pain, and whether this other experience is of intrinsic value. A person seized by periodic episodes of intense physical pain may nevertheless have important experience during the pain-free intervals (the Wertenbacker case); so may a person seized by intense psychological distress (Virginia Woolf). On the other hand, a person subjected to low-grade but unremitting physical or emotional pain (say, chronic headache or permanent endogenous depression) may have no experience not infected by the pain. Hume remarks on the man who is

> cursed with such an incurable depravity or gloominess of temper as must poison all enjoyment and render him equally miserable as if he had been loaded with the most grievous misfortunes.[28]

Suicide, he says, cannot be held against such a man.

Accordance with Fundamental Interests

In general, we regard an act as rational only if it is in accord with what we might call one's "ground-projects" or basic interests, which themselves arise from one's most abiding, fundamental values.[29] Sometimes these "ground-projects" or fundamental interests are self-centered ones, in the sense that they are concerned with the acquisition or arrangement of things for the benefit of ourselves; some-

[27]Seneca, *Letters* (*op. cit.* II/7), Letter 77, p. 125.

[28]Hume, "Essay on Suicide" (*op. cit.* I/49) p. 567.

[29]The notion of *ground project* is developed by Bernard Williams in "Persons, Character and Morality," in *The Identities of Persons,* Amelie Oksenberg Rorty, ed. (Berkeley and Los Angeles: University of California Press, 1976), pp. 197–216.

times, however, they are altruistic, and concerned with the benefit of someone or something else. Thus, an individual's ground-projects may involve acquiring a bigger house, getting a better job, or learning various skills (though for some people such projects may be superficial ones only); they may also involve working for a cause, initiating reforms, or other projects of social improvement. They may even be malevolent; what is at immediate issue here is the rationality of an act, not its moral character.

An act which conflicts with the satisfaction of one's ground-projects or fundamental goals is usually held to be irrational; an act intended to satisfy them is not. To put this another way, an act can be said to be rational in the sense that it is an effective means to a given end; the moral character of the end is not at issue.[30] For instance, if a person has been working for years, say, for a liberal political cause, has attended party meetings and organized campaigns, but votes for the conservative candidate when there is no politically expedient reason to do so, we say that that person has acted ''irrationally''; we would also say that he acts irrationally if he does not vote at all. In fact, he acts rationally only if he votes for the liberal candidate, since it is the success of the candidate which is his goal. If a person has multiple but conflicting ground-projects, we will say that it is rational to act to satisfy the most basic of these. Suicide, since it puts an end to life, appears to thwart the satisfaction of all one's basic projects or ground interests, and so appears to be irrational in every case.

It is true that one cannot satisfy certain kinds of interests if one is dead, and the satisfaction of many ground-projects requires the continuing existence of the agent. One cannot satisfy one's project to live in a bigger house if one does not live, nor can one perfect one's skills when dead. But not all ground-projects require the continued existence of the agent: one's most important project may be essentially altruistic or centered on others, and can perhaps be satisfied even if one is dead. So, for instance, parents whose fundamental goals include putting their children through college can have this ground-project satisfied, even if they are no longer alive. One's ground-projects can sometimes even be satisfied if one kills oneself for them, as for instance in the parent who kills himself in order to donate an organ and thus ensure the survival of his child. We have already mentioned a number of cases of self-sacrificial and martyrdom suicide, including Cato and Captain Oates, in which an individual relinquishes his life in order that his fundamental goals with respect to someone else or some cause be satisfied.

Suicides which might appear to satisfy an individual's basic goals, however, are often said to be irrational on psychological grounds. For instance, as Margolis points out, although General Custer clearly entertained a fundamental interest in the success of his forces at Little Bighorn, his bravery is sometimes viewed as the symptom of a pronounced death wish, and therefore irrational.[31] Norman Morrison, the Quaker who burned himself to death to protest the Vietnam War, was said by some of the press to be insane.[32] Criticism of religious martyrs is often conducted in

---

[30]This is the Rawlsian value-free notion of rationality, originally a purely economic notion; rationality is ''taking the most effective means to given ends.'' John Rawls, *A Theory of Justice* (Cambridge, Mass.: Belknap/Harvard, 1971), p. 14.

[31]Joseph Margolis, *Negativities* (Columbus, Ohio: Charles E. Merrill, 1973), p. 24.

[32]Pretzel, describing the death of Norman Morrison (see Chapter II, footnote 78), concludes that we do not have adequate data to determine whether this self-immolation should count as a rational suicide.

this way: self-sacrificial acts are frequently said to be impelled by hidden death wishes, neurotic desires to manipulate others, delusions of grandeur, or by outright psychosis. In many cases, no doubt, these claims are right. But this does not mean, of course, that it is always irrational to die for a cause. Even in the presence of obvious psychopathology, one might not want to call an act irrational when it serves its agent's fundamental ends.

One might object that to be dead precludes appreciation of the satisfaction of one's ground-projects or interests, and that therefore suicide can never be rational. An argument of this sort is hinted at by Choron in reporting the death of Paul Lafargue, son-in-law of Karl Marx, a physician who had become increasingly active in support of the socialist revolution in Russia. Lafargue had long planned to kill himself when he reached the age of seventy; he did so in 1911. Choron writes:

> There is considerable irony in Lafargue's suicide, for had he waited another six years (and there is no indication that he could not have lived that long), he would have seen the triumph of his cause in Russia in November 1917.[33]

But it is obvious that although his suicide precludes Lafargue's knowing or appreciating the fact that his guiding interest in the success of social revolution was satisfied, that interest was nevertheless in fact satisfied, whether Lafargue was alive or not. And since Lafargue's interest was in the triumph of the revolution, not in his appreciation of it, there appears to be no reason to think that Lafargue's suicide ran counter to his own most basic interests. According to this criterion, it cannot be said to have been an irrational act.

Furthermore, there may be cases in which not the life but the death of the agent is required to promote the ground-projects which he has himself adopted. One thinks for instance of Socrates, facing the hemlock. Given his fundamental commitment to preserving the laws of Athens, to escape execution would be to thwart satisfaction of those interests. Hence, he allows himself to be killed. Similarly, only by suicide could Saul satisfy his fundamental interests in protecting him from humiliation and torture by the Philistines, and thus preserving the dignity and honor of the Jews. Likewise, only by suicide could Cato promote his interests in the freedom of his people. The figures and their cases are familiar; now we also see the sense in which their suicides are the *rational* consequences of their commitment to certain abiding purposes. Suicide is, in these cases, the only effective means of achieving their paramount ends. Bernard Williams writes:

> It is worth noting here that there is no contradiction in the idea of a man's dying for a ground-project: quite the reverse, since if death really is necessary for the project, then to live would be to live with it unsatisfied, something which, if it really is his ground-project, he has no reason to do.[34]

Suicide may also be rational if it is the only effective means by which one can avoid change in the ends one has—even if those ends would be changed by oneself. For instance, imagine a person whose fundamental ground-project is to live his life

---

[33]Choron, *Suicide* (*op. cit.* i/2), p. 101. Lafargue's suicide was a joint one with his wife, Karl Marx's daughter.

[34]Williams, "Persons, Character and Morality," (*op. cit.* IV/29) p. 209.

in a way █████ ..., generous, and humane: it is central to him to be morally good. But now ████ ...se, as Dan Wikler suggests,[35] that such a person is captured by the Nazis, and ..s commanded to do a certain morally repugnant task. He is convinced by their psychologist that if he goes ahead and does it, the psychologist will turn him into the kind of person who enjoys doing morally repugnant things—just the kind of person he earlier least wanted to be.

Would suicide to avoid forcible alterations of his fundamental ground-projects be rational? This is a very difficult question to answer; we must remember that it is closely connected with the issue of predicting one's reactions to future events. We have not held that it is irrational to act on the basis of preferences one does not now have but predictably will have in the future. The business executive who falls from favor may not now, as we suggested in earlier analogous cases, find satisfaction in the notion of selling shoes for a living; but he may (predictably, if he knows himself well enough) find satisfactions in life as a shoe salesman in the future. There, we said that it would be irrational to discount future preferences and commit suicide now; here we seem to be saying that future preferences may (and should) be rationally discounted, and that suicide to avoid Nazi reprogramming can indeed be the rational choice.

Is there a conflict here? Only an apparent one, I think; the difficulty lies in the fact that in the one case, it is a genuinely *fundamental* ground-project—living a life which is morally good—which is at risk. In the other, the character of one's occupation may not be a matter of fundamental ground-project, though obtaining satisfaction from one's employment may be. If the erstwhile business executive were a person to whom executive status is genuinely central, we might grant that the choice of suicide when executive status is irrevocably closed to him might be the rational choice; but such cases are rare. The person for whom living a morally good life is central, on the other hand, cannot lightly discard this commitment as just another evanescent goal.

This notion permits us to see that suicide may be rational, insofar as it permits satisfaction of one's goals or fundamental interests, even for individuals who do not have commitments to other persons or groups, or to institutions, principles, or causes. Some individuals' primary goals or interests are connected with other persons and things; for some individuals, however, the most fundamental interest involves self-understanding, self-revelation, and perhaps self-perfection. This is not to be confused with naive interests in self-protection or the usual prudential interests in avoiding harm; rather, these interests arise when the individual finds himself and his own character the focus of his major concerns. It is a trait we admire in novelists, poets, and religious visionaries; it is a trait that is shared, perhaps, by many lesser folk. But there is a familiar problem: if one's basic goals are self-centered, can suicide ever be rational, when that self will no longer exist?

In one type of case this seems immediately obvious: the case in which the individual's basic goal or concern is in some way connected with the act of dying, so that suicide will bring about this experience. This focus is common among the Romantics, especially Novalis and Rilke, and it is inherited to some degree by the Existentialist movement; death in these traditions is sometimes described as a central, culminating event, a kind of final "peak experience." James Hillman, a contemporary psychoanalyst who shares the view that death is the most important

---

[35]Private communication.

and culminating event in life, but also holds that death is followed by a personal afterlife, writes:

The impulse to death need not be conceived as an anti-life movement; it may be a demand for an encounter with absolute reality, a demand for a fuller life through the death experience.[36]

This need not involve the kind of misleading metaphor described by Joyce Carol Oates, though of course such misleading metaphors are prevalent; if one's metaphysical or religious conceptions lead one to believe that this culminating experience can be attained through suicide, and if, furthermore, attaining that experience is the central focus of one's life, then suicide in order to attain it would seem to count as a rational action. Whether life continues afterward or not is irrelevant once this utmost experience has been achieved.

However, religious and poetic lore aside, the real issue concerns whether suicide can be a rational choice for someone whose interests and fundamental goals are self-centered. One is inclined to think not. But there are cases when self-interests of this sort will be undermined or thwarted if death does not intervene, and in these cases suicide may be the rational choice. The Nazi-reprogramming case is one such circumstance. But there may be others on a much less conspicuous scale. Imagine, for instance, a pianist for whom perfection of keyboard technique has been his central, abiding interest since early youth. As this pianist ages and arthritis sets in, he finds it increasingly difficult to play well. If he kills himself, of course, his interests are not furthered, since he no longer exists as the referent of his piano-playing interests. But if he does not commit suicide and the arthritis becomes increasingly crippling, his long-term self-interest in perfection of his piano style will be increasingly undermined. No Nazi reprogramming is involved; the villain here is age.

Of course, he might simply stop playing the piano; this would be to live with an interest unsatisfied. Better still, he might succeed in releasing himself from piano playing as a central interest; still better, he might adopt another interest, say, composing, or writing music-theory books, and in this way avoid continued frustration of his original interests. Robert Schumann transferred his interests to composing after a finger sling he had devised jammed his right hand early in his performing career.

This, of course, is all well and proper for interests which are replaceable, or which can be relinquished. But we are talking about central interests and fundamental ground-projects, not peripheral ones; *fundamental* self-referential interests cannot be simply dropped, replaced, or forgotten whenever circumstances arise which make their satisfaction impossible. For instance, the maintenance of honor may be a central interest for some people, as it clearly was in classical Rome and in Japan. For some, it may be possible to discard one's interest in honor when one's honor is compromised, but if the interest is central, or if it is the product of long-term cultural influences, to discard it will not be easy. Or, imagine a person whose fundamental interests involve achieving a clear view of the world, or unimpaired rationality: when such a person feels insanity coming on, suicide may be the rational

---

[36] James Hillman, *Suicide and the Soul* (New York: Harper & Row, 1964), p. 63; emphasis his.

choice, as Plotinus recommended[37] and Virginia Woolf practiced.[38] If these cases are accepted, still others will occur. For instance, if it is correct to describe Ernest Hemingway's macho, tough-guy image as a central self-interest, then even the incursions of middle age might begin to thwart satisfaction of that interest. His suicide is generally viewed as pathological, in part a failure of the psychiatric sciences but in part also the product of his inflexibility in changing roles; under our criteria, however, it may count as rational.[39]

This is a general point about the rationality or irrationality of altering one's life circumstances, activities, and goals in response to setbacks or hindrances, mishaps, unfortunate events, unfulfilled expectations, and so forth. It is almost universally assumed that to do so is rational; that is, the rational thing to do in the face of some unavoidable and irreversible setback is to alter one's life so as to accommodate oneself to the change. But the suggestion here is that if the concerns, interests, and fundamental ground-projects which one may be forced to relinquish are genuinely central, it may not be rational to let them go. These are the cases in which suicide may be a rational alternative.

This argument can be applied to distinct groups of people, particularly the aged. To those individuals for whom independence, status as contributing members of society, and/or the ability to experience intensely are central interests, old age will quite likely prove to be a condition which hinders satisfaction of their most basic interests. For some of these individuals, the original basic interests may prove not to be so basic after all, and may be fairly readily replaceable. Some older people find new satisfaction in being nurtured, in occupying a position as senior but not executive member of the family, or in active reminiscence of their earlier years. These are the individuals who "adjust well" to major life changes. But for some, abandonment of one's earlier concerns for autonomy, self-reliance, and activity may prove impossible, or categorically distasteful, and for these individuals the mental and physical limitations of old age may serve only to thwart their most basic interests. Of course, in many cases, it may be very hard to distinguish these situations from those in which individuals are fearful or defensive about altering relatively peripheral interests; this is the kind of distinction which continuing counseling might facilitate. But not all cases of refusal to "adjust" involve merely peripheral interests; in some cases it is much more the central interests which are at stake, and to thwart these is to thwart what it is that the individual essentially lives for. "The worst death for anyone is to lose the center of his being," Hemingway had said, "Retirement is the filthiest word in the English language."[40]

We are often tempted to claim that the preservation of one's own life is the

---

[37]Plotinus, *Enneads* I.4 and I.9 (*op. cit.* I/133), see esp. note 1, pp. 324–35.

[38]Quentin Bell's *Virginia Woolf: A Biography* (New York: Harcourt Brace Jovanovich, 1972), provides the text of the note Virginia Woolf left for her husband Leonard on the morning she drowned herself: "I feel certain I am going mad again. I feel we can't go through another of those terrible times. And I shan't recover this time. I begin to hear voices, and I can't concentrate. So I am doing what seems the best thing to do . . ." (p. 226)

[39]Szasz, in his "The Ethics of Suicide," (*op. cit.* i/10) says that Hemingway was "demeaned" by the "psychiatric indignities inflicted on him" (p. 13). Also see Pretzel, "Philosophical and Ethical Considerations of Suicide Prevention," (*op. cit.* II/78) pp. 31–32, and Maris, *Pathways to Suicide* (*op. cit.*, i/2).

[40]A. E. Hotchner, *Papa Hemingway* (New York: Random House, 1966), p. 228.

most fundamental and basic of all ground projects; this is, no doubt, in part what is intended by the claim that self-preservation is man's most fundamental instinct and law. But it is quite obvious that some individuals place other projects and concerns above their interests in self-preservation. This becomes clear in forced-choice tests, as for instance the apostasy-or-torture choice offered many early Christians. Some chose one, some the other, but we may assume that when confronted with this choice, each individual revealed what at heart were his or her most basic goals: some wished to stay alive, some wished to see God. Similar forced-choice situations may reveal, in any case of apparent multiple ground interests, which one is really more fundamental. If one's basic ground-projects can be furthered only by one's own death, or if they will be thwarted by one's remaining alive, suicide in these cases appears to be the rational choice.

Of course, suicide to accomplish a ground-project is rational only if that ground-project can be fulfilled regardless of one's own existence. However, many ground-projects we think of as independent of our own existence may not really be so. For instance, I may have dedicated my life to writing an article which could, in fact, be completed equally well by someone else; if so, the article is a ground-project which is independent of my own existence. If, for whatever reasons, my own suicide would implement the completion of this article (by somebody else), while my staying alive would impede it, I would not be irrational, at least on these grounds, to kill myself. But, as John Perry (working on his own article) says, "I want not merely that this article be completed, but that it be completed by me."[41] Our involvement in even the most noble of projects often tends to be quite personal in this way, even though we are often unwilling or unable to admit it; but it is just this fact of personal involvement that precludes suicide as a rational choice in the accomplishment of that goal.

Finally, as David Wood points out,[42] suicide may also be rational even when it is not a means for accomplishment of some goal. He distinguishes between *instrumental suicide,* which is intended to bring about certain effects, and what he calls *expressive suicide,* in which the meaning of the act is its whole purpose. As an example, he suggests the suicide (by jumping) of an architect who pioneered high-rise apartments, and realizes too late what he has done. The suicide will not accomplish the demolition of the highrises, nor prevent future entrepreneurs from building them. Nor will the suicide prevent future harms to this person (he will not be condemned, or rejected from the Architects' Society; and his remorse will diminish with time), or preclude forcible alterations in his fundamental ground-projects (his project remains, as it was, to contribute to the quality of human life). His suicide may not accomplish any good, or forestall any evil. Yet because of its capacity to express the central concern of this particular man, we may see it as a rational act. Not all expressive suicides are rational acts; they may suffer, as Wood suggests, from lack of genuine feeling, or from irrelevance of suicide as form of expression. But some acts of suicide may escape these difficulties, and even though not performed in order to produce some benefit or avoid some substantial harm, nevertheless count as rational acts.

[41]John Perry, "The Importance of Being Identical," in Rorty, ed., *The Identities of Persons (op. cit.* IV/29), pp. 67–90; see p. 79.

[42]David Wood, "Suicide as Instrument and Expression," in Battin and Mayo, eds., *Suicide: The Philosophical Issues, (op. cit.* i/10) pp. 151–60.

One last issue presents itself in considering the concept of "rational suicide." In cases in which suicide, whether because it prevents harms, accomplishes goals, or expresses what is central to a human being, is a rational choice, is it always also rational to choose to remain alive? Is suicide, if it is rational in given circumstances, sometimes *the* rational choice, or is it always merely *a* rational choice among others? Clearly, when strategies other than suicide will equally well prevent harms, accomplish goals, or express a person's deepest convictions, staying alive and using these other strategies will be an at least equally rational choice. But where other strategies will not succeed, suicide may be the only rational thing to do. This issue will have crucial practical consequences for the theory of rational suicide.

CHAPTER 5

Paternalism and Suicide

Whether the impending suicide would be rational or not, the usual response to suicide threats and attempts is prevention. This may mean prophylactic counseling, persuasion, or restraint prior to an attempt, immediate intervention in an attempt once it has begun, or resuscitation after an attempt has been made. All of these, except for genuinely nondirective counseling, involve some abridgement of the individual's liberty or freedom of action. This is almost always said to be justified on paternalistic grounds: preventing someone from suicide is warranted because suicide is not in that person's best interests. What is best for that person (though the suicide attempt shows that he is deeply confused at the moment) is continuing life.

Paternalistic Intervention in Suicide

According to Dworkin, paternalism may be roughly defined as the abridgement of an individual's liberty or other rights in order to promote his or her interests, good, happiness, needs, values, or welfare.[1] We restrain the child from touching a hot stove; we oblige the motorcyclist to wear a helmet when riding on the highway. For their own good, we do not allow people to duel, to prescribe their own medications, or to purchase air for scuba diving unless they meet specific qualifications. And we do not allow them to commit suicide.

Paternalistic interference in an individual's actions is typically said to be appropriate in two kinds of circumstances. What has come to be known as "soft" or "weak" paternalism permits interference when the individual is disturbed, emotionally upset, irrational, immature, ill, inadequately informed, insane, or for other reasons has impaired mental capacity. Weak paternalism would permit intervention

[1]Dworkin, "Paternalism" (*op. cit.* 1/41).

in any suicide which does not meet the "nonimpairment" criteria outlined in the previous chapter, including almost all cases of what we typically call "suicide." Second, "hard" or "strong" paternalism further permits intervention in an individual's actions not only when his mental capacities are impaired, but when the harm which would otherwise occur to him would be very great. Thus, strong paternalism will permit intervention in suicides which fail to meet the two "satisfaction of interests" criteria also outlined above. It is also assumed that the more seriously impaired the choice and the more severe and permanent the harm it will produce, the stronger the paternalistic interference may be.

In supporting paternalistic suicide intervention on the grounds that suicide is irrationally chosen, most writers point to a variety of symptoms of irrationality: ambivalence, emotional disturbance, clinical mental illness, clinical physical illness (where it is severe enough to warp thinking processes), depression, and a number of other indicators detectable by the psychiatrist's repertoire of diagnostic instruments. In general, although this may seem to oversimplify the matter, the assertion that suicide is irrationally chosen is the contention of those who espouse the medical model of suicide: irrationality is the symptom of underlying mental illness. The claim that suicide is a very great harm—that it brings about death, which does not serve the individual's genuine interests—is the underlying claim advanced by those adopting the "cry-for-help" model. In this case, we may recognize that suicide attempts are not necessarily irrational: they are a sophisticated and often effective, although risky, strategy for altering the circumstances of one's life. But we also see that it is not death but something else which is intended: revenge, attention, love. Here, the paternalist's job is to listen carefully to what the suicidal individual wants—help in changing his life—and then to intervene to prevent an act which would thwart those interests. Again, I do not wish to suggest that the medical-model and cry-for-help schools of suicide theory are entirely distinct or that their methods are incompatible, but these two approaches do provide different bases for paternalistic intervention. In practice, of course, we tend to lump the two together, and advocate intervention on either basis. Thus, we often say that suicide prevention is legitimate if either the choice of suicide is irrationally made, or if death seems not to be what the individual really wants.

The Justification of Paternalism

Paternalistic abridgement of an individual's liberty is said to be justified on various grounds. Some authors stress the notion of "future-oriented consent": although the individual now objects to whatever interference is made in his actions, later (when he comes to his senses and/or discovers the harm he might have done himself) he will be grateful that the interference was made. This kind of justification is often used in cases of forcible religious "deprogramming," confinement while drunk, judicial refusal to allow someone under indictment to argue his own case, and various similar cases. It may seem to be an attractive justification for paternalistic intervention in suicide, particularly since many persons who have made serious suicide attempts later express extreme gratitude for the saving of their lives. Indeed, many prevented or rescued suicides make no further attempts. But this is not true of all; some suicide attempters repeat their attempts, and a sizeable proportion of those who do eventually kill themselves have made earlier, unsuccessful attempts. One might wish to interpret repeated suicide attempts as a continuing display of nonconsent to paternalistic interference, although many such cases can perhaps more plausibly be interpreted as a continuation of the impaired condition which presumably led both to the first attempt and to the subsequent ones. One might rely on a hypothetical future consent which would be available if the present impairment were removed, even though the individual in fact continues to repeat his attempts; but this is to assume that there will be future consent, rather than to produce it as justification for paternalistic interventions already being made. In any case, although such stories appear rarely in the suicide-treatment literature, many professionals have seen cases in which an individual resuscitated after an attempt expresses extreme bitterness over the interruption, and vows to repeat the attempt again.

Paternalistic intervention is also often said to be justified because it preserves for the individual a wider range of freedom. Thus one may paternalistically prevent someone from selling himself into slavery, or from entering a contract in which his freedom would be very severely curtailed. However, this argument presents philosophic difficulties: not all forms of paternalism we accept seem to have this effect. To prevent a small child from touching a hot stove is hardly to preserve a "wider range of freedom." But with reference to suicide a special problem arises: unlike slavery or restrictive contracts, suicide cannot be said to place the individual in an unfree state: on the no-afterlife model we are assuming here, it places him in no state at all. His liberties are not curtailed; he is simply not available for action at all.

Finally, paternalistic interference is sometimes said to be justified just when it is what would be chosen by a fully rational individual. A fully rational individual would not choose to drive a car without fastening his seatbelt, scuba-dive unless qualified to purchase air, or operate dangerous equipment without safety glasses. Coercing these activities is appropriate, since they are what the fully rational individual would choose. Consent to such laws and practices, Dworkin argues, is like subscribing to a "social insurance policy";[2] it will protect us, too, if we are in a position to require it. But clearly, this form of justification will not license all paternalistic interference in suicide, for some suicide, as we have argued in a previous chapter, may be the product of rational choice. The fully rational individual would hardly subscribe to a social-insurance policy preventing him from acting on his own rational choice.

Whatever basis of justification is adopted, paternalistic intervention in suicide presents a number of difficult practical questions. One, for instance, concerns the degree of interference in an individual's liberty which may be licensed on paternalistic grounds. While counseling before an attempt or resuscitation during an attempt may be appropriate, is continuing involuntary commitment, for instance, justified to prevent future such attempts? What about surveillance, involuntary medication, or ongoing psychiatric management? Answers to questions such as these would require a full theory of the limits of paternalistic intervention, with particular attention to the point at which infringement of an individual's liberty becomes a major harm of its own.

In extreme cases, very strong interference in a person's liberties is often said to be justified. Since in suicide the decision to die is always seriously impaired, and the harm the activity causes—death—is maximal, the degree of interference in a person's liberty may be very, very great. Thus, it is claimed, not only counseling or persuasion may be appropriate in the early stages of suicide prevention, but also threats, surveillance, physical restraint, and involuntary incarceration. Interference

---

[2]*Ibid.*, p. 78.

with an attempt in progress may involve invasion of privacy, police arrest, and forcible medical treatment; resuscitation after an attempt may involve forcible medication, involuntary hospitalization, and even temporary or permanent commitment to a mental institution.[3] Although most suicide-prevention services are not this invasive of an individual's liberty, all these practices do occur. Furthermore, all occur within the apparent sanction of the law.

A second practical problem in paternalistic interference concerns accurately predicting a suicide attempt, and, if the attempt occurs, whether or not it will be fatal. This is what we might call the "fallibility of paternalism" issue. In the Introduction to this book, we've discussed the false-positive problem in connection with treatment strategies which involve identifying persons of "high suicide potential" either on the basis of prodromal clues like explicit threats or giving away property, or on the basis of conditions like recent bereavement, unemployment, social isolation, etc. If the methods of suicide prediction are not perfectly reliable, the paternalist may find himself interfering with the liberty of persons who would not in fact have committed suicide.[4]

A third practical problem involves what we might call the "inefficiency of paternalism" issue. Here, the problem is that paternalistic intervention, however genuinely intended, may have paradoxical effects. For instance, David Reynolds and Norman Farberow, in their book *Suicide: Inside and Out,* have argued that the more restrictive forms of suicide intervention—in this case, hospitalization under suicide precautions—may actually increase rather than decrease the likelihood of suicide.[5] Reynolds, a reporter, had himself admitted incognito to a hospital in order to study suicide prevention techniques; he ended up, apparently as a result of the suggestivity of these practices, making a genuine (though unsuccessful) suicide attempt. Some workers also believe that preventive counseling increases rather than decreases the likelihood of suicide by making it an issue of ongoing concern.

Still other practical issues involve the difficulties of ascertaining, in any given case, whether either of the criteria for paternalistic intervention—impairment or harm—is satisfied. These are the problems of evidence, arising in cases of doubt. Suppose, for instance, that a woman, about whom you know nothing, is discovered unconscious, with the gas turned on or an empty bottle of pills by her side. How, in this case, do you establish that her decision to die was an irrationally made one, or that death will constitute a harm? Clearly, given the evidence available, you cannot do so in any fully satisfactory way. There will be certain external clues: the woman may be young and apparently healthy, or quite old and in clearly deteriorating health. Yet even clues of this sort are not altogether reliable: a young woman may have a good reason for her choice, while an older one is merely temporarily depressed. There may be a note, though even the most elaborate, self-explanatory note may not be reliable. Third parties may be able to provide some information about circumstances, motives, and such; yet such information itself may be inaccurate or biased. Even supposing an adequate justification for paternalistic intervention in general it is very often unclear whether such procedures will be appropriate in a particular case.

---

[3]Descriptions of such practices can be found in Szasz, "The Ethics of Suicide" (*op. cit.* i/10).

[4]See Introduction, pp. 12–16.

[5]David K. Reynolds and Norman L. Farberow, *Suicide: Inside and Out* (Berkeley: University of California Press, 1976).

A Paternalistic Policy for Suicide Prevention

Because the evidence is so often lacking, I think we must recommend temporary intervention in a situation like this: that is, resuscitation followed by enough psychiatric examination or counseling to establish more clearly the character of the case. When in doubt, it is often said, "err on the side of life"; if the intervention has been unwarranted the individual can always try again. A completed suicide, however, cannot be reversed.

This approach to particular cases can be generalized as an overall public policy. Since most cases of suicide in contemporary western culture are neither the product of intelligent choice nor designed to serve the individual's true interests, it is probable that any random suicide one encounters will be irrational. Thus, it will be reasonable for the otherwise uninformed onlooker to expect that this, like most suicides, will be a proper subject for paternalistic intervention. Consequently, the onlooker ought to try to save every suicide, at least where there is any substantial degree of doubt. The practical public policy which these considerations seem to recommend is intervention in all except the most clearly rational cases.

However, while I think we must accept this paternalistic policy in cases of doubt, it is not without certain qualms. To begin with, suicide is said not to be an easy thing, and to lightly suggest that the individual can always "try again" masks a certain callousness toward the person who may have urgent reason for ending his life. Second, while it may be the case at present that most suicides in our culture are not rational, this may not necessarily continue to be the case. The time may be quickly approaching in which a larger proportion of the self-caused deaths in this society will be recognized as matters of rational choice. Thus, we should hesitate to recommend any policy for paternalistic intervention which might prove inflexible in the face of changing needs. But there is an advantage to a policy such as this which I think outweighs its deficiencies: by supporting a policy under which all cases except the most clearly rational are routinely treated by "erring on the side of life," we tend to undercut the unduly large role and responsibility which onlookers might otherwise be assigned. In the end, the onlooker has very little real way of deciding whether the suicide of another person is in fact a rational one, particularly from ambiguous outward clues, and to make the *onlooker* responsible for deciding whether an individual shall live or can be allowed to die seems an extremely undesirable course.

This latter point is one of considerable importance. It is true that when the evidence is skimpy, an onlooker may be unable to determine whether a given case of suicide should count as rational. But even the best-informed onlooker may tend to make such an assessment in a faulty way, importing onto the situation his own conceptions of the conditions under which suicide might be a rational choice. The person with a strong religious background, for instance, might regard suicide as "irrational" (since, among other things, he believes it invites damnation) under almost any conditions at all. The person whose sensitivity to physical pain is very great, however, may find suicide the clearly rational choice even early in the course of an incapacitating or terminal illness. But since the rationality or irrationality of suicide, as we have characterized it, is a function not only of circumstances but of the suiciding individual's values, beliefs, goals, commitments, and other interests—not those of the onlooker—only an onlooker who is extremely intimately informed or who shares these views will be able to approximate a correct determination.[6] This would be true, of course, for any major choice; but the difficulties in the case of suicide are clearly magnified. In the end, most cases of suicide are cases of doubt, and we tend to assuage our doubts about the rationality or irrationality of a given suicide by supplying our own evaluation of the facts. It is precisely this which true paternalism does not permit.

A policy restricted to true paternalism in suicide intervention, but which enjoins onlookers to "err on the side of life" in cases of doubt, would have what I take to be an additional salutary effect. It would encourage those contemplating suicide in a rational way to make public their reasons, as well as the relevant values, beliefs, and goals, well in advance. This is not as bizarre as it sounds; it simply invites persons to consider carefully, "in advance of need," in what sorts of situations they probably would not wish to continue to live, and to convey these notions to others around them. This may be done formally, by making a statement to one's physician or one's attorney, or informally, by ongoing discussions with one's family and friends. To be sure, this is difficult in a society still subject to a strong suicide taboo. Nevertheless, there are examples: Jo Roman, the New York artist who ended her life rather than succumb to breast cancer, had made clear her views on the rationality of suicide in terminal illness for at least fifteen years in advance, and when the situation arose composed a book and videotape describing and defending her choice.[7] Similarly, Wallace Proctor, a retired dermatologist with Parkinson's Disease, paid a call to the district attorney in advance of his suicide to indicate clearly the circumstances of the case and the rational nature of his choice, and to assure the law that there would be no foul play involved.[8] Of course, the person afflicted with ambivalence, depression, emotional disturbance, or other uncertainty will have extreme trouble in announcing and defending such intentions coherently and clearly in advance; but these, under the paternalistic account advanced here, are just the suicides it will be appropriate to prevent.

This may seem to conflict with the claim, to be examined later, that under a conception of suicide as a right, it is the preventers who must supply justification for intervention, not the prospective suicide a defense. But I think there is no conflict here; although intervention will be appropriate in many and perhaps most cases, justification of intervention is often easily supplied. The person who contemplates rational suicide, on the other hand, need not supply any further justification for his right to do so, but will nevertheless be encouraged to show in advance that his suicide is a suicide of rational choice. Thus the burden of discriminating between rational and irrational suicides is shifted away from onlookers, upon whom it cannot properly depend.

This policy does not decide, however, what course of action is appropriate in those cases where a purely paternalistic policy would not authorize interference in a suicide, but considerations of the welfare of others would. Suppose, for instance, that a person who is painfully and terminally ill has rationally chosen to die; but that the spouse, for reasons of religious belief, cannot at all accept such a choice: suicide

---

[6]See Jerome Motto's discussion of the difficulties the psychiatrist encounters in assessing the character of a person's projected suicide in "The Right to Suicide: A Psychiatrist's View," (*op. cit.* IV/8).

[7]See accounts of the suicide of Jo Roman in *The New York Times,* June 17, 1979, and in subsequent Letters to the Editor. Her videotape was aired on PBS in most parts of the United States on June 16, 1980. There is considerable controversy over whether her suicide was a rational one.

[8]See Chapter 1, p. 58.

of the one will mean destruction of the psychic equilibrium of the other. Or suppose a person who rationally chooses to die in order to support a crucial cause will thereby leave unsupported several dependent children (this latter question arises in connection with a great deal of parasuicidal activity, such as high-risk exploration or sports, volunteering for military duty, etc.). Lebacqz and Engelhardt, as one party to this debate, suggest that suicide-preventive interference, although no longer properly speaking paternalistic, will be appropriate in some cases such as these:

> . . . we must ask about those cases in which a competent adult chooses to die, but others have reason to think that the demands of justice would be violated by the suicide (i.e., that it is wrong and that the person seeking suicide is not relieved of her obligations to others because illness prevents their discharge). In such circumstances, persons have a right to intervene to prevent the act in order to protect their rights or the rights of others.[9]

But Landsberg, as we saw at the outset of Chapter Two, holds that one's own choice concerning the termination of one's life is "far too personal" to be decided with reference to others. Here, the obligations of the paternalist are clear enough—to refrain from intervention—but the paternalistic posture as a whole may give way to larger considerations of rights and duties of individuals within society as a whole. A complete and satisfactory policy for paternalistic intervention in suicide can be provided only when a larger theory of the relations between the individual and society is accepted.

We began this chapter by observing that suicide-prevention activities are usually justified on two paternalistic grounds: impairment and harm. We have seen, however, that in some cases suicide is rationally chosen and death is not a harm. In such cases, *paternalistic* prevention of the suicide is impossible, since genuine paternalism serves, rather than thwarts, the individual's interest, and prevention would only serve the interests of onlookers or of others in the society as a whole. In these cases, paternalism does not call for suicide prevention, but forbids it.

Paternalistic Facilitation of Suicide

To point out that there are some situations in which genuine paternalism forbids intervention in suicide is only half the issue; such situations present a still more acute problem for the paternalist. To see this, we must notice that paternalistic interference in a person's liberty may take two major forms: that in which certain actions are restricted or prevented, and that in which certain actions are enforced. Thus, paternalism may involve not only restraining someone from an act which it is irrational for him to do; it may involve encouraging or forcing him to perform an act which he otherwise would not do. In discussions of paternalism, examples of restraint-paternalism and what we might call "directive" or "facilitative" paternalism are typically intermixed: we speak of paternalism both in restraining someone from smoking cigarettes or from diving without a scuba license, and in requiring someone to use a motorcycle helmet, buy automobile insurance, or spend a portion of his income on social security. Legal paternalism tends to confine itself to

[9]Lebacqz and Engelhardt, "Suicide," (*op. cit.* II/6), p. 693.

restraint requirements; directive paternalism appears to be much more common in educational, domestic, and religious-group situations. Of course, the distinction between restraint paternalism and directive paternalism may not always be sharp: to prohibit someone from diving without a scuba license is to oblige him to obtain a scuba license if he dives, and so forth. Nevertheless, we are familiar in domestic contexts with innumerable examples of paternalism best described as directive: making one's spouse or children take vitamins, go to the dentist, or wear an overcoat when it rains.

It is just this sort of directive, action-enforcing paternalism which presents unrecognized but acute problems for the issues in suicide. If suicide is in some cases the rational choice from the point of view of the welfare of the individual whose death it would be, the consistent directive paternalist will wish to encourage, facilitate, or enforce this action. After all, the individual may not fully recognize that suicide is the rational choice, or he may be caught in hesitation produced by various religious, social, or philosophical arguments against suicide, by irrelevant legal prohibitions, or by misinformation, superstition, and the like. This is the individual of whom Philippa Foot writes:

> . . . someone may cling to life when we would say confidently that it would be better for him if he died, and he may admit it too.[10]

To kill this person, even on the grounds that he is better off dead, might violate other moral canons; to encourage his suicide, however, even though it may violate his liberty to do as he chooses, may be seen as helping him to do what is in his own best interests.

Thus, just as there are circumstances in which genuine paternalism requires onlookers to prevent an irrational suicide, there may be circumstances in which the same paternalistic principles require us to promote a rational suicide which would not otherwise be undertaken. This is, one might say, the particular embarrassment of paternalism when it is used to justify suicide prevention: it backfires and argues for the facilitation of rational suicide as well.

Of course, the more coercive the paternalistically "directive" or "facilitative" measures, the less likely it is that a "decision" to end one's life will be voluntary, and so the less likely that the term "suicide" will apply. But to suggest that encouraged or facilitated suicide is not really suicide and so outside the scope of our problem and interests, is to overlook both a theoretical and an empirical point: (1) that self-killing as the result of forcible coercion is nevertheless still voluntary, since the victim always has the option to refuse to kill himself and settle for the consequences (even though these may involve being killed),[11] and (2) that a good deal of what we actually do recognize as suicide is the product of suggestion, innuendo, veiled threat, deliberate maltreatment, and other forms of coercion, even though they may not be recognized as such by either the coercer or the victim. The

[10]Foot, "Euthanasia" (*op. cit.* III/8) pp. 89–90.

[11]It may of course be objected that forcibly coerced action is involuntary, and that I do not voluntarily give my wallet to the thief who demands, "Your money or your life." Certainly I do not voluntarily give it to him in the same way that I contribute, say, a sum of money to the Red Cross, i.e., as one among a number of possible options which include keeping it in good conscience and in good health. But when coerced I do nevertheless make a genuine choice between the two options offered me: being robbed, or being dead, and to this extent giving my wallet to the thief is a voluntary act.

notion of "suicide facilitation" is by no means self-contradictory, even when the means are quite strong, although there are certainly cases when the *moral* considerations appropriate to murder will apply. For instance, a middleaged English woman was convicted some years ago of banging her elderly mother's head against the commode in an effort to get her to commit suicide; we can correctly speak of this bizarre and unfortunate case as one of "suicide facilitation," though one in which the moral condemnation associated with murder surely applies.

But not all means of suicide facilitation are so rough, nor is it clear that they are always wrong. Since we do not now generally recognize the moral legitimacy of any paternalistic suicide facilitation, we do not generally consider what sorts of mechanisms might be involved, and how severe an invasion of an individual's liberty—for his own good—we might be willing to allow. In almost all jurisdictions, the law places quite severe penalties on what may be even fairly mild forms of suicide facilitation, regardless of whether the suicide can be said to be rational or not; it penalizes suggestion, provision of means, and other forms of solicitation which are often grouped under the rubric of "assisted suicide."[12] More coercive forms of suicide facilitation, including force, duress, and deception, are typically treated as murder. But this may disguise from us those situations in which paternalistic suicide facilitation may be morally appropriate—if any paternalistic interference in suicide ever is—and which should perhaps be subject to more careful, thoughtful scrutiny. If the prevention of irrational suicide can be justified on paternalistic grounds, it is difficult to see why, apart from the very real risks of abuse, facilitation of rational suicide cannot also be so.

Mechanisms of Suicide Facilitation

The mechanisms for facilitating rational suicide may be quite mild: they may consist, for instance, of reassurance, support, intercession with third parties who intend to prevent the suicide, or simply frank discussion of the situation which confronts the individual. Indeed, facilitation may consist only in helping to undo the hesitation produced by antiquated antisuicide arguments, by superstition, or fear; this is perhaps what Szasz has in mind when he says that counseling may give the prospective suicide "the strength to die."[13] This kind of mild encouragement toward suicide is particularly relevant in cases of terminal illness and may be viewed as an antidote to the common assumption that the patient ought to "hang on" as long as he possibly can. But we can also discern two stronger mechanisms of suicide facilitation which serve to bring about a rational decision to end one's life when one would not otherwise do so.

CIRCUMSTANTIAL MANIPULATION. The first of these we may call "circumstantial manipulation." Since the rationality or irrationality of an individual's decision to kill himself is in part a function of his circumstances—his health, living conditions, political environment, opportunities for enjoyable or fulfilling activities—altering these circumstances may make what would have been an irrational and undesired choice of suicide a rational and desired one. Here, what the

---

[12]Francis, "Assisting Suicide: A Problem for the Criminal Law" (*op. cit.* i/37).

[13]Szasz, "The Ethics of Suicide" (*op. cit.* i/10), p. 189.

manipulator does is to alter the victim's immediate and/or long-range circumstances in such a way that the victim himself chooses death as preferable to continued life.

Manipulation of this sort may happen in an obvious way, as for instance in sustained torture. Where blatant circumstantial manipulation of this sort is intended to result in suicide, we call it coercion, and consider it a form of murder. No doubt much more frequent, however, is the small, not very visible, often even inadvertent kind of manipulation that occurs in domestic situations, where what the manipulator does is to ''arrange things'' so that suicide becomes the reasonable, even attractive choice for his victim.[14] For instance, negligent family members may fail to change the bedsheets of an incontinent bedridden patient, or in other ways provide poor or hostile nursing care. Or, they may make suicide an easy choice by providing drugs or other instruments, by ensuring privacy, and in other ways altering the circumstances so that the choice becomes more convenient and attractive than it had been before.

Of course, suicide will not be the rational choice if these circumstances are likely to change or if they can be altered in some way. Where adverse circumstances are the result of coercion or manipulation by some other person or group, the obvious *rational* response would be to resist or attack the perpetrator in an effort to stop the manipulation and improve the circumstances. Thus, the incontinent bedridden patient's rational move is to complain to friends or authorities that his bedsheets are unchanged and that the care he is given is cruel, or that his family is urging or coercing him into suicide by providing the means.

In some cases, however, resistance to circumstantial manipulation may not be possible. In severe forms, the victim may be unable to elude his torturers, and suicide may in fact be the only way of escape. In less severe forms, it may be impossible to detect the more subtle ways of ''making suicide an easy choice.'' Perhaps such cases are rare. But if we recognize the notion of rational suicide, we must also recognize that in such cases, suicide may be the only rational choice for the victim, whether he is coerced and whether his circumstances have been deliberately worsened or not. Where the victim can identify the perpetrator and retaliate in some effective way, to do so is clearly the more rational choice, but manipulation is not always easy to detect, and even when it is, its perpetrators are not always easy to stop.

IDEOLOGICAL MANIPULATION. The rationality of suicide is also in part a function of one's beliefs and values, and these, like circumstances, can also change. Suicide, as we've seen, is irrational if it is chosen in an impaired way if it violates one's fundamental beliefs and values, but it is rational when it is in accord with one's most fundamental beliefs and values. For instance, Stoic thinkers held slavery to be a condition so degrading that death was to be preferred to it, and those who took their lives to avoid slavery (Cato, for instance) regarded themselves and were regarded by others as having made a fully rational choice.[15] These fundamental

---

[14]It is Virgil Aldrich who suggests the use of the phrase ''arrange things'' in connection with manipulation into suicide. It is well to notice, however, that terms like ''arrange things'' and ''manipulation'' suggest conscious intentionality on the part of the ''arranger'' or ''manipulator,'' though conscious intentionality need not always be a feature in these cases.

[15]See, e.g., Seneca, *Letters* (*op. cit.* II/7), Letters 70, 77, and 78 on preferring death to slavery, and Plutarch's *Lives of the Noble Greeks and Romans* on the death of Cato the Younger. This view is not confined to Stoicism; see Josephus, *The Jewish War*, VII 320–419 (*op. cit.* I/10) on the mass suicide at Masada.

beliefs, of course, vary from one society and era to another: though loss of virginity or chastity was a basis for rational suicide in early medieval times,[16] the contemporary rape victim does not typically consider sexual assault a reason to kill herself, even though it may cause very severe emotional distress. Nor does contemporary western society countenance suicide in bereavement, for honor, or to avoid poverty, insanity, or disgrace, although all these have been recognized as grounds for suicide in various cultures at earlier times.[17]

Once we see that the beliefs and values on which the rationality of suicide in part depends can vary from one individual or historical era to another, we also recognize that such ideology can change. Ideological change may occur as part of the natural evolution of a culture, or such changes can be engineered. The contemporary world is already well familiar with deliberate attitude and values manipulation, from the gentle impress of advertising to the intensive programming and conditioning associated with various religious and political groups. If our attitudes and values in other areas can be deliberately changed, it is not at all unreasonable to think that our conceptions of the conditions under which suicide would be the rational choice can be changed too. One can imagine, for instance, a culture which encourages renewed attention to the notions current among the early Scandinavians, the American Indians, and many other groups, that physical decline is ignominious, and that death—if it does not occur in battle or other heroic pursuits—should be taken upon oneself before old age or debilitating illness can destroy the integrity of the body. One can imagine loyal children telling their aging, faltering parents both of the horrors of nursing homes and of the heroism of the ninety-year-old woman of Cos, who gathered her innumerable descendants around her and took the hemlock amid their farewells. These are forms of ideological manipulation, and their effect is to get someone who would not otherwise have done so to choose suicide—in a clearly voluntary way.

PURE AND IMPURE PATERNALISM. Not all apparently paternalistic interference in an individual's liberty, however, serves only the interests of the individual involved; it may and very often does serve other interests as well. Infringement in an individual's liberty wholly for his own sake we call "pure" paternalism; however, actual examples are oddly difficult to find, and many of the more common examples of paternalism are "impure" or "other-interested" in that they also serve the interests of other persons, institutions, or society at large. For instance, laws requiring motorists to wear seatbelts serve the interests of the motorists themselves, by reducing injury; but they also serve the interests of other specific persons (e.g., family members who are spared grief) and other persons in the public at large (e.g., those for whom insurance costs are minimized and available medical care

---

[16]See, e.g., St. Ambrose, "Concerning Virgins" (*Select Works and Letters,* in *A Select Library of Nicene and Post-Nicene Fathers of the Christian Church,* ed. Philip Schaff and Henry Wace; Grand Rapids, Mich.: Wm. B. Eerdmans Publishing Co., 1955, X, 386–387) and Eusebius, *Ecclesiastical History (op. cit.* I/107), Chapter 12, for accounts of Christian women who committed suicide rather than be violated by the Romans. Support for this view ends, however, with St. Augustine's repudiation of suicide as an alternative to sexual defilement, *City of God (op. cit.* I/19), Book I, Chapters 16–28.

[17]See Fedden, *Suicide (op. cit.* i/11) for an account of suicides for bereavement, insanity, honor, poverty, and disgrace in western and nonwestern cultures. Note also that bereavement suicides are familiar to us in the Hindu practice of *suttee,* and honor suicides in the Japanese practices of *seppuku* or *harakiri* and in *junshi.* See also the group of articles on suicide in various cultures in the *Encyclopedia of Religion and Ethics (op. cit.* I/1), Vol. XII.

maximized). Similar considerations pertain to other sorts of legal and domestic paternalism, both restrictive and directive: laws restricting the sale of scuba air to qualified divers protect the interests not only of the divers but of the rescue workers who would otherwise have to retrieve them and the society which pays for rescue operations; laws prohibiting self-prescription of antibiotic drugs serve not only the interests of the ill person by protecting him from medical error, but of the community at large by protecting it from the development of antibiotic-resistant strains of bacteria.

Although it is not always acknowledged, paternalistic suicide prevention is often impure. For instance, one might describe the resuscitation of the suiciding mother of four small children as at least partly other-interested, since continuing life may be not only in her own interest, but also in that of the four children and of the society which would have to support them as well. The suicide attempts of convicted murderer Gary Gilmore in Utah in 1977 were obviously interrupted not out of pure paternalistic concern for Gilmore's own interests or welfare, since he was resuscitated only in order to be executed by firing squad, but presumably out of social interests involving the maintenance of legal procedure, prison security, and the administration of justice; indeed, Gilmore's resuscitation apparently was not paternalistically motivated at all. Similar distinctions can be made between pure and impure suicide *facilitation*. One may encourage one's spouse to end the pain of an extended terminal illness, both for that person's own sake, and to spare oneself and the rest of the family the continuing agony of watching a loved one die. The warden who looks aside as a severely deranged mental patient ends his life serves not only the patient but the interests of society in decreased medical expenses and increased hospital space. But if impure paternalism is accepted in suicide prevention, we may seem to be committed to accepting it in suicide facilitation as well.

Thus, paternalistic intervention in suicide is a two-edged sword; while it is the most common basis for our many activities in suicide prevention, it seems to require the facilitation of suicide in many other kinds of cases. This is true both for suicide facilitation which is purely paternalistic, performed wholly for the good of the person who chooses suicide, and for impurely paternalistic facilitation, serving the interests of others.

Whether the acceptance of suicide facilitation practices in purely and impurely paternalistic cases would lead to increases in nonpaternalistic facilitation ("concealed murder," we might call it) is the issue addressed by the so-called wedge argument, sometimes also called the "slippery slope" or the "camel's nose under the tent." According to the wedge argument, to permit practices of a particular sort—say, abortion or voluntary euthanasia—even though they may in themselves be morally permissible, may lead causally or serve as a precedent for other practices which are not morally permissible: say, infanticide or involuntary euthanasia. When applied to suicide, the wedge argument holds that to permit or paternalistically encourage certain morally permissible forms of suicide—say, suicide in terminal illness or in extreme old age—may lead causally or set a precedent for other kinds of suicide-facilitation which are not morally permissible, like the English woman's banging her elderly mother's head on the commode. The wedge argument is most often pursued with reference to the euthanasia program in Nazi Germany, mentioned in our earlier section on social darwinism. The euthanasia program apparently began with a somewhat paternalistically motivated program for ending the lives of suffering incurables, but moved very rapidly to thrift-euthanasia and then to wholesale political and racial slaughter on a completely nonpaternalistic basis.

Whether permissive attitudes towards suicide would have equally grim results is the question lurking in the background here.

Before considering the evidence for this sort of claim, however, let us look for a moment at another sort of application of the issues in paternalism: the problem of distinguishing paternalistic and nonpaternalistic facilitation in mass suicide situations. Then we will explore the implications of the paternalist position for future social policy, particularly with regard to the ill, the elderly, and other special groups.

Paternalism in Mass Suicide

In May of the year 73 A.D., Eleazar exhorted his followers at Masada, who faced imminent capture by the Romans, to commit mass suicide rather than surrender:

> . . . neither did Eleazar himself contemplate flight, nor did he intend to permit any other to do so. Seeing the wall consuming in the flames, unable to devise any further means of deliverance or gallant endeavor, and setting before his eyes what the Romans, if victorious, would inflict on them, their children and their wives, he deliberated on the death of all. And, judging, as matters stood, this course the best . . .[18]

Capture by the Romans would have meant torture and death for the men, rape and slavery for the women, slavery and often death for the children. The men, embracing their wives and their children in tearful farewells, killed them; each man then lay beside his slaughtered family and proffered his own throat to one of the ten men chosen by lot to dispatch the rest; the ten, each in turn determined by lot, offered his throat to the next. The solitary survivor set fire to the garrison and fell upon his sword. Nine hundred and sixty people died in this mass suicide.

During the Second World War, the directress of an orthodox Jewish girls' school in a Nazi-occupied city came to understand that her girls, ranging in age from twelve to eighteen, had been kept from extermination in order to provide sexual services for the Gestapo. When the Gestapo announced its intention to avail themselves of these services—ordering the directress to see that the girls were washed and prepared for defloration by "pure Aryan youth"—she called an assembly and distributed poison to each of the students, teachers, and herself. The ninety-three maidens, as they have come to be called, swallowed the poison, recited a final prayer, and died undefiled.[19]

In both the Masada and the girls'-school cases, the position or authority of a single individual is employed to "encourage" or coerce others under his or her direction into suicide. What is crucial about these cases, though, is that in both the motivation appears largely paternalistic: the suicides of the inhabitants of Masada and the Jewish schoolgirls are engineered in order to protect them from harm of a

---

[18]Josephus, *The Jewish War* VII (6) 320–321 (*op. cit.* I/10) on the mass suicide at Masada, 73 A.D. Compare *Jewish War* III (33) 316–391, on the smaller mass suicide at Jotapata, from which Josephus escaped by trickery.

[19]See Hillel Bavli's poem, "The Letter of the Ninety-Three Maidens," in Azriel Eisenberg, ed., *Modern Jewish Life in Literature* (New York: United Synagogue Commission on Jewish Education, 1952), pp. 122–23; and Sholem Asch's fictional account, "A Child Leads the Way," in *Tales of My People*, tr. Meyer Levin (New York: G. P. Putnam's Sons, 1948), pp. 193–202. Also see Chapter 1, pp. 32–33 of this volume on Kiddush Hashem.

very serious sort, and are not intended to serve other extraneous social purposes or to satisfy the personal needs of the leader. Complete data may of course be lacking, but the historical accounts suggest that these mass suicides are prime cases of paternalistic suicide facilitation, precisely the kind of thing in which, according to our earlier discussion, the directive paternalist ought to engage. The circumstances also suggest that mass suicide, like individual suicide, may sometimes be described as rational, and that suicide in groups as well as by individuals may sometimes meet the rationality conditions outlined above. In neither the Masada nor the girls'-school cases is there evidence of pathology or disruption of the reasoning processes, misinformation, or distorted worldviews; in both the suicides serve to avoid severe physical harm and to prevent permanent thwarting of fundamental goals. Again, we are limited by lack of substantial evidence, but it is at least plausible to interpret these cases in this way.

Of course, there have been numerous cases of mass suicide performed at the orders of powerful or charismatic leaders whose intent was not primarily paternalistic; the suicides of over nine hundred members of the People's Temple in Jonestown, Guyana, on November 18, 1978 is an example.[20] Jones controlled the group with both physical coercion and deliberate misinformation, forcing them to undergo frequent mass suicide "rehearsals"; it is evident that the suicide decisions of most of the members were not reached with unimpaired reasoning or adequate information. It is also clear that the suicides did not serve the interests of the members of the group, and that Jim Jones' role in producing them was not paternalistic but self-aggrandizing.

However, even with a case in which there is ample evidence of both killing and forced suicide of a number of members, we must in theory be prepared to consider whether at least some of these suicides were rational in the sense we have outlined above, and thus whether Jones' action may nevertheless have been to some degree paternalistic. If the restrictions of camp life and lack of direct contact with the outside world did not interfere with the normal reasoning capacities of some of the members, and permitted fairly accurate information both about the circumstances of the group and other lifestyle alternatives elsewhere for its members, some members, if not all, may have chosen suicide as the rational alternative to disruption of a highly valued communal way of life which was apparently about to be destroyed by outside interference. More likely, this particular mass suicide was a symptom of what Joost Meerloo, describing mass suicide in general, terms "collective psychotic behavior,"[21] exhibited in response to the sustained coercive pressures imposed by Jones and his armed guards on the people of the commune. Clearly, resolution of the facts about this particular case will require much more information about the beliefs, value structures, and psychological conditions of the individuals

---

[20]Accounts of the Guyana mass suicide are available in most major newspapers in the days immediately following the event, that is, in the last week of November and the first weeks of December 1978. Other accounts include Charles A. Krause and the staff of the *Washington Post, Guyana Massacre* (New York: Berkeley Publishing Corp., 1978), and Tim Cahill, "In the Valley of the Shadow of Death," *Rolling Stone*, January 25, 1979, pp. 48–57. Joseph Richman has provided a suicidologist's analysis of this event in his talk "Mass Suicide as a Family Affair: The People's Temple in Guyana," presented at the 12th annual meeting of the American Association of Suicidology, May 12, 1979; see also Richard H. Seiden, "Reverend Jones on Suicide," *Suicide and Life-Threatening Behavior*, 9, no. 2 (Summer 1979), 116–19.

[21]Joost A. M. Meerloo, *Suicide and Mass Suicide* (*op. cit.* II/34), p. 72.

involved than may ever become available; yet we cannot ignore the philosophical views involved. As David Wood puts it:

> *It is easy to suppose that the object of one's repugnance [to the Jonestown suicides] is the mere fact of mass suicide. But it is more plausibly related to the mixture of coercion and indoctrination involved. If it were reported that the members of a recently discovered primitive tribe had collectively committed suicide to avoid what they realized was the inevitable destruction of their way of life, we would not feel repugnance so much as sorrow, misery, and shame.*[22]

Furthermore, not even the fact that "coercion and indoctrination" were involved in facilitating these suicides will assure us that such facilitation was morally repugnant, for we permit coercion and indoctrination, sometimes on a very thoroughgoing scale, in the prevention of suicide. That is just what paternalism is, the overriding of a person's liberties by coercing or indoctrinating or in other ways bringing him to refrain from doing, or forcing him to do, something he would otherwise not have done. We distinguish paternalism from murder in suicide facilitation by whether it is for the sake of the person involved.

Paternalism and Social Engineering

A much more common variant of mass suicide involves deliberate social engineering. By this means, suicide is fomented among certain kinds of individuals, social groups, or classes on a continuing basis; and although the deaths are neither simultaneous nor the product of group action, large numbers of people may choose to end their lives. We've already mentioned the principal mechanisms by which such suicide-facilitating social engineering works; it may use circumstantial manipulation, or ideological manipulation, or, more often, both. Such social engineering is sometimes malevolent and designed only to further the interests of the person or group responsible for the engineering, as in the social-darwinist policies practiced in Nazi Germany. However, social-engineering tactics and policies may also work to facilitate rational suicide in what is essentially an impure or even purely paternalistic way. Under these latter schemes, particular groups or types of individuals are encouraged to end their own lives *for their own benefit,* though this may happen to serve the welfare of society as well.

Such policies are not now openly practiced within western culture; they have, however, been a major component of both western and nonwestern societies in the past. In classical Greek medicine, for instance, the physician who found a case hopeless would routinely suggest suicide if he could not treat the disease or ease its symptoms; it was also his office to supply the appropriate lethal drugs.[23] Traditional Hindu culture, as we've mentioned, advocated self-drowning or self-immolation of those afflicted with leprosy and similar incurable, contagious diseases. Thomas More's *Utopia* similarly envisions a general policy of encouraging suicide where it will benefit the individual and the society: the inhabitants of Utopia will be given careful medical attention, but

---

[22]Wood, "Suicide as Instrument and Expression," (*op. cit.* IV/41), p. 158.

[23]Introduction, footnote 59.

if a person suffers from a disease which is both incurable and continually excruciating, the priests and magistrates come and urge him to make the decision not to nourish such a painful disease any longer. He is now unequal to all the duties of life, a burden to himself and to others, having really outlived himself. They tell him not to hesitate to die when life is such a torment, but in confidence of a better life after death, to deliver himself from the scourge and imprisonment of living or let others release him. This, they say, he would do wisely, for by death he would lose nothing but suffering.[24]

A contemporary version of the same vision is presented by the English jurist Mary Rose Barrington, who, as we mentioned earlier, argues in favor of the widespread acceptance and routine practice of suicide among the very elderly and terminally ill. She says:

. . . if we can bring ourselves to choose our time for acceptance [of death], so much the better for us, for our family, for our friends, and for society.[25]

The encouragement of self-senicide would be impurely paternalistic; it would serve dual, but not incompatible, purposes. It would benefit society, as reflected in a view where refusal to end one's life is seen as the selfish choice:

What if a time came when, no longer able to look after oneself, the decision to live on for the maximum number of years were considered a mark of heedless egoism? What if it were to be thought that dulce et decorum est pro familia mori?[26]

But it would also serve the interests of those whose deaths are involved.

Death taken in one's own time, and with a sense of purpose, may in fact be far more bearable than the process of waiting to be arbitrarily extinguished.[27]

Using the impurely paternalistic model, the social engineer may encourage or facilitate suicide, either of individuals or of given groups, wherever both individual and social interests could be served. Of course, such practices can be genuinely paternalistic only if the suicide decision Barrington advocates meets adequate criteria for rationality, or can be correctly said to be in the interest of the person who is to die. But if ending one's life is rational and in the interest of an extremely old or terminally ill person, then social policies which encourage this practice cannot be objected to on grounds that they sacrifice the individual to the welfare of society, since like many other impurely paternalistic practices, such policies may serve both the individual and society at one time. Such policies might be described as the contemporary version of traditional institutional senicide practices found so ubiquitously distributed in cultures around the earth: although the deaths of elderly persons are seen as an advantage to the society, and a necessary one where the economy is marginal and existence uncertain, they are also seen as serving the interests of the persons who die.

---

[24]Thomas More, *Utopia*, Book II, "Their Care of the Sick and Euthanasia," tr. and ed. H. V. S. Ogden (Northbrook, Ill.: AHM Publishing Corp., Crofts Classics, 1949), p. 57.

[25]Barrington, "Apologia for Suicide," (*op. cit.* i/54), p. 102.

[26]*Ibid.*, p. 97.

[27]*Ibid.*, p. 99.

To recognize the possibility of paternalistic encouragement of rational suicide is to open the theoretical way for medical, psychiatric, religious, and public social policies designed to facilitate mass or customary suicide in particular social groups. In fact, Robert Kastenbaum argues that suicide will become, within a few years, the preferred mode of death, not only, as we've seen, because it permits control over the place, time, duration, and style of death, but because it permits one to make a final contribution to the welfare of society as a whole.

> *Elders and any other individuals who accept the judgment of their culture that they are used up, unproductive, expendable, etc., might be strongly motivated to attain a last moment of stature through voluntary termination of life. This process might become fairly rigid and institutionalized. Self-termination might be clearly expected of a person who finds him- or herself in a particular situation. Or it might remain as an option; one does not have to commit suicide, but the strong, virtuous, socially-conscious person would. For many individuals, the choice of going out beautifully, boldly, and in the national interest might appeal more than lingering on the fringes as a secondary or resented figure.* [28]

But although we may recognize the theoretical possibility of paternalistic suicide facilitation among various groups, we may also scoff at the notion that such developments could occur. And yet, if we look at contemporary society, we can already see considerable evidence of change in areas relevant to precisely this sort of social engineering. To detect such change is not to find evidence of deliberate facilitation or manipulation, but it is to show the kinds of change in association with which we might expect increases in paternalistic suicide facilitation to occur. These are all changes by which persons who would not otherwise have done so, might be brought to rationally choose suicide as that course of action best serving their own interests.

In the first place, we may note various kinds of circumstantial change relevant to the practice of rational suicide. Some are changes that might decrease the incidence of suicide: the development of more effective methods of pain relief, for instance, and institutions like Hospice. But others tend on the whole to worsen the conditions of certain individuals or groups: here, one might cite our increasing tendency to confine elderly persons in nursing homes, the increasing expense of institutional care, the loss of social roles for the elderly, and the increasingly difficult financial circumstances of those living on marginal or fixed incomes. One might also mention increasing loss of autonomy in the seriously ill, as "heroic" practices in medicine become increasingly mechanized; new abilities to maintain seriously injured or birth-defective persons in marginal states, and so forth. Gerontologists and patients'-rights advocates have been pointing to the inhumane consequences of such circumstantial changes for some time, and such observations are hardly new; what is new, however, is attention to their role in rational suicide. Increasingly poor conditions in a society which is becoming to accept a notion of rational suicide may mean an increasing likelihood that suicide will be the individual's choice.

We can also diagnose in contemporary society several significant ideological changes. For instance, we notice a profusion of recent literary accounts favorable to suicide and assisted suicide in terminal illness cases—real-life stories of one partner

---

[28]Kastenbaum, "Suicide as the Preferred Way of Death," (*op. cit.* i/54), p. 439.

assisting the other in obtaining and taking a lethal drug to avoid the ravages of cancer.[29] We observe increasingly frequent court decisions favoring patients' rights to refuse medical treatment, even when refusal will mean death.[30] We notice public accounts of suicides conceived of and conducted as rational: the Henry and Elizabeth Van Dusen, Wallace Proctor, and Jo Roman cases, to mention a few.[31] And we observe that some religious groups have begun to devote attention to the issue of whether suicide may be, in certain kinds of terminal circumstances, an act of religious conscience, even though Christianity has not allowed it for the past fifteen hundred years.[32] Almost all of these cases involve suicide in the face of painful terminal illness, and that illness is very often cancer. If we were to diagnose our own ideological changes with regard to suicide, we would probably say that they involve a very recent move—by no means universal, but already widely evident—from the view that there is *no* good reason for suicide to the view that there is at least one adequate reason for suicide: extreme and irremediable pain in terminal illness.

The transition may not seem to be a very large one. But we have no reason to think it is complete, and we may perhaps predict the direction in which it will continue by noticing the kinds of reasons which are typically given to justify killing and nonprolongation of life in several closely-associated phenomena: euthanasia, abortion, infanticide of defective newborns, and noninitiation or withdrawal of treatment in chronic or terminal illness cases. Extreme pain is one such reason. So is extreme physical dependence, sometimes called "degradation"; this is often cited as a reason for discontinuing long-term tube feeding or maintenance on life-support systems, nonresuscitation, and hospital "no-code" procedures.[33] Financial burdens are now also sometimes mentioned, even by the Catholic Church: the expense of a protracted chronic or terminal illness may count among the reasons to withhold heroic treatment, even when the patient will die instead.[34] Expense is also often a

---

[29]Wertenbacker, *Death of a Man* (*op. cit.* III/16); West, *The Woman Said Yes* (*op. cit.* IV/23); Humphrey with Wickett, *Jean's Way* (*op. cit.* IV/23).

[30]See accounts of a number of these cases, including *In re Yetter, Saikewicz,* and *Perlmutter,* in Alan Sullivan's "A Constitutional Right to Suicide," (*op. cit.* i/43).

[31]For an account of the deaths of Henry P. Van Dusen, former president of Union Theological Seminary, and his wife Elizabeth, leaders in American theological life, see *The New York Times,* February 26, 1975, p. 1. At the time of their deaths, Mr. Van Dusen was 77 and Mrs. Van Dusen 80; he had had a disabling stroke five years before, and she had serious arthritis. They left a letter explaining their intentions and saying, "We still feel this is the best way and the right way to go."

For accounts of the suicides of Jo Roman and Wallace Proctor, see footnotes 7 and 8 of this chapter.

[32]See, e.g., a pastoral letter of the Presbyterian Senior Services, The Presbytery of New York City, March 9, 1976, which concludes that "it is clear that for some Christians, as a last resort in the gravest of situations, suicide may be an act of their Christian conscience."

[33]Decisions which support the assertions made here are difficult to document in detail. However, the court in the Karen Ann Quinlan case observes: "... it is perfectly apparent from the testimony we have quoted . . . , and indeed so clear as almost to be judicially noticeable, that humane decisions against resuscitative or maintenance therapy are frequently a recognized *de facto* response in the medical world to the irreversible, terminal, pain-ridden patient, especially with familial consent. And these cases, of course, are far short of "brain death." (*Matter of Quinlan* 355A.2d 647 at 667)

[34]The text of Pope Pius XII's 1958 statement on medical resuscitation, "The Prolongation of Life," is available in Stanley Joel Reiser, Arthur J. Dyck, and William J. Curran, eds., *Ethics in Medicine* (*op.*

consideration in decisions to withhold or terminate *ordinary* treatment, especially in the elderly and in defective newborns.[35] Still another consideration coming to the fore in current life-vs.-death decisions is that of impact on the immediate family: one now hears as a justification for passive and active euthanasia, abortion, infanticide, and withdrawal of treatment in the chronically or terminally ill the claim that this will "spare the family" the agony of watching someone die a protracted and painful death, or enter a seriously deficient life. Considerations regarding scarce medical resources are also sometimes heard, together with those involving the care burden placed on medical personnel and family members by someone suffering a lengthy, difficult illness, or with a severe birth defect. Finally, we now also recognize religious reasons for voluntary death when life could be continued: the Jehovah's Witnesses blood transfusion cases appear to establish the right of an individual to relinquish his life in order to protect his religious beliefs, at least where this does not infringe on the rights of others.[36]

Except for pain, none of these considerations are now generally recognized as reasons for *suicide*. But they are already recognized as reasons which may justify the killing of others and the nonprolongation of one's own life, and it is highly plausible to expect that they will soon be recognized as relevant in suicide decisions too.

These alterations in the prevailing ideology all involve medical and quasi-medical situations. They would begin to allow what we might call "euthanatic" suicide, or a choice of death in preference to prolonged and painful death. As circumstantial changes make the conditions of those who are faced with dying increasingly difficult, there is reason to think the attractiveness of euthanatic suicide as an alternative will increase. But there are no *a priori* checks on the breadth of such extensions of the concept of rational suicide, and no reason why future extensions must be limited to euthanatic medical situations. As we've said, such conditions as dishonor, slavery, and loss of chastity have been considered suicide-warranting conditions in western culture in the past; widowhood and public dishonor have assumed such roles in the East, and it seems merely naive to assume that these conditions, or others we now find equally implausible reasons for suicide, could not come to be regarded so in the future. This is particularly obvious if we keep in mind the possibility of circumstantial manipulation and of both inadvertent and deliberate ideological engineering. The motivation for such manipulation and engineering, in a society confronted with scarcities and fearful of an increasingly

---

cit. II/57), pp. 501–504. The physician is not obligated to use "extraordinary means" (including, e.g., respirators) to sustain the biological life of someone who is "virtually dead." Considerations to be made in individual cases include whether an attempt at resuscitation is "such a burden for the family that one cannot in all conscience impose it upon them," and is usually interpreted to include both financial and emotional burdens.

[35] Again, though particular decisions on such bases are difficult to document, see the symposia "Spina Bifida" and "Infants and Ethics" (both in *The Hastings Center Report*, vol. 7, no. 4, August 1977 and vol. 8, no. 1, February 1978, respectively) and many other articles in this and other bioethics and medicolegal journals for a sense of the kinds of considerations which are made with respect to life-vs.-death choices.

[36] *Erickson v. Dilgard* (252 N.Y.S.2d 705) held that an adult patient had the right to refuse a blood transfusion even if medical opinion was to the effect that the patient's decision not to accept blood was tantamount to the taking of the patient's own life; *Application of President and Directors of Georgetown College* (331F.2d 1000 (1964)) authorized an unwanted transfusion to a patient who objected on religious grounds, but apparently because she was the mother of a 7-month-old child.

large "nonproductive" population, may be very strong. Old age, insanity, poverty, and criminality have also been regarded as grounds for rational suicide in the past; given a society afraid of demands from increasingly large geriatric, ghetto, and institutional populations, we can see how interest in producing circumstantial and ideological changes in order to encourage such people to choose the "reasonable" way out might be very strong.

It is crucial to remember that such pressures need not be malevolent on the part of the manipulator. Manipulation into suicide can be purely paternalistic, where one pleads with a person to "consider yourself" and end a life which the paternalist perceives as hopelessly burdensome.[37] One can, after all, sincerely believe that another person would be better off dead, particularly if that person is suffering in an extended and irreversible way. But such pressures may be impurely paternalistic as well: one imagines a counselor advising an old or ill person to spare *both* himself and his family the agony of an extended decline, even though this person would not have considered or attempted suicide on his own, and would have been willing to suffer the physical distress. Can he resist such pressures? Not, perhaps, in a climate in which suicide is "the rational thing to do" in circumstances such as these. To resist, indeed, might earn him the epithets now applied to the person who does choose suicide: coward, sociopath, deviant, lunatic, apostate. He has, after all, refused to do what is rational, and what is believed to be not only in his own interests but in those of people he loves.

Of course, the paternalistic facilitation of suicide can be engineered only under a prevailing notion of *rational* suicide. True paternalism requires, as we've seen, an attention to the values, beliefs, and goals of the person whose liberty is to be abridged on his own behalf, not the values, beliefs or goals of the paternalist. But in this sort of ideological manipulation, that individual's values, beliefs, and goals are changed so that direct paternalistic intervention, if he does not undertake suicide by himself, now becomes appropriate. Manipulation of this sort does not involve driving one's victims into insanity or torturing them into irrationality; rather, it consists in providing a basis for the making of a *reasonable* decision about the ending of one's life, and in providing the criteria upon which that decision is to be made. The choice itself remains essentially free. Furthermore, in a suicide-permissive society, the choice of suicide would be protected by law, religion, and custom, and would be recognized as evidence of sound mental health. But the circumstances of the choice have been restructured so that choosing now involves weighing not only one's own interests but those of others. Where the costs of death will be less for oneself and for others than the costs of remaining alive, suicide will be the rational—and socially favored—choice. Indeed, perhaps the choice is not so free after all; if paternalism involves the abridgement of liberty, this is where one's liberty falls.

As we've said, there is no reason to think that such questions must remain confined to medical situations or what we might call euthanatic suicide. Not only do these considerations apply to nonterminal as well as terminal illness cases (consider, for instance, the pain, dependence, expense, impact on the family, and use of scarce

---

[37]Diogenes Laertius relates that when Antisthenes was mortally ill, Diogenes brought him a dagger, offering it to Antisthenes to release himself from his pains. Antisthenes declined, saying he wanted release from his pains, not from life; Diogenes Laertius observes "it was thought that he showed some weakness in bearing his malady through love of life." (*Lives of Eminent Philosophers:* VI. 18-19, on Antisthenes, tr. R. D. Hicks, Cambridge: Harvard Univ. Press, 1965, vol. ii, p. 21) Tales of paternalistic assistance in suicide are common in Stoic Greece and Rome.

medical resources in connection with nonterminal conditions like renal failure, quadriplegia, or severe arthritis), but they will also apply to medical conditions where there is no illness as such at all: retardation, genetic deficiency, abnormal personality, and old age. One can even imagine that continuing ideological redefinition might invite us to regard life as not worth living, and the interests of others as critical, in a much wider variety of nonmedical situations: chronic unemployment, widowhood, poverty, social isolation, criminal conviction, and so forth. Such claims may seem alarmist. But all these conditions have been promoted as suicide-warranting at some time in the past, and they are all also very often associated with social dependence. After Hitler, we are, I hope, beyond extermination of unwanted or dependent groups. But we may not be beyond encouraging *as rational* the self-elimination of those whom we perceive to constitute a burden to themselves and to others, and I think that this is where the risk in the facilitation of suicide lies. Yet it would seem to be something our canons regarding paternalism and rational activity must in consistency permit, and it is by no means philosophically clear that it would be wrong.

This issue is a difficult one for thinkers molded by scientific and cultural twentieth-century attitudes insisting on the psychopathology and immorality of suicide. Most crucial, perhaps, is the fact that, although paternalistic and socially interested prevention of suicide is very widely practiced, the facilitation or encouragement of suicide, if it occurs at all, must take place without social support or regulation of any kind. It is the lack of cultural regulation of the facilitation of suicide, in cases where that may be warranted, which might be identified as the most dangerous legacy of the suicide taboo.

Paternalism and the Mentally Ill

The issues presented by paternalism are seen at their starkest, no doubt, with reference to suicide in the severely mentally ill. This is an extremely difficult and discomforting problem, to which we alluded in Chapter 4. The first part of the problem is this: in cases in which suicide is clearly irrationally chosen, but death is not a harm, paternalist principles may favor permitting the suicide on grounds that it is the evidently reasonable choice. British geneticist Eliot Slater, for instance, argues that suicide ought not be prevented among patients who are "irretrievably psychotic" and who attempt repeatedly to end their lives, both for social-benefits reasons and also on paternalistic grounds. Rather, he says, we should allow the suicide to occur, because it is what will serve the patient's interests best:

> What—to take the argument to its logical extreme—are the humane considerations we should bear in mind in treating the irretrievably psychotic patient who has repeatedly shown his determination to die? An account of such a patient has been given by Watkins, Gilbert, and Bass in the American Journal of Psychiatry only a few months ago. This man made eight separate and desperate attempts at suicide by slashing himself, jumping from a height and running with his head full tilt against a wall. The authors refer to other such patients, and comment that as supervision and control are increased, more and more ingenious methods of evading them are used, such as aspirating torn up paper tissues and tearing the blood vessels with the fingers. They say, "It is only by constant alertness on the part of the staff that the determined patient may be prevented from killing himself." What this means is that the invasion of his privacy must be complete. The patient must be stripped down to the state in which there is absolutely nothing of him, not one of his bodily or mental functions, which can

be his to call his own. I ask you, what right do we have to debase and degrade both the patient and his custodians to this level? What harm would be done if, by the accident of a blind eye, the patient did make away with himself?[38]

It is true of course that pharmaceutical psychiatry has made enormous progress in the cure and amelioration of severe mental illness, and that the prognosis, particularly in conditions like reactive depression, is often quite good. But it is simply not true that all mental illness can be cured, or that the mentally ill can be protected from psychic or physical pain. If "irretrievable" psychotic conditions are often as searingly painful as many authors claim, then death, by comparison, may not always be a harm. However, the irretrievably psychotic individual cannot, by definition, *rationally* choose to die. Yet we might agree that a decision to die, however irrationally reached, could be in accord both with his fundamental interests and his perceived ones, as evidenced by his repeated attempts to die. Hence, the paternalist must allow the suicide to occur, even though it is an irrational choice.

But there is a second aspect of this problem. The choice of the irretrievably psychotic person to die may be irrationally made, but, under the assumption that all choices in psychosis are *ipso facto* irrationally made, the choice *not* to die may also be an irrational one. Thus it too becomes a candidate for paternalistic overriding. We cannot simply assume that the psychotic's choice for suicide is irrational while his choice against it would not be so; if the psychosis itself is the basis for claiming that the decision is impaired, it applies equally well to choices of dying and to choices of staying alive. Furthermore, we may have no way of determining what that person's unimpaired choice would be—to stay alive in such conditions, or to die—and so no firm basis for paternalistic intervention. But to refrain from intervening in an irrational choice to stay alive (although there may be other good reasons for such restraint, for instance the possibility of abuse) is itself a paternalistic stance, and should be recognized as such.

The issue of paternalism with reference to suicide in the severely mentally ill is by no means an easy one. While some individuals may be determined to die because the anguish of a psychotic condition is so great, other psychotics may intend to end their lives because they expect to become birds, or Santa Claus, or God. We might be tempted to say that because we know these latter expectations to be false, we cannot allow these suicides to occur. But other individuals may stay alive because they believe the King of France has ordered them to, or because they know where to find the rainbow's pot of gold; unfortunately, we know that these expectations too are false. We might try to distinguish between those persons who, although severely and irretrievably mentally ill, "rationally" desire death because the anguish of their condition is so great, and those who desire death for various "irrational" or unrealistic reasons; we might also distinguish between those whose desire to stay alive is rational in this same sense, and those whose desire is not; the paternalist might then permit or foment suicide in cases where death is "rationally" desired or where there is an "irrational" desire to stay alive, but forestall suicide in the other two cases. But this would be hasty, and the actual facts of such problems are much more complex than can be suggested here. What is clear is that the obligations of the paternalist *qua* paternalist towards suicide among the severely mentally ill ought to be earnestly reexamined; fear of abuse and of reckless "clearing out the asylums" ought not disguise the issues the true paternalist must face.

[38]Slater, "Choosing the Time to Die" (*op. cit.* II/75), p. 202.

CHAPTER 6

Suicide
and Rights

Claims that suicide is wrong because life is of intrinsic value, or because suicide harms others, or because permissible attitudes towards suicide may lead to coercion and abuse, are opposed by the view that a person nevertheless has the *right* to end his life if he so chooses, and that this right overrides other objections to suicide we have raised. Furthermore, the person's right to suicide precludes paternalistic intervention if it would impede the exercise of this right. In this chapter we shall consider the view that suicide is a matter of right.

There are two things we should notice about this view. First, to say that the right to suicide overrides other objections to suicide does not show these objections to be erroneous or unfounded. For instance, to say that the right to suicide overrides the inherent value of human life is not to say that human life is not of value—it may be of great value, great enough so that one person may not destroy *another's* life; it is only to say that the value of human life is not so great that one may not bring one's *own* life to an end. Similarly, to say that the right to suicide overrides objections which may be made on grounds of harms to others is not to say that such harms do not occur or should not be noticed. Nor is to say that the right to suicide overrides the risk of abuse and manipulation to say that these risks are not real, but only that we ought not compromise the choices of some individuals in order to protect others. Thus, to entertain the notion that suicide is a right is not to render superfluous the earlier considerations we have made.

Second, under the more common versions of the view that suicide is a right, it is said to be a right held by *all* persons. Many ethical theorists, even of nonlibertarian stripe, grant that persons whose lives are hopelessly blighted by intolerable, incurable illness or pain have a right to end their lives; under the present view, however, all persons have this right—even those who are young, healthy, and prospering—though of course persons whose lives are blighted may be much more likely to choose to exercise this right.

First, however, we must consider whether there is such a right.

Suicide as a Right

The claim that suicide is a right is hardly new. Schopenhauer, for instance, although he held that suicide is always metaphysically foolish, asserts that man nevertheless has a right to end his life:

> *it is quite obvious that there is nothing in the world to which every man has a more unassailable title than to his own life and person.*[1]

Indeed, although the terminology of rights is of much later usage, the notion that an individual is entitled to end his life if he chooses is already at work in a great many classical Greek and Roman sources. In a metaphor used by several Stoic writers, Cicero says:

> *An actor need not remain on the stage until the very end of the play; if he wins applause in those acts in which he appears, he will have done well enough. In life, too, a man can perform his part wisely without staying on the stage until the play is finished.*[2]

Josephus' Eleazar speaks of suicide as a "privilege";[3] so does Seneca, who holds that a man may exercise this privilege "as soon as Fortune seems to be playing him false."[4] Although the Stoics condemn frivolous suicide, they do in general hold that man has a right to end his life if its disadvantages outweigh its advantages. They also hold that the right to determine the precise circumstances and style of one's own death is among one's most fundamental rights, least easily overridden by the claims of others. Seneca says:

> *Every man ought to make his life acceptable to others besides himself, but his death to himself alone. The best form of death is the one we like.*[5]

The most forceful assertions that suicide is a right occur after the many centuries of the medieval Church's strict opposition to suicide; of particularly strong impact was Rousseau's novel *Heloise* (1761), where Saint-Preux asserts that to rid oneself of the "misery of life" is "the most simple of nature's rights of which no man of sense yet ever entertained a doubt."[6] Among the Romantic thinkers and the philosophers influenced by them, suicide in any circumstances is seen as an ultimate human right. Nietzsche is representative in insisting: "Suicide is man's right and privilege."[7]

[1]Schopenhauer, "On Suicide" (*op. cit.* I/131), p. 25.

[2]Cicero, *On Old Age* VII (*op. cit.* I/42), p. 241.

[3]Josephus, *The Jewish War* VII 325 (*op. cit.* I/10), p. 597.

[4]Seneca, *Letters* (*op. cit.* II/7), Letter 70, p. 63.

[5]*Ibid.*, Letter 70, p. 63.

[6]Rousseau, *Julie, or the New Heloise* (*op. cit.* I/72), Letter 114, p. 175.

[7]Nietzsche, *The Dawn of Day* (*Morgenrote*), original edition, 1881. (Stuttgart: Kroner Verlag, 1953), p. 210.

Such claims may seem to be of historical interest only. But it is important to see that a crucial philosophical point hangs on them, one with far-reaching consequences for our contemporary views of suicide. It is this: when we construe suicide as a *right,* the strategies change for determining when it is or is not morally permissible. In the earlier chapters of this book, we have considered various moral canons which prohibit suicide; most of these allow certain cases of suicide as exceptions. For instance, following Aristotle, we might say that suicide violates one's obligation to the community; but, as we've seen, exceptions will be made in cases where suicide benefits the state. Plato and Augustine claim that one has a prior obligation to obey the command of God; both acknowledge as exceptions, however, instances (like Socrates and Samson) in which God requires rather than forbids the ending of one's life. Kant held that suicide is forbidden because one has an obligation to respect the humanity in one's own person; apparently he too, though otherwise strictly impermissive of suicide, recognized an exception in the case of Cato. According to these views, suicide is in general wrong; certain special cases are permitted as exceptions.

But when we interpret suicide as a right, the strategy changes. Here, one begins by assuming suicide to be (at least) a *prima facie* right, but then considers circumstances in which this initial right may be overriden. This tactic might succeed in religious argumentation: one could assume that human beings have a right to end their lives (in virtue, say, of their responsibilities for self-determination under the doctrine of free will), but that God's edicts override this right by prohibiting suicide in all but certain (rare) kinds of cases. Or, to use a similar strategy in reinterpreting the Aristotelian point, we might assume that all persons have a right to end their lives, but that for those persons whose deaths would constitute an injury to the state, this right is overridden. In fact, this latter kind of analysis is sometimes used in contemporary discussions of the morality of suicide, even when the right to suicide is said to be overridden for almost everyone: in these analyses, emphasis is typically placed on the injury which exercising one's right to suicide would cause to other individuals and to society: this is the basis for overriding that right after all. Thus, to grant that persons have a right to suicide is not to say that they may kill themselves whenever they wish; one can advocate a rights-based analysis of suicide and yet hold that this right, unlike most other rights, is one which is almost always overridden. Before we can consider the implications of construing suicide as a right, however, we must first discover whether such a notion is intelligible at all.

We can, I think, distinguish several different ways in which the claim that suicide is a "right" might be understood. According to one, widespread in popular culture, the right to suicide is understood as a kind of property right; this view is based on a conception of one's own life as belonging to oneself, rather than, say, to the state or to God. The second view, perhaps equally widespread, sees suicide as a right in virtue of one's general freedom to act as one wishes, provided only that one does not thereby harm others or violate moral rules. Third, in an interesting but needless to say controversial view, one may treat suicide as a *natural* right, one among the fundamental liberties of man. In all these views, an individual has the right to end his life provided there are no overriding considerations; what is of interest, then, are the circumstances in which rights of these sorts are overrideable by other claims.

"It's my life": The Argument from Private Ownership

A frequent theme in a number of historical eras is the notion that an individual's life is "his own"; this supports the argument that the individual may therefore do as he wishes with his life, even if he wishes to end it in suicide. In the classical literature, this notion has been understood on the model of freedom from slavery; indeed, for the Stoics, suicide is the *proof* that one is not a slave.[8] Enlightenment and eighteenth-century thinkers, in contrast, interpret this notion as supporting a counterargument to the medieval religious claim that suicide is wrong because man's life belongs to God. As H. J. McClosky puts it, the argument for a right to suicide is Locke's traditional view, that man is the property of God, "turned on its head":

> it is akin to saying that the man who is a decider, a chooser who has a will of his own, possesses himself, is his own 'property', and as such, has property rights in and to his person. His autonomy is his most precious possession, and gives him his property right in and to himself.[9]

Survivals of the medieval anti-suicide argument from divine ownership still occur in contemporary authors; the Russian emigré Berdyaev, for instance, writes:

> People who do not think [that suicide is murder] make much of the fact that a murderer takes a life which does not belong to him. Their argument turns on the proposition that since my life is my own, I can take it without committing murder in the same way that I can take my own money without being a thief. But this argument is false and superficial. My life is not solely my own, it does not belong to me absolutely, it belongs to God first. He is the absolute owner; my life also belongs to my friends, to my family, to society, and finally to the entire world which has need of me. Absolute private ownership is a false principle, generally speaking.[10]

But the argument from private ownership, denied by Berdyaev in order to argue against suicide, can also be used in its positive form to argue against suicide. For instance, a seventy-four-year-old Washington, D.C. man with Parkinson's Disease was told by his physician, after a serious suicide attempt, that if he didn't "want his life" he "might as well give it to a useful cause," and enjoined on that basis to refrain from further suicide attempts but to volunteer as a subject for potentially dangerous medical research.[11] Here, the physician's underlying argument, similar in character to the religious analogies considered in Chapter One, suggests that although one has the right to dispose of one's property if one wishes, one ought to give it to someone or some cause which can make further use of it, like an outgrown coat, rather than destroy it altogether.

[8]See Seneca's description of the Spartan boy, p. 80, above.

[9]H. J. McClosky, "The Right to Life," *Mind*, Vol. 84, no. 332 (July, 1975), pp. 416–17.

[10]Nicholas Berdyaev, "On Suicide," *Approach: A Literary Quarterly*, No. 43 (Spring 1962), pp. 6–27. Reprinted from *Christianisme Social: Revue Internationale et Sociale pour un monde chrétien*, 1953. Tr. Elizabeth Bellenson and Helen Fowler; citation from p. 15.

[11]Victor Hasenoehrl, private conversation.

More frequently, however, the conception of one's life as one's own is used to argue in favor of libertarian practices with respect to suicide. This argument has received extensive public exposure in recent years in Brian Clark's play entitled "Whose Life Is It, Anyway?"; it involves a quadriplegic's determined quest for freedom from the medical measures forcing him to continue his life.[12]

But the private-property argument is not without its conceptual difficulties. One might object that life, unlike land, money, livestock, articles of clothing or household goods, is not the kind of thing that can be *property,* for nontransferable property is not property at all. Kluge considers the following reply:

> *What we own—in any full-blooded sense of that term—we can disown, give away, sell, or otherwise dispose of so that it becomes the property of someone else. We cannot do this with our lives. Therefore, whatever the unique relationship this bears to us, it cannot be one of ownership.*[13]

We do, perhaps metaphorically, speak of selling oneself into slavery or devoting oneself to a cause as "giving one's life" to someone else; we certainly speak of self-sacrificial heroes as having "given their lives." We speak of "trading" our lives for certain benefits, of "relinquishing" them, "discarding" them, and even of "throwing one's life away." These locutions strongly suggest an underlying metaphor of life as an item of disposable property. But, it could be argued, the analogy on which the private ownership argument for suicide is based is an unsound one, at least assuming a no-afterlife metaphysics: in ordinary property-destruction cases the owner of the property continues to exist (and be benefitted or harmed) after he destroys his property, whereas in suicide the owner *is* his destroyed property. "It's *my* life," we might point out, bears a misleading grammatical resemblance to "it's *my* whistle" or "it's *my* house," since the possessor of a life will not survive the surrender of his property, but the possessor of a whistle or a house will.

There is no doubt that the notion of one's life as "one's own" is widely current in libertarian popular thinking; interestingly, it is an argument one very often hears from adolescents and young adults. Nevertheless, it is not at all clear that the underlying notion of one's life as one's private property is philosophically coherent. "It's *my* life" may express an important sentiment, but not necessarily that one's life is an item among one's belongings.

The Argument from Freedom

A closer approach to the notion implicit in the sentiment "it's *my* life," I think, can be achieved by considering suicide not as a property right, but as a right generated by one's natural freedoms. Here, one may end one's life in virtue of one's liberty to do as one chooses, provided that one's actions do not harm others or infringe on their rights and provided that there are no contravening obligations or duties. Where there are, one's right is said to be *overridden.*

[12]Brian Clark, "Whose Life Is It, Anyway?" (New York: Dodd, Mead, 1978).

[13]Kluge, *The Practice of Death (op. cit.* I/46), p. 119.

There are three major conceptions of rights under which we might interpret the notion of a right to suicide: the Hobbesian notion of liberty rights; the notion of rights which involves claims to noninterference; and what is sometimes referred to as the notion of welfare rights. I will call them all "simple" rights, as distinguished from the natural rights we will consider later. In the first of these conceptions of rights, to say that a person has a right to do something means that he has no obligation not to do it: if Jones has a right to visit a fortune-teller, then Jones has no obligation or duty not to visit a fortune-teller, although there may be other good reasons (e.g., prudence) for him not to do so. In the second basic conception of rights, to have a right means not only that the person has no obligation not to do the act, but that other persons have corresponding obligations not to interfere. If Jones has a right to sail to Bermuda, then you and I have no right to prevent him from getting into his boat. The third conception of rights incorporates the previous two, but imposes still stronger claims: it involves positive provisos that others, at least where they can do so without serious risk to themselves and without violating other moral canons, are to assist in the exercise of that right. If Jones has been captured by robbers and lashed to a tree, his right to freedom from unlawful restraint, if it is a welfare-right, obliges us to release him, if we can do so without risking capture ourselves and without violating other moral rules. To say that we have a *right* to suicide, then, might be to say any one of these things: that a person has no obligation not to kill himself (as he might, for instance, if he has dependent children), that other persons have no basis for interference in any attempt he may make at suicide (and thus, that suicide-prevention social and police services, if legitimate at all, require special justification), or that other persons (though not necessarily any specific persons) have an obligation not only not to interfere but to assist him in killing himself, if that should be his choice.

Of contemporary authors who treat suicide as a right at all, most take it as a liberty-right, some as a right which imposes claims upon others. What presents continuing philosophical problems is the matter of determining when, and under what circumstances, the right to suicide can be overridden. The psychiatrist Jerome Motto, for instance, asserts:

> From a psychiatric point of view, the question as to whether a person has the right to cope with the pain in his world by killing himself can be answered without hesitation. He does have that right . . . The problem we struggle with is not whether the individual has the right to suicide; rather, we have a two-fold dilemma stemming from the fact that he does have it. Firstly, what is the extent to which the exercise of that right should be subject to limitations? Secondly, when the right is exercised, how can we eliminate the social stigma now attached to it?[14]

Bioethicists Lebacqz and Engelhardt argue that

> Since arguments in principle against suicide do not succeed, there is a prima facie right to kill oneself. The question of suicide thus becomes a question of distributive justice—of balancing this right against the legitimate claims of others.[15]

[14]Motto, "The Right to Suicide: A Psychiatrist's View" (*op. cit.* IV/8), p. 213.

[15]Lebacqz and Engelhardt, "Suicide," (*op. cit.* II/6), p. 669.

Some simple rights are fairly easily overridden—my *prima facie* right to pick my nose, say, is quickly overridden by the sensibilities of the other diners at the table; other simple rights are not—my right to plant a vegetable garden is not overridden by my neighbor's preference for looking at flowers. Of course, arbitrating the way in which duties, obligations, and the consequences of actions override rights of various sorts is the stuff of ordinary moral life, and while some cases are easy, others are not. But they may be particularly difficult with respect to suicide. Is an eighteen-year-old girl's *prima facie* right to suicide overridden by the devastating consequences her death would have for her parents, and by their fundamental interest in watching her grow? Perhaps so. Is an eighty-one-year-old woman's right to suicide instead of death by terminal cancer overridden by her adult children's rigid religious convictions? Perhaps not. But these cases raise one of the central problems posed by treating suicide as a right: what conditions or circumstances, exactly, would override this right?

Nor is this the only sort of problem posed by treating suicide as a right. A second major issue concerns claims for noninterference and assistance on the part of others. Suppose, for instance, that Jones has a right to suicide, and that his right is not overridden by any other considerations. Does this entail that Smith has an obligation to stay out of Jones' way as he ends his life? More strongly, might Smith have an obligation to help Jones do the deed? In some relatively simple cases, we may be able to posit successful answers to questions such as these, but this is far from producing a coherent and complete set of principles governing overridings and obligations on the part of others. This is not to say that the notion of suicide as a right is not a philosophically useful one, but that if we choose to use it, a good part of the philosophical work still remains to be done.

However, there are several pitfalls in treating suicide as a right. First and most important, to treat suicide as a right which can be overridden by other duties and obligations to other persons may provide unequal treatment for individuals whose grounds for suicide are the same, but who differ in their surrounding circumstances or their relationships to others. Of two persons afflicted with an identical terminal illness, for instance, one might have a right to suicide while the other's right is overridden, if one is free from family relationships and the other is not, even though the reasons for the suicide might be the same. Second, to treat suicide as a right may grant equal license to those whose reasons for suicide are not equally good. If suicide is a right overrideable primarily on the basis of duties and obligations to others, two potential suicides whose interpersonal relationships and commitments to others are similar may have the same right, or lack thereof, to kill themselves, even though they have vastly different reasons for doing so. Furthermore, the person who chooses suicide on rational grounds and the person whose reasons are superficial or pathological might seem not only to have equal rights to end their lives, but equal claims to noninterference or assistance in doing so. Third, to treat suicide as a right, regardless of which model of rights we accept, may seem to impose obligations on others in a uniform way regardless of their own individual characteristics and sensitivities. If suicide is conceived of as a liberty-right, no person, however close, would be said to have an obligation to intervene or to assist. If suicide is understood as a welfare right, then other persons generally might be said to have an obligation to help the individual to his end.

No doubt these pitfalls could be avoided with a complex system of rights, overridings, and obligations which would not give such simplistic results. But as a complex system is developed, it will begin to take more substantial account of the grounds upon which rights, overridings, and obligations with respect to suicide might be based. Developing a complex system would indeed reveal the real deficiency of the view of suicide as a right which we have considered so far: it does nothing to identify the grounds upon which such a right is based. If suicide is a right simply as a function of one's freedom to do as one chooses, then it will be very difficult to show why, in any case in which others are at all adversely affected, the right to suicide is not always almost immediately overridden, and how it could ever impose claims for assistance upon others. Suicide might be a right, but only a right as substantial as the right to pick one's nose: something you may do just if nobody minds. But if a "right" to suicide is only this strong, we have somehow not done justice to those traditional assertions with which we began. Clearly, something much stronger is meant.

There is still another problem with the view that suicide is a simple right. As James Bogen points out, an account of suicide in terms of rights, duties, and obligations may not really answer the moral questions in suicide: it may tell us what we are allowed to do, but not what we *ought* to do.[16] To establish that I have a right to suicide does not establish that my committing suicide is a good or bad thing to do, any more than establishing that I have a right to vote for a certain candidate establishes that that is a good way to cast my vote.

However, there is still another way of treating suicide as a right which may overcome these problems to some extent: it is to consider suicide as a *natural* right. This may bring with it some preliminary answer to the question of how readily a right to suicide can be overridden, and, further, some indication—however tentative—of when suicide may be a good thing to do. After all, the kinds of things to which we believe we have *natural* rights are things we believe important to have and, on the whole, good to do.

Suicide as a Natural Right

Thus, a third way in which we might understand the claim that suicide is a right is to group suicide among the fundamental or natural rights of man. These more basic rights, as distinct from the simple rights one has as a function of one's freedom to do as one chooses, are rights of the sort identified in the classical manifestoes: the American Constitution and its Bill of Rights, the French Declaration of the Rights of Man, the Communist Manifesto, and the 1948 U.N. Declaration of Human Rights, among others. The rights listed, of course, vary from one manifesto to another, variously including rights to life, liberty, ownership of property; freedom of assembly, speech, and worship; rights to education, employment, political representation, and medical care. However, although the manifestoes vary considerably in their contents, the conception underlying them is similar: they declare that certain universal, general, fundamental rights are held by individuals in virtue of their being human. Although in practice violations do occur, at least in theory natural rights cannot be easily overridden, and then only for some compelling reason of the public interest.

Could suicide be a *natural* right? This would place it on a par with the rights to life, liberty, freedom of speech and worship, political representation, and the pursuit of happiness, equally deserving of protection where this right threatens to be

---

[16]James Bogen, "Suicide and Virtue," in Battin and Mayo, eds., *Suicide: The Philosophical Issues*, (*op. cit.* i/10), pp. 286-292.

abridged. It would demand recognition in law, custom, medicine, and religion, as another pillar of an enlightened, moral society. The right to die when and how one wishes, and for reasons of one's own choosing, would be as basic as the right to live.

Two principal problems are encountered with this way of construing the right to suicide. First, there is no precedent for the claim; in particular, none of the great human-rights manifestoes mentions any "right to suicide." Recent legislation in some U.S. states does establish a so-called "right to die"; however, use of this latter expression is restricted to medical situations which involve only the withholding of heroic means of prolonging the lives of those already terminally ill. The right to die, as it is used in this legislation, is the right only not to have one's dying prolonged; it is not the right to end an otherwise continuing life. Thus, that there is, in some jurisdictions, a legal right to die by refusing treatment in terminal illness does not establish that there is a larger right to suicide. Of course, that a right to suicide is mentioned in none of the major manifestoes, nor in legislation, does not show that there is no such right; it can perhaps be established on other, independent grounds.

A second principal objection to construing suicide as a natural right is that this view cannot take adequate account of the pathology involved in most actual suicide cases. It can hardly be disputed that there is pathology involved in much, or perhaps even most, suicide which is reported and studied today. But this does not disprove the existence of such a right; it may mean only that the exercise of this right will often be subject to paternalistic constraints of the sort we have discussed above. After all, we regularly countenance the abridgement of other natural rights in non-normal or pathological circumstances, as for instance when we limit the liberty, freedom of speech, right of association, and even the pursuit of happiness among the criminal and mentally ill.

These two objections aside, we may wonder what positive evidence there is for the existence of such a right. To base it on the larger right of autonomy or self-determination may be merely to treat it as a simple right, a position which in the end might prove quite weak. Alternatively, the right to end one's life might be said to be self-evident: a natural, fundamental right which cannot and need not be derived from other rights, interests, or duties. Or, it may be based on a larger, positive right; this is the view advanced by Rousseau's Saint-Preux, who finds it rooted in the general, fundamental right to pursue one's own good.

> The more I reflect, the more I am convinced that the question may be reduced to this fundamental proposition: Every man has a right by nature to pursue what he thinks good, and avoid what he thinks evil, in all respects which are not injurious to others. When our life, therefore, becomes a misery to ourselves, and is of advantage to no one, we are at liberty to put an end to our being. If there is any such thing as a clear and self-evident principle, certainly this is one.[17]

But while Rousseau's text, like that of many other thinkers, asserts the self-evidence of the right to suicide, other thinkers just as strongly assert the self-evidence of the contrary principle: that suicide is forbidden. Pursuing this line of thought, Wittgenstein writes:

[17]Rousseau, *Julie, or the New Heloise* (*op. cit.* I/72), Letter 114, p. 167.

If suicide is allowed then everything is allowed. If anything is not allowed then suicide is not allowed. This throws a light on the nature of ethics, for suicide is, so to speak, the elementary sin.[18]

What is extraordinary about the issue of suicide is the self-certainty with which both sides are argued: the one, that suicide is an individual's natural right; the other, not only that it is not a natural right, but is strictly forbidden. Furthermore, the thinkers on both sides appeal to the self-evidence of their positions. Yet, since the right in question is said to be self-evident, further justification of it presumably cannot be given—in much the same way that further justification was said to be superfluous for the fundamental principle of the value of life. Consequently, if conflicting principles are urged as self-evident, it may appear that this dispute cannot be resolved. Let us look, however, at the kinds of arguments put forward by those concerned with the right to end one's life.

THE RIGHT TO SUICIDE AND THE RIGHT TO LIFE. But, perhaps suicide is incompatible with the natural right to life; if so, this would suggest that a right to suicide cannot also be a natural right, and is perhaps not a right at all. This issue is addressed by various thinkers, including Joel Feinberg[19] and Antony Flew.[20] Feinberg points out that the Jeffersonian tradition in political theory, embodied in such documents as the U.S. Bill of Rights, describes the right to life not only as universal but also as *inalienable;* that is, it cannot be abrogated by any individual or institution, presumably including oneself. But if one cannot surrender or waive one's right to life, then, it may seem, one does not have a right to end one's life. This argument suggests there is no such thing as a right to suicide.

However, we may object that, although the right to life is inalienable, there is attached to this right no requirement that it be exercised.[21] If, setting aside for the moment the right to life, we inspect the list of other rights which, under our prevailing assumption of the natural-rights framework, are generally held to be natural rights—liberty, property, fraternity, the pursuit of happiness, freedom of worship, free speech—I think it will be apparent that in no case, except perhaps liberty, is it suggested that an individual is required to exercise the right. The right to worship is a natural right, let us say, but does not preclude not worshipping at all. The right to property does not require one to own anything; one can elect poverty if one wishes. In short, a right is something neither necessary nor obligatory, but optional; it is what one may do if one chooses. If the right to life is a natural right, then it guarantees an individual the right to live if he chooses, but does not obligate or compel him to do so. Another way to put this is to say that the natural right to life, along with other natural rights like liberty, free association, and freedom of worship, are *rights* only, not duties: there is no duty to worship, to associate with one's fellows, or to speak freely, and there is no duty to live.

[18]Ludwig Wittgenstein, *Notebooks 1914–1916*. Tr. G. E. M. Anscombe, R. Rhees, and G. H. Von Wright (Oxford: Clarendon, 1961), p. 91e. He concludes this paragraph, however, the last entry in his notebooks of 1914–16, by conjecturing "Or is even suicide in itself neither good nor evil?"

[19]Feinberg, "Voluntary Euthanasia and the Inalienable Right to Life" (*op. cit.* II/54).

[20]Antony Flew, "The Right to Death," MSS, University of Reading.

[21]Feinberg, "Voluntary Euthanasia and the Inalienable Right to Life" (*op. cit.* II/54), pp. 104ff.

However, this invites the reply that a distinction is to be made between natural rights which are discretionary, such as free speech, and those which are mandatory, like liberty, education, and, for Hegelians, the right to punishment. Children have a right to education, this position claims, but attendance at school is not simply a matter of their or their parents' discretion; it is required. Man has a natural right to liberty, Mill argued, but even where abridgement of liberty is self-respecting only, as in selling oneself into slavery, an individual has no right to preclude his own freedom.[22] Similarly, one could argue that the right to life is a natural right, but unlike such discretionary rights as free speech, free assembly, or freedom of worship, it must be exercised: one has a duty to remain alive.

But the case for the existence of mandatory *rights* (to be distinguished from generally recognized duties) is a weak one. This is because one can always claim that the exercise of certain rights is required only to prevent abuses of them; these rights are not in themselves duties. For instance, although compulsory school attendance may make it appear that the right to education is mandatory, compulsory attendance policies may not in fact reflect any moral obligation on the part of children to attend school, but serve to prevent infringements on children's rights to attend school, both by virtue of the children's own immature judgment, and coercion by adults who would prefer to use children's labor or companionship for their own ends. The argument that the right to life is mandatory, similarly, can always be countered by the claim—an important one, as we have seen in our discussion of "facilitated" suicide—that exercise of this right is essential to guarantee it for all. If some people were to fail to exercise their right to life and choose instead to die, so this argument goes, the possibilities of coercion and abuse towards others would become enormous. Thus, the fact that we insist that people stay alive does not show that they have no right to end their lives, but only that we regard the consequences of allowing them to exercise their right to do so as potentially disastrous for others. Indeed, this might be regarded as an example of a natural right routinely overridden to serve some "compelling reason of the public interest."

We should also point out that the individual who chooses to die does not lose his or her *right* to life. To commit suicide is not to abridge one's right to life; it is to abridge one's life. Similarly, though slaves no longer have freedom, they have a right to freedom, albeit often unrecognized by the societies within which they live. Refusal to worship, own property, vote, or speak freely does not abridge one's rights to do these things, and it would be misleading to speak of persons who refuse as having waived, abrogated, relinquished, or surrendered their rights to do them. A person may, of course, lose some or perhaps all of his rights. But this does not occur through non-exercise of them, but rather through some other circumstances, such as by contract or as a consequence of misdeed: one may lose one's right to financial independence by becoming married, or, as proponents of capital punishment claim, one's right to life by committing murder. Thus, refusal to exercise one's right to life by committing suicide does not entail that one loses that right. If this is so, a right to kill oneself may be compatible even with the *inalienable* right to life.

Perhaps the analogy between the right to life and other inalienable natural rights is weak, since failure to exercise it at one time precludes any further enjoyment of it: effective suicide prevents any opportunity for future exercise of the right to life. But effective suicide does not terminate one's *right* to life; if an individual

---

[22]This thesis is argued in John Stuart Mill's *On Liberty* (1859); however, Mill does not discuss suicide in this text.

who had committed suicide were to become alive again, we would be unlikely to say that he no longer had any right to live. Of course, earlier historical periods have not seen the matter quite this way; suicide has been a capital offense in most of late medieval and early modern Europe, and those whose suicide attempts were ineffective were put to death as a penalty.[23] The contemporary suicide attempter, on the other hand, is with very few exceptions no longer subject to criminal penalties, but is resuscitated and encouraged to live.

THE BASIS OF A NATURAL RIGHT TO SUICIDE.   That the natural right to life need not be exercised does not entail, however, that suicide is a natural right; this must be independently established. But to justify the natural rights is a notoriously difficult and disputatious task. As we've noted, the principal manifestoes do not agree even on the less contentious items, and argumentation among philosophers about the foundations of natural rights are unending. Nevertheless, I think we can sketch the outlines of a defense of suicide as a natural right.

One might assume, as I have proposed elsewhere, an account of fundamental or natural rights as grounded in human dignity.[24] This view considers persons to have natural or fundamental rights to do or have certain sorts of things just because things of that sort tend to promote human dignity. Perhaps this notion of dignity is vague, but it is also, as Ronald Dworkin puts it, "powerful,"[25] and we can intuitively grasp the way in which such things as liberty, freedom of speech, education, freedom of association, and other basic rights tend on the whole to promote human dignity. On the other hand, we do not have *natural* rights to things like alcoholism, because alcoholism on the whole does not promote human dignity, even though we may be free (i.e., have a simple right) to become alcoholic if we wish, provided it harms no one and contravenes no other obligation. This sort of view, and I think it is a plausible one, would suggest that suicide is in fact a matter of natural right because it tends, on the whole, to promote human dignity.[26]

This assertion may seem to fly in the face of the most evident fact. Clearly, suicide as we know it does *not* tend on the whole to promote human dignity; it is a dismal, pathetic affair. Consider, for instance, the ubiquitous "get-even" suicides, consciously or subconsciously intended to produce guilt, remorse, or injury to another person; obviously, suicide of this sort displays human nature at its least sublime. Or, again, consider the suicide of isolation: the elderly man, living alone in a shabby rented room, without family, without friends, without social contacts of any real kind. To claim that suicide is a natural right because it tends on the whole to promote human dignity clearly misdescribes these cases, and encourages us to overlook the very real tragedies that are played out here.

---

[23]See Alvarez's quotation of a disturbing description of the hanging of a suicide attempter in London, circa 1860, in *The Savage God* (*op. cit.* i/16), p. 43; this chapter reprinted as "The Background" in Battin and Mayo, eds., *Suicide: The Philosophical Issues* (*op. cit.* i/10), quotation pp. 7-8.

[24]See my "Suicide: A Fundamental Human Right?" in Battin and Mayo, eds., *Suicide: The Philosophical Issues* (*op. cit.* i/10), pp. 267-85. Some of the material in this section is taken from that article, although the account of rights given differs slightly.

[25]Ronald Dworkin, *Taking Rights Seriously* (Cambridge, Mass.: Harvard University Press, 1977, 1978), p. 198. Dworkin bases his account of rights in two independent notions, the "vague but powerful idea of human dignity," and the "more familiar idea of political equality."

[26]This account appears to bear some resemblance to Jean Baechler's defense of suicide as "an inalienable human privilege" (*Suicides, op. cit.* i/32, p. 34) based on the right to freedom, the right to happiness, and the right to dignity (p. 50). See especially his chapter 2, "The Humanity of Suicide," pp. 38-52.

But, as we've said earlier and ought to repeat often, the fact that suicide in this culture is very strongly associated with depression, disturbance, or mental illness does not prove that the connection is necessary, or that a person must be ill to consider such a thing. Were it not for the cultural taboo and the inherited notions of suicide as crime and as sin, suicide might indeed be a much more common and accepted event than it now is. Barrington, we saw, thinks that suicide might be a boon to those afflicted by terminal illness or old age; Kastenbaum speculates that it could become the *preferred* way of death. In such worlds, the pathological cases we now see would represent only a tiny, aberrant fraction of the whole.

But can *suicide* in fact promote human dignity, as would have to be the case to consider suicide a natural right? This is a question, I think, for sustained, careful, and unbiased thought. One might begin by mentioning certain exemplary names: Cato, Socrates, Charlotte Perkins Gilman, Szmul Zygielbojm, and Captain Oates. One might attend carefully to the notion of rational suicide, and the ways in which one's values may sometimes take precedence over the continuation of one's life. One might consider whether some self-deaths could not be understood, paradoxically, as a kind of "self-preservation," a kind of self-respect and protection of one's fundamental interests. "I am what I have been," suicides sometimes seem to say, "but cannot be any more." They are based, as it were, on a self-ideal: a conception of one's own value and worth, beneath which one is not willing to slip. Of course, one's self-ideal may be distorted by depression, psychosis, or other illnesses of the mind, but then again, it may be realistic, sensitive, and intact, and form at least part of the basis of the notion of human dignity with which we began. Whether the threat to one's self-ideal is from physical illness and pain, as in euthanatic suicide, or from the destruction of other persons or values upon which one's life is centrally focused, as in self-sacrificial suicide, or from a fundamental refusal to submit to the conditions of life in a degraded world, as in suicides of principle and social protest, the import is the same: one chooses death instead of further life, because further life would bring with it a compromise of that dignity without which one cannot consent to live.

But, again, what about the cases in which suicide is clearly the product of pathology, as are the majority of cases with which we are familiar today? Here, I think, the answer, as we've seen, is simple: here, the right to suicide, although a fundamental human right, is overridden, because the individual is not competent to exercise it in a way that might achieve its end. As we've said, we regularly countenance abridgement of other fundamental rights in cases of pathology or disturbance. For example, although we find that liberty, in general, promotes human dignity, and man can achieve full stature only if he is free, we nevertheless confine those who are criminal, incompetent by reason of very young or old age, or insane. But if we permit the abridgement of other natural human rights in circumstances like these, there is no reason why we should not permit the abridgement of the right to suicide in certain circumstances too. These abridgements might curtail suicide among the depressed or temporarily disturbed, while permitting it, for instance, among the terminally ill.

Let us recall David Wood's example of the suicide of the architect who pioneered highrise apartment buildings and has regretted what he has done.[27] Is this a suicide of dignity, and so one to which he has a fundamental right? Or is it a suicide like most of those with which we are empirically familiar, the product of a dis-

[27]See the final section of Chapter 4.

turbed, irrational mind? We can imagine the case either way: as the final, desperate act of self-loathing, occurring as the confused climax of long years of self-reproach; but we can also imagine it as a considered, courageous statement of principle, a dignified final act transcending one's own defeat. If it is the former, we can imagine reminding the man that he has obligations to his family, his friends, his gods, and himself, and doing what we can to prevent the act. But if the latter, such objections seem petty, and the interference perverse: we can only admire his attainment of a difficult human ideal. Can one imagine telling Cato that he ought not kill himself because his accounts are incomplete or because it would disrupt the activities of his slaves? We admire acts of dignity in other realms, but sometimes forget that they can—though perhaps not often—occur in suicide too.

Of course, to claim that a person has a right to end his life because to do so would further human dignity is not to claim that that person may not also have duties to live, and/or duties which presuppose living. Socrates weighed his choice of death against his duties to his two small sons and reaffirmed his choice; St. Paul weighed his duties to the Church against his desire to see Christ, and stayed alive. Many of the duties generated by human relationships would seem to preclude suicide; many of the arguments against suicide which we have considered in this book are attempts to argue for duties which presuppose living, and hence are thought to justify legal and cultural suicide prohibitions which assure that the duty of living is performed by all. But it is not clear how strong duties to others must be in order to override a *natural* right to suicide. Furthermore, just as some of a person's interests can be satisfied without his continuing to live, so some of a person's duties can also be fulfilled despite his death: payment of debts, for example. Some duties may be overridden by various other considerations: the duty to provide conjugal companionship, for example, may be overridden by the right to avoid pain. On the other hand, the right to suicide may be so strong that other duties very rarely touch it at all. If there is a *natural* right to end one's life when one chooses, one of the most substantial and crucial areas of normative ethics would become the weighing of other duties against this right.

Rights and the Role of Others

Whether suicide is a right is not merely an abstract question; crucial practical consequences depend upon it. If a given act is a matter of right, then any abridgement of that right calls for justification; exercise of it does not. For instance, any abridgement of the right to liberty calls for justification (e.g., the need for military draft in time of war), whereas any exercise of the right to liberty does not. If there is a right to end one's life when one so chooses, then justification must be provided in order to interfere with an individual's plans for suicide. This would be true whether those who interfere are help-line volunteers, police, psychiatrists, legislators formulating legal sanctions against suicide, insurance companies withholding death benefits to survivors of suicide,[28] health insurance plans refusing coverage in cases

[28]See Chapter Two, footnote 13, on life and health insurance policies in connection with suicide. One justification for the two-year exclusion clauses now common in life-insurance policies might be to protect the insurers against persons who deliberately insure themselves and then commit suicide in order to have their beneficiaries collect the proceeds, but such clauses do not take account of other nonfraudulent

of injury during an incomplete suicide attempt, or hospital, prison, military, or other institutional personnel who seek to interrupt the suicide attempts of individuals in their care. Any person or institution seeking to prevent an individual from taking his life would have to be able to provide good reason for doing so. This would be just as true in emergency situations as at other times.

This is not to require, of course, that a complete and explicit statement of justification be produced prior to any interference, at least in emergency situations or first-time attempts; one might advocate a policy, as we described in Chapter Five, whereby temporary intervention is permitted just in order to discover the circumstances of the case. Further intervention would be appropriate in cases where suicide is not autonomously chosen or where the individual has obligations (say, to dependent children) strong enough to override his rights; intervention would also be appropriate in cases where the evidence is inadequate. In principle, however, justification for intervention in any suicide attempt would always be required, and the individual considered free to do as he chooses unless such justification can be found.

As things now stand, just the reverse assumption is made. Suicide interveners do not have to justify their actions either before the fact or after, whereas persons who wish to end their lives—if they are ever permitted to do so—are in general expected to provide adequate justification for their choice. That it is not a legal wrong to prevent a suicide presupposes that suicide is not a right. The assumption is that practice of suicide requires special justification, whereas suppression of it does not. But if suicide is a right, the prospective suicide cannot be required to produce a reason for his actions. The only issues which remain concern whether the right may be overridden for one reason or another.

Furthermore, a right may not only impose upon others an obligation to refrain from interference, but also one to render assistance. In a recent paper, Peter Williams argues that there cannot be such a thing as a right to die (he has in mind euthanasia situations) because there is no corresponding duty on the part of others to do the killing.[29] But this is precisely the issue. If there is a right to die (which can be exercised either in euthanasia or suicide), this means that there may also be an obligation on the part of others—though one which we do not now legally or morally recognize—either to perform euthanasia for the individual, or to assist him in his own self-killing. If the right is a natural right, the obligations it imposes on others may be still stronger. In the most extreme example, consider the case of the quadriplegic, who because of the complete and permanent paralysis of all his limbs is unable to terminate his own life. If we agree that this person has no obligation to continue to endure his condition or, more strongly, has the right, like anyone else, to end his life if he so chooses, we must confront an additional issue: does someone else—whether physician, family member, friend, or state official—have an obligation to administer to this person the means of death he chooses? If we acknowledge the right, we must be prepared to acknowledge a corresponding duty, and if we hold that suicide is a fundamental right, we must be prepared to ensure that the duty is

---

grounds for suicide which might arise within a two-year period. It may be reasonable to expect insurance companies to protect themselves with exclusion clauses against financially-motivated suicide, but perhaps not clauses based on a stipulated length of time. It is not at all clear that this sort of justification would apply in cases of health insurance.

[29]Peter Williams, "Rights and the Alleged Rights of Innocents to be Killed," *Ethics* 87 (1977), 383–94.

met. Of course, not all rights give rise to corresponding obligations on the part of others to provide means for satisfaction of that right: U.S. citizens, for example, have a right to interstate travel, but this fact does not obligate the government or any individuals to provide it. On the other hand, U.S. citizens also have a right to legal counsel; here, in contrast, the state does assume the obligation to provide counsel, in the form of public defenders, for those who cannot obtain it for themselves.

Thus, if the right to end one's life is in fact a right, we must still settle the issue of whether it is a simple liberty-right or a natural right, and whether it does not or does impose obligations on others. This point has been rarely explored in recent philosophy; most authors who recognize a right to suicide treat it as a liberty-right only, one not imposing obligations. But there are some historical precedents for treating suicide as a right which does impose obligations of assistance upon others: the Roman citizen could expect his slave to hold the sword upon which he would fall, and the Roman city at Marseilles maintained a public supply of poisons for use in suicide, to which it granted access to any citizen who could present an adequate set of reasons for his suicide to the Senate.[30] Nor have such notions been confined to ancient Rome. The Sorbonne physician Binet-Sanglé called in 1919 for the establishment of public thanatoria or euthanasia parlors where the client could choose from among electrocution, poison, gases, narcotics, and a variety of other means a method of reaching an "individually styled" death.[31] Doris Portwood, on the other hand, resists what we might call this bureaucratization of suicide but claims that aging and ill persons have a right to assistance in suicide from their intimates and friends.[32] Of course, the existence of such practices and claims does not entail that entitlement to assistance in suicide is a matter of moral right, but they should encourage us to reexamine our beliefs and practices in this regard.

In 1961, Nobel physicist Percy Bridgman, then almost 80 years old and suffering from terminal cancer, shot himself. He left the following final note:

It isn't decent for society to make a man do this thing himself. Probably this is the last day I will be able to do it myself.[33]

Bridgman's case may serve well to test the range of moral views on the role of others in suicide. If we adopt the traditional religious or social arguments against suicide or the stricter versions of the view that life is of value, Bridgman did himself, his family, and his society wrong. If, on the other hand, we adopt the stronger versions of the thesis that suicide is a right, society failed Bridgman in its final obligation, as Bridgman himself clearly believed. Of course, the relationship between the rights of individuals and the obligations of others is a complex issue, but this is no reason to ignore Bridgman's claim.

---

[30]Valerius Maximus, *Memorabilia,* Book II, Chapter 6, recounts an aged woman's appearance before the magistrates to request permission to commit suicide.

[31]Dr. Binet-Sanglé, *L'Art de Mourir. Défense et Technique du Suicide Secondé.* (Paris: Albin Michel, 1919). See especially Part II, Chapter II, "Choix du Procédé, euthanasique."

[32]Doris Portwood, *Commonsense Suicide (op. cit.* II/16).

[33]Percy Bridgman, letter in *Bulletin of the Atomic Scientists,* quoted by Max Delbrück, "Education for Suicide," interview in *Prism,* a publication of the American Medical Association, 2 (1974), 20.

Conclusion: Suicide and Moral Rules

This book began by detaching itself from the prevalent scientific view of suicide, which considers it an event caused by psychological or social forces beyond the control of the individual to whom they occur. Our purpose was to reassess the underlying moral issues in suicide. We've examined traditional religious answers to these questions; most of these arguments led only inadequately to the conclusion that suicide is never right, and led us to speculate that they arise from Christianity's need to curb the believer's haste to achieve a beatific afterlife. The traditional, largely consequentialist social arguments against suicide, we found, tend to reverse themselves, producing arguments favoring suicide when social benefits are thereby attained. Objections to suicide based on the value of life itself, which may have seemed the most thoroughgoing objections to suicide, dissolve in many cases. In short, the traditional arguments against suicide do not establish that it is wrong.

Approaching these issues as they tend to be formulated in contemporary discussion, we then considered whether suicide might ever be a rational act. Even if most suicide as it is now practiced does not meet these criteria, we found no reason to think that suicide cannot in principle be a rational choice. But if suicide can be rational, then an additional, difficult problem confronts us: the principle of paternalism, now most commonly used to justify suicide-prevention activities, would require encouragement of suicide when it is a rational act.

This is a disturbing result. But perhaps its impact is blunted by considering suicide as a right, something which the individual is ultimately entitled to choose or reject, and we considered several possible interpretations of this view. Finally, we considered what consequences such a view would have concerning the roles of others in discouraging or encouraging a person's attempt to bring about his own death. Perhaps we have not reached as many answers as we'd like; perhaps the philosophical problem of suicide is far more complex than we may have thought. But I think we can begin to see the dimensions of the issues in suicide and what has been concealed by taboo.

Even without answers, I think we can discern the form in which a solution to these problems may begin, however slowly, to be achieved. Suicide, we must remember, is a form of killing. But what we need to observe is that we already have access to quite precise moral rules about killing which have developed within western culture since its beginning. These are not rules about suicide as such; they are rules about the killing of other human beings, with various motivations and in various circumstances. These practical moral rules regulating killing are for the most part codified in law, where statutes distinguish among first-degree murder, second-degree murder, manslaughter, and excusable and justifiable homicide; they are also preserved in custom, literature, religion, and are reflected in our everyday moral attitudes. They determine our conceptions of what rights we do and do not have, and what those rights entail about the obligations of others. Of course, the rules concerning killing coexist with and incorporate other moral canons, such as those concerning regard for human life, respect for autonomy, and duties to preserve the social group. We find killing excusable in some cases, inexcusable in others, and permissible or perhaps required in still others. In some areas, the moral rules concerning killing are not entirely clear, or are undergoing fairly rapid change: those concerning abortion and euthanasia are examples. And some individuals dissent from particular portions of the generally accepted rules: this is particularly evident with regard to capital punishment. Nevertheless, our practical moral rules concerning the killing of others are, in general, quite precise, and the substance of them is familiar to all competent members of the culture. They might be conceived of as cultural guidelines which direct the course of our everyday behavior; while some of us do violate them, the vast majority of us do not.

But we have no conceptual distinctions or practical moral rules of this sort concerning suicide, only an absolute (though perhaps crumbling) ban. As Richard Walton points out, the concept of suicide is "crude" by comparison with the concept of murder;[1] our tendency has been to treat all suicides as uniformly wrong. Many nonwestern and primitive societies do have highly developed practical moral rules regarding suicide as well as the killing of others: this is the case in societies which practice institutional suicide or permit suicide for certain kinds of personal reasons. The west, however, has no set of moral rules concerning suicide; this is why the philosophical problems surrounding suicide are so pressing in western philosophy, but do not arise with much force in nonwestern systems of thought. It may be that contemporary western society is very slowly beginning to develop the first germs of a set of practical moral rules for suicide. As we have suggested, very recent patients'-rights advocacy and right-to-die legislation are beginning to open the way for recognition of the rationality and moral permissibility of euthanatic suicide in cases of painful terminal illness. Some writers, as we have seen, are beginning to suggest that suicide, or rather self-senicide, may become permissible, preferred, or even expected in old age. But suicide in terminal illness and old age is still far from being adequately covered by practical moral rules, and there are many kinds of noneuthanatic suicide for which we have no specific moral rules at all, only the ban. These areas include suicide in mental incapacity or mental illness, in criminal recidivism or in long-term or life imprisonment, from religious motives, for public dishonor, after the death of a spouse, and even cases like suicide from boredom or for sport. Other cultures contain quite specific rules governing suicide in most of

[1]Richard E. Walton, "Socrates' Alleged Suicide," paper delivered at the Northwest Conference on Philosophy, University of Victoria, Victoria, B.C., November 1978, p. 2, and in a longer, unpublished version of this paper, pp. 1–3, University of Montana, Missoula, Montana.

these cases, sometimes permitting, sometimes requiring, sometimes forbidding it; western post-Christian culture, in contrast, issues only a blanket prohibition. Most dangerous perhaps is the lack of any cultural or other regulation of the ways in which suicide can be encouraged, assisted, or promoted by others, for it is here that the largest potential for abuse is to be found. Yet not to permit suicide or to discourage it when it is clearly the only good and desired option is an abuse in itself as well.

The Christian prohibition against suicide was developed, largely by Augustine, to combat self-killing in a particular type of situation: religious zealotry, fired by the hope of immediate martyred entrance into heaven. That ban, however, was not really designed to regulate suicides due to physical or emotional suffering, old age, altruism towards others, personal or societal honor, illness, and the like, and the earlier Platonic position which did govern these cases (however summarily) was misinterpreted and forgotten. The result is that western society has evolved without developing a reasonable, equitable, and humane set of laws and practices regarding the ending of one's own life, though it has done so with respect to ending the lives of others; eastern society, as a continuing legacy of colonialism, has simply adopted the modern western view. Of course, within western society there is dissent from particular provisions of the laws and practices concerning killing of others, as no doubt there would be dissent from particular portions of any laws, conventions, customs, or practices which might arise to regulate self-killing. But to claim that there is or might be dissent from particular portions of a general set of practical moral rules concerning suicide is not to say that we should not consider, or attempt to codify, any such set of rules.

This is not to advocate the establishment of committees or legislative boards for the formulation of such rules; first, most members would themselves be molded within the prevailing scientific and cultural assumptions regarding suicide, and the initial policies devised by such groups would therefore probably only reflect the prevailing taboo. Or, more dangerously, they might be covertly coercive, designed to produce suicide among socially unwanted or costly groups. Nevertheless, one might well begin to articulate morally satisfactory rules by attending to the other moral canons we accept, particularly those concerning autonomy and mercy, and the assumptions we make about the value and purposes of life.

Of course, a set of expressed moral rules governing suicide would be likely to change over time, due perhaps both to societal changes in underlying values and to new pressure for consistency with other moral canons. But we are quite accustomed to changes in our expressed moral rules. With regard to the killing of others, for instance, we do not now permit killing for revenge, though western society once did, and we do now sometimes permit abortion though at other times western society did not. The fact that rules concerning killing or suicide may develop and evolve over time is no reason not to have them, particularly where such rules might serve to prevent abuse.

Particularly instrumental in any attempt to elaborate or codify a set of moral rules concerning suicide might be the strategy of construing suicide as a *right*. As we've said, rights-based accounts of suicide so far proposed leave two major sorts of problems unresolved: what other factors can override this right, and what claims for noninterference and assistance this right might impose upon other persons. For this reason, a rights-based account of suicide may have seemed to be an uninformative and unhelpful one. But I think this conclusion is mistaken. After all, consider the history. Twentieth-century philosophers have devoted considerable effort to refining and elaborating notions of rights and natural rights inherited from earlier philosophical times; our legal system too, based as it is on a Lockean/Jeffersonian natural-rights foundation, has given rise to an elaborate fabric of precedent and policy governing rights and obligations in everyday life. But throughout much of this time, suicide has been regarded largely as a sin, a sickness, and a crime, and has been subject to a very strong taboo. Consequently, suicide has been overlooked or rejected from among the kinds of cases to be covered in devising a coherent and complete set of principles governing rights and obligations; that is why it poses such an interesting test. This does not mean that suicide *is* a right, but rather suggests that quite substantial philosophical and practical progress in our treatment of suicide might be made by encouraging ourselves to reconsider suicide in this way.

My own view of the underlying moral issues in suicide and the moral rules into which they should be formulated tends to be an autonomist one, viewing suicide as potentially rational and dignity-promoting in many more cases than we now recognize. At the same time, I applaud the sincere efforts of suicide-prevention workers and researchers to prevent suicide which is irrationally or pathologically chosen, and welcome those voices who remind us of the value of life. But I am disturbed by the fact that, according to a consequentialist view, many sorts of self- and other-benefiting suicide may seem to be not only permissible but obligatory; by the fact that Kantian deontologism may seem to make suicide required in certain kinds of cases; and by the fact that genuinely paternalist considerations properly employed in the prevention of suicide also favor the promoting of suicide when it is the rational thing to do. I think these facts in part account for the strength of the suicide taboo operative in western culture; the taboo gives us a way of ignoring the difficult conclusions to which our ethical principles lead us. Is suicide not only morally permissible or a supererogatory option, but in some cases morally *required?* I think we must look carefully at this issue and bear in mind that our society has not evolved a measured, considered set of moral rules, laws, and customs concerning suicide. This, I think, is cause for philosophic and practical alarm.

Index

Gail Downward